THE
FORGERS

THE FORGOTTEN STORY OF THE
HOLOCAUST'S MOST AUDACIOUS
RESCUE OPERATION

ROGER MOORHOUSE

BASIC BOOKS
New York

Basic Books

Hachette Book Group

1290 Avenue of the Americas, New York, NY 10104

www.basicbooks.com

Printed in Canada

First Edition: October 2023

Published by Basic Books, an imprint of Perseus Books, LLC, a subsidiary of Hachette Book Group, Inc. The Basic Books name and logo is a trademark of the Hachette Book Group.

The Hachette Speakers Bureau provides a wide range of authors for speaking events. To find out more, go to hachettespeakersbureau.com or email HachetteSpeakers@hbgusa.com.

The publisher is not responsible for websites (or their content) that are not owned by the publisher.

Print book interior design by Jeff Williams

Library of Congress Cataloging-in-Publication Data

Names: Moorhouse, Roger, author.
Title: The forgers : the forgotten story of the Holocaust's most audacious rescue operation / Roger Moorhouse.
Other titles: Forgotten story of the Holocaust's most audacious rescue operation
Identifiers: LCCN 2023016628 | ISBN 9781541619852 (hardback) | ISBN 9781541619845 (ebook)
Subjects: LCSH: Grupa Ładosia. | World War, 1939–1945—Jews—Rescue—Poland. | World War, 1939–1945—Jews—Rescue—Switzerland. | World War, 1939–1945—Underground movements—Poland. | Holocaust, Jewish (1939–1945)—Poland. | Identification cards—Forgeries—Poland. | Forgery—Poland—History—20th century. | Identification cards—Forgeries—Switzerland. | Forgery—Switzerland—History—20th century. | Diplomatic and consular service, Polish—Switzerland.
Classification: LCC D804.6 .M667 2023 | DDC 940.53/1835—dc23/eng/20230609
LC record available at https://lccn.loc.gov/2023016628

ISBNs: 9781541619852 (hardcover), 9781541619845 (ebook)

MRQ-C

10 9 8 7 6 5 4 3 2 1

To the victims of the Holocaust,
and all those who endeavored to help them

CONTENTS

FOREWORD

Embassy receptions can be curious events. They are conventionally rather formal; conversation is often stilted, the wine indifferent. Yet occasionally they can serve as the springboard for something of more substance. In May 2017, the newly appointed Polish ambassador to Switzerland, Dr. Jakub Kumoch, was hosting a reception at the embassy in Bern, when—in a chance conversation with a Jewish guest—he was informed that the embassy building was a "holy place." Intrigued, the ambassador probed further and was told that, in that same building on Elfenstrasse, his wartime predecessor had masterminded an ingenious effort to save Jews from the Holocaust by providing them with forged Latin American passports. With that, a seed was sown.

The story of that wartime predecessor, Aleksander Ładoś, had hitherto essentially been forgotten. The surviving members of the Ładoś Group, his coconspirators, had disappeared into obscurity in the postwar period, and—scattered by the vicissitudes of life—none of them had left memoirs or diaries of the time. As if to deepen the silence, those whom they had helped save from the death camps generally had no idea of their existence. Given the veil of secrecy that was necessarily drawn around the operation, the recipients ordinarily had little idea who had supplied their false identity documents.

At the ambassador's instigation, embassy staff began researching the activities of their wartime predecessors, scouring the wealth of Holocaust memoirs as well as archives in Switzerland, Poland, Germany, Britain, and the United States looking for references to their clandestine work. The story that emerged from that research surprised everyone involved. Ładoś and his colleagues—his legation counselor Stefan Ryniewicz, consul Konstanty Rokicki, attaché Juliusz Kühl, as well as Jewish activists Abraham Silberschein and Chaim Eiss—presided over one of the most ambitious rescue schemes of the Holocaust, producing false identity documents for an estimated eight to ten thousand individuals and helping over eight hundred to survive. Their activities would span wartime Europe and resonate far beyond, to the United States and Latin America. The recipients included citizens of more than fifteen countries.

Given this scale, the discovery of the story of the Ładoś Group is highly significant. Of course, it has a profound human importance and not just to those, probably many thousands today, who owe their lives to a Ładoś passport. No less significantly, it is a genuinely new contribution to our collective knowledge, an addition to history's endless puzzle, and a challenge to some entrenched popular assumptions about the history of the Holocaust.

For a long time, the study of the Nazi genocide against the Jews has been shaped by the tripartite classification of "perpetrators, bystanders, and victims." Of course, this was intended merely as an analytical tool, a framework rather than a rigid instruction. But it nonetheless allowed little space for the discussion of those more marginal groups—such as rescuers—who stood beyond that triad. More importantly, it tended to encourage the assumption that Jews faced the Holocaust entirely alone.

Of course, a number of individual rescuers of Jews have been recognized, spurred no doubt by the popularity of the story of Oskar Schindler and the film of his life, *Schindler's List*. There were others, not least among them Raoul Wallenberg, the Swedish diplomat who saved thousands of Jewish lives in wartime Budapest. Less well-known are the examples of Henryk Sławik, a Polish diplomat who helped thousands of Jews by issuing false baptismal certificates; Irena Sendler, a Polish social worker who smuggled Jewish children out of the Warsaw ghetto; and Sebastián de Romero Radigales, a Spanish diplomat who saved several hundred Jews in Greece by issuing false papers. The list could go on. In all, the category of "Righteous Among the Nations"—the honorific title awarded by the State of Israel to those non-Jews who risked their lives to save Jews during the Holocaust—contains over twenty-seven thousand names.

Notwithstanding such efforts by brave individuals, the assumption of Jewish "aloneness" in the Holocaust was not entirely misplaced. As this book demonstrates, though nominally sympathetic, the outside world was not prepared to do anything material to assist Jews in their efforts to escape the German genocide. Consequently, governmental attempts to aid the Jews were almost entirely absent, hindered by strategic concerns, more pressing priorities, and old-fashioned anti-Semitism. Contrary to the popular assumption of many—itself a backward projection of our modern pieties—outside governments were not held back from assisting the Jews by ignorance of the facts or by insuperable logistical challenges; they were held back mainly by their own indifference to Jewish suffering.

In stark contrast, the wartime efforts of the Polish government-in-exile and its diplomats to advocate for Europe's Jews stand out as exemplary. Of course, they had a vested interest. Despite the difficulties in minority relations that Poland experienced in the interwar years, the Polish government-in-exile viewed Polish Jews as Polish citizens first and foremost and did what it could to protect them. Consequently, it would be these Polish officials who would be instrumental not only in endeavoring to tell the world the truth of the genocide against the Jews already in 1942, but also in trying thereafter to find ways of mitigating its hideous consequences—as witnessed in their wholehearted support for the Ładoś passport operation. European Jewry had few outside allies during the Holocaust, but the Polish exile government was undoubtedly one.

This book seeks to explain that complex relationship and to place the activities of the Ładoś Group within the wider context of the Holocaust and of inter-Allied diplomacy. It is a story of a conspiracy of forgers, of venal officials, of underground couriers, of inept spies, and—of course—of some of the many desperate Jewish victims of the Germans seeking a way out of the maelstrom. The story of the Ładoś Group is a rare thing: a genuinely new contribution to a well-trodden subject. It expands our understanding not only of the nefarious machinery of the Holocaust but of the brave individuals who sought to resist it. It also shows us that Europe's Jews did not stand entirely alone.

PROLOGUE

"HE WHO SAVES ONE LIFE . . ."

ON THE NIGHT OF SEPTEMBER 27, 1944, HEINZ LICHTEN-stern went to see his family for the last time. He had done his best to save them. He had left Germany for Holland, not long after Adolf Hitler had come to power, making a new life for them in Amsterdam. When the Germans invaded west in 1940, he had entrusted the family's wealth to a non-Jewish friend in an effort to avoid the expected forced confiscations of Jewish assets. He had even arranged for false identity papers to be prepared, in the hope that some sort of exit route from the gathering horror could be secured. But now, after a short stay in the ghetto at Theresienstadt in Bohemia, he realized that he had come to the end of the road. He had been informed that he would be deported the following morning. The deportation notice reminded him that he should appear punctually, with minimal luggage but with work clothes, blankets, and underwear. Failure to comply would incur official sanction.[1]

In justifying the impending deportation, the notice spoke of overcrowding in the ghetto and the need to mobilize able-bodied men for a six-week period of labor service. The camp authorities requested five thousand men, who were to be sent in two batches "within the shortest period"; only the most "urgent and justi-fied" exemptions would be granted. The men would be selected, the notice stipulated, only on the basis of age and regardless of the position that an individual might hold. By way of assuaging the fears of family members, it was suggested that postal contact with the deported would be established within a short time.[2]

Despite all the promises, euphemisms, and obfuscations, Heinz had a reasonable inkling of what deportation meant. He didn't know the destination. The deportees had been told merely that they were needed for labor "in the Reich," and part of him, perhaps, would have wanted to believe that it was true, that they really were being sent for labor and that they would return. But in his heart, he would have suspected the worst. Like many Jews, he had heard the rumors. He would, no doubt, have already heard of Auschwitz, a place spoken of in whispers, a place from which no one ever seemed to return. To make matters worse, he knew that his family would follow him in due course, and that he would be unable to help or protect them anymore. So it was that Heinz hurried to the barrack block where his wife and children were housed to say his last goodbyes. He tried to put on a brave face, to convince his wife that all would be well and impress upon the children to be good and to take care of their mother. But when he got there, overwhelmed with the knowledge that he was being sent to meet his fate, he simply lay down on the bunk, held the children tight, and sobbed uncontrollably. His daughter, nine-year-old Ruth, had never seen her father cry.[3]

The following morning, Heinz duly appeared in the *Schleuse*, the courtyard outside the camp's "Hamburg" barrack, wearing his shabby coat with its yellow star and carrying his few permitted possessions. The *Schleuse*, according to one eyewitness, was "a di-abolical chaos," where those being prepared for deportation were thrown together, isolated from the rest of the camp for a day or two and surrounded by the remaining detritus of their lives—backpacks, suitcases, bedrolls, plates, and dishes—until they were ready to depart. The deportees would be registered and ticked off the list, their possessions checked through. They were required to hand over to the German guards their ghetto identity cards as well as any remaining ration coupons or other official papers. They were promised that new identity documents would be issued when they reached their destination.[4]

While they were waiting, the deportees had time to think—to curse their fate or to consider some way out. It was possible to appeal against one's deportation on grounds of health or incapacity. Trying to exploit networks of patronage, bribery, and influence might secure another few days of life in the familiar surroundings of the ghetto. Appeals were heard, in the first instance, by the soldiers who guarded the *Schleuse*. Thereafter, an appeal would be passed on to the Jewish administration of the camp—the euphemistically named Transport Management Department—and from there upward, perhaps, all the way to the camp commandant himself, *SS-Sturmbannführer* Karl Rahm, a thirty-seven-year-old Austrian with a quick temper and a penchant for violence. Rahm was often present at the deportations and could sometimes be receptive to a direct appeal. The risk was that, if he was not amenable, the applicant could be slapped and kicked and sent back into the *Schleuse* with only bruises to show for their efforts.[5]

It was during this time that one of Heinz's fellow prisoners reminded him that he still had the Paraguayan passport that he had sourced back in Holland. Heinz had always considered that the passport would be of little use; it hadn't saved him from being deported from Westerbork in the Netherlands to Theresienstadt, so why should it save him now? But, he reasoned, if there was a last opportunity to try to use it, it was today. Girding himself, he approached a nearby soldier. Braced for a spittle-flecked tirade, he reached into his coat pocket and pulled out the passport: a slightly crumpled facsimile of the original, headed with the words "Au Nom de la République de Paraguay" and bearing his portrait photograph and personal details, as well as those of his wife and children. After a brief read of the document and a suspicious glance at its bearer, the soldier took Heinz—and the passport—to a superior, who repeated the exercise.[6]

The record shows that a train left Theresienstadt that morning, bound for Auschwitz, with only 2,499 men aboard instead of the required 2,500. Most of them were gassed upon arrival. Heinz, however, was allowed to return to his barrack block and to his family, bearing a small slip of pink onionskin paper that showed his name, his camp number, and the word *ausgeschieden*— or "withdrawn." His Paraguayan passport had saved his life.[7]

Heinz Lichtenstern would never find out where that passport had come from. To the end of his life it was merely a curiosity, an incidental detail in the story of his miraculous survival. He would never know that it was part of a much wider operation—involving Polish diplomats, Jewish activists, couriers, and a compliant Swiss honorary consul—that would produce Latin American passports and identity documents for as many as ten thousand people in an attempt to save Jewish lives from the Holocaust. His was but a small part of a thoroughly remarkable story, one that has remained untold until now.[8]

1

EMPTY SYMPATHIES

THE HOTEL ROYAL WAS ONE OF THE GRANDEST IN EUROPE. It had been built in 1909, and the British King Edward VII—no stranger to luxury—had promised to be one of its first guests. It never hosted its would-be patron, who died the following year, but the royal title stuck. With its elegant balconied facade, manicured lawns, and parkland giving commanding views across Lake Geneva toward Lausanne, the hotel dominated the resort town of Évian-les-Bains and was an established address for Europe's wealthy elite.

In the hot, troubled summer of 1938, however, it was not the concerns of the rich that dominated the thoughts of the guests at Évian; it was the fate of some of the least fortunate: Europe's growing numbers of refugees, specifically the Jews of Germany, who were beginning to feel the full force of Nazi persecution. The spike in the number of Jews fleeing Hitler's "Greater Germany," which had followed the Anschluss with Austria earlier that year, had finally forced the outside world to take notice of their plight. Germany's Jews had been technically stateless since the promulgation of the Nuremberg Laws of September 1935, which had rendered Jews merely as "subjects" of the German state, with no citizenship rights. By 1938, around half of the German Jewish population had already fled—mainly to France, Holland, and Palestine—but when, following the annexation of Austria, an additional two hundred thousand Jews fell under Nazi rule, US president Franklin D. Roosevelt called a conference to discuss how the international community should respond to the crisis.

Gathered at Évian were representatives of some thirty-two nations, primarily from Europe and the Americas—including the United States, Britain, and France, as well as Mexico and Argentina—and observers from more than twenty voluntary organizations and international bodies such as the World Jewish Congress and the League of Nations. They were bureaucrats, diplomats, and ministers sent to discuss one of the most pressing issues of the day. Yet, they can scarcely have imagined how many individual fates would ultimately hinge upon their deliberations.

There were a few notable absences. Germany itself had not been invited. This was considered preferable, as the US secretary of state Cordell Hull put it, to having "to negotiate with a felon." Fascist Italy declined to attend, as did the Soviet Union, which did not see such "capitalist squabbling" as its responsibility. Other absentees included Poland and Romania, both of which already had large Jewish populations—and blemished reputations in their treatment of Jews—and so were considered unlikely to collaborate in easing the problem.[1]

Given the illustrious list of participants, one might have imagined that the conference was well-placed to seriously address the issue that had provoked its calling. Yet, there was a basic problem. For all the piety on display, none of the participant nations actually wanted to open their doors to Jewish refugees from Hitler's Germany. They were content to express sympathy for the plight of German Jews and to discuss what others should perhaps do to help, but they were fundamentally unwilling to do anything themselves.

The lead in this approach had been taken by Roosevelt. The US president's invitation to would-be participants had reassured them that no country would be expected to change its existing immigration regulations and no concrete action on behalf of the refugees was being proposed. Rather, the conference was foreseen merely as the start of a dialogue. Opening proceedings at 4 p.m. on July 6, the American representative—Myron Taylor, a bluff New York industrialist and friend of the president—set the tone for much that was to follow. He referred earnestly to the ongoing "migration problem," which, he acknowledged, was "increasing daily," exacerbated by the international economic slump. Yet, he refrained from either mentioning the Jews specifically or explaining why so many of them were so desperate to leave Germany. It was as if a general crisis of migration was afflicting Hitler's Third Reich and its cause could not be fathomed. Taylor then admitted that there was not much that could be done. "We must admit frankly," he said, "that this problem of political refugees is so vast and so complex" that all that was realistically possible for the meeting was to set in motion the long-term processes that might lead to its eventual amelioration. He closed by proudly announcing that the quota of German refugees that the United States would accept for that year would be 27,370. The inattentive delegates present might have imagined that that figure represented an increase over previous years. In truth, it was simply an amalgamation of the existing German and Austrian quotas.[2]

The American stance must have delighted the other delegates. If the United States, which had called the conference, could retreat behind empty platitudes and mendacity, so could they. Thus relieved of the requirement to actually do anything more than talk, the delegates lined up the following day to praise Roosevelt's humanitarian vision, to express their profoundest sympathies for the dreadful plight of the refugees, and to explain why their own specific circumstances made it impossible for them to allow any increase in Jewish immigration. Belgium, for instance, regretted that it already had a large number of refugees in its territory; the Netherlands, too, stated that it could admit refugees only in "exceptional cases." Sweden's representative, meanwhile, expressed his regrets that his homeland was "not a country of immigration" and declared hopefully that "if tangible and effective results are to be obtained," then "emigration must be so arranged that it is directed to countries outside Europe."[3]

This did not go down well among the representatives of those non-European countries present, all of which had excuses of their own for restricting Jewish immigration. The Ecuadorean representative protested that his was above all "an agricultural country," which had little use for urbanized laborers and intellectuals. The Peruvian and Uruguayan delegates agreed, suggesting that they would prefer to take in agricultural workers who could more easily be "assimilated into the . . . farming and stock-breeding communities." The Colombian representative echoed those desires and sought to place the onus of responsibility back on the European nations: "It is not enough to assert that France, the United Kingdom and the Netherlands have . . . already reached saturation point," he argued, when their colonial possessions offered so much more potential. "*Messieurs les francais, Messieurs les anglais, Messieurs les hollandaise*, it is for you to act first," he declared.[4]

Some representatives were rather more blunt. The Australian delegate, trade minister Sir Thomas White, stated unequivocally that non-British immigration was unwanted. The country had "no real racial problems," he explained, and was "not desirous" of importing them. The Swiss representative, Dr. Heinrich Rothmund, head of police at the Swiss Justice Department, made it clear that, despite Switzerland's comparative generosity in accepting Jewish immigration in previous years, Swiss resources were "not unlimited," and so the country would now be closing its doors.

Switzerland, Rothmund went on, would henceforth act solely as a "country of transit," providing only temporary residence to those actively preparing to depart to a permanent place of refuge. As a result, he said, it would be imposing "very stringent control" over further Jewish immigration.[5]

Amid the chorus of negativity at Évian, only one country offered what appeared to be an optimistic message. The Dominican Republic, represented by Virgilio Trujillo Molina—the brother of the nation's violent and corrupt dictator, Rafael Trujillo—made what posterity has often viewed as a startling offer, stating that his country, with its "large areas of fertile, well-irrigated land," would provide "specially advantageous concessions to Austrian and German exiles." But all was not as it seemed. Trujillo's offer was so hedged with conditions about applicants being of unimpeachable character and meeting certain legal stipulations that only a handful of immigrants would ever be admitted. It was essentially a publicity stunt, an attempt to garner some positive international headlines after the so-called Parsley Massacre of the previous year, in which some twenty thousand Haitians had been brutally killed by Dominican security forces.[6]

After the delegates had all had their say and the various subcommittees had met, discussed, and deliberated, the conference was brought to an end with a final plenary meeting on Friday, July 15. As chairman, Myron Taylor was the first to speak, praising the "spirit of cooperation" that he had perceived and urging that the work of the newly established Intergovernmental Committee on Refugees should continue "without interruption," so that the hopes of the desperate should not be dashed. According to British government records, Taylor had wanted to include a condemnation of Germany in his closing address, but he had been dissuaded from doing so by the British delegation, under instructions from the foreign secretary Viscount Halifax. Clearly it would not do to criticize the Germans directly.[7]

Taylor was followed by Lord Winterton, the British representative, who, after expressing his satisfaction with the "very encouraging outcome" of the meeting, surprised everyone by breaking his own instruction not to mention Palestine. For many of those present, especially those representing Zionist interest groups, Palestine appeared to be a natural solution to the problem being discussed, but Winterton had failed to mention the territory—under British mandate control—in his earlier statement because of explicit instructions from the Foreign Office. However, in his closing comments, he relented, acknowledging that "some quarters" believed that the issue of Jewish emigration "could be solved if only the gates of Palestine were thrown open to Jewish immigrants without restriction." It was a suggestion, he said, that was "wholly untenable," owing to the small size of the territory and the "prevailing conditions" there—a euphemism for the sizable Arab presence—which made large-scale Jewish immigration problematic.[8]

By way of compensation, Winterton announced an alternative possibility. The British colony of Kenya, he said, was under "active consideration" for the "small-scale settlement of Jewish refugees." What precise form that plan might take he was not yet in a position to say, but he stressed that any process of settlement must be a gradual one. There was to be "no question" of mass immigration. With that, he closed, praising the "harmonious conclusion" of proceedings.[9]

For those present at Évian, the conference appeared to have been broadly satisfactory. The problem of Jewish emigration had been aired and discussed, and a framework had been established to monitor it in the future. The delegates were satisfied: they had played golf, gambled in the casinos, and enjoyed a gala supper of sole meunière. Crucially, no country had been forced to act against its will, and the clamor of voices demanding that something must be done had been temporarily stilled. Moreover, with the establishment of the Intergovernmental Committee on

Refugees, a mechanism for the eventual alleviation of the suffering of German Jewry had been set up. Little wonder, perhaps, that Lord Winterton would laud the conference's anodyne resolutions as "a very encouraging outcome."[10]

Yet, for any Jews present at Évian or reading about the proceedings in the newspapers, it must have seemed like so much hot air. Though the representatives at the conference had wrung their hands and expressed their sympathies, they had done little more than provide excuses and squabble about who should make the most effort to accommodate Jewish refugees. It was all thoroughly unedifying. According to Golda Meir, the future prime minister of Israel who was present at Évian as an "observer from Palestine," the conference achieved nothing except words. She watched the proceedings with "a mixture of sorrow, rage, frustration and horror" and wanted to scream at the delegates, to remind them that the "numbers" and "quotas" that they referred to were human beings.[11]

The world's press broadly agreed with that negative assessment. *Time* magazine regretted that though "all nations present expressed sympathy" for the Jews, "few offered to allow them within their borders." William Shirer, the American CBS correspondent in Berlin, concurred, expressing his doubt that "much will be done" and lamenting that the British, French, and Americans were seemingly unwilling to offend Hitler. "It's an absurd situation," he noted in his diary. "They want to appease the man who is responsible for their problem."[12]

German newspapers, in contrast, had a field day, pointing out the hypocrisy of the democracies in criticizing German actions against people whom they were themselves unwilling to aid. The Nazi Party newspaper, the *Völkischer Beobachter*, carried the headline "No One Wants to Have Them," and the *Danziger Vorposten* even suggested that the conference at Évian had justified German policies against the Jews. Later that year, at the annual Nuremberg rally, Hitler lambasted the democratic world's failure to help the Jews: "No help," he mocked, "just moralizing."[13]

IT WOULD BE UNFAIR, OF COURSE, TO CRITICIZE THE DELE-gates at Évian too strongly. After all, they could not see the future; they could not have known what horrors history had in store for the unfortunates whose fates they had momentarily considered. Nonetheless, their empty sympathies did nothing to ease the situation, and it did not take long for what had become known as "the Jewish question" to return to center stage. The same month as the performative hand-wringing in Évian, the arrival of a new Nazi gauleiter in Vienna, Josef Bürckel—who publicly declared that the former Austrian capital was "overfilled with Jews"—sparked a renewed panic. In response, some Austrian Jews stormed the British legation, begging for visas, but British officials, though sympathetic, were very limited in their options. Since the Anschluss in March, Britain had tightened its rules regarding the issuing of visas to refugees, imposing a new visa requirement on Germans and Austrians and banning the issuing of temporary visas. Appeals to the Dominions were also largely fruitless. The Colonial Office in London was just as dismissive of the idea of Jewish emigration to Australia or India as the representatives at Évian had been, citing "climactic conditions," hostile native populations, or meager employment prospects. Palestine, too, was out of the question. As one British Secret Intelligence Service (SIS) agent would later recall: "There were very few chances of giving anybody a visa for Palestine in those days. It was all about trying to keep the numbers down."[14]

In response, some British officials in Vienna—led by the passport control officer (and SIS agent) Thomas Kendrick—decided to bend the rules. Embarking on a humanitarian mission, Kendrick employed a number of tricks to get the desperate out of Vienna: from simply issuing visas to those who did not meet the criteria to providing false baptismal certificates and even smuggling people out of the country in his diplomatic car. Among those Kendrick saved was a young George Weidenfeld, who would go on to found the Weidenfeld & Nicolson publishing house, as well as two brothers—Georg and Johann Schwarz—who, once in Britain, would change their surnames to Kendrick in recognition of their savior. It was estimated that Kendrick and his staff issued as many as two hundred identity documents per day that summer.[15]

Nonetheless, few would be so fortunate as to find an easy way out. One contemporary recalled Austrian Jews being illegally dumped over the frontier or living in small boats on the Danube, drifting from port to port, desperate to avoid official scrutiny. Meanwhile, the fate of the German steamship *Ariadne* demonstrated that, if anything, international attitudes toward Jewish refugees had already hardened. That summer, Finnish authorities put a temporary stop on visa applications after it was discovered that the Finnish embassy in Vienna had been issuing visas to Austrian Jews without due process. When on August 17 the *Ariadne* reached Helsinki with some fifty-three Austrian Jews on board, they were refused permission to disembark, despite some of them having the necessary paperwork for an onward passage to the United States. No exceptions were granted. A pregnant passenger was permitted to disembark in order to give birth in a Helsinki hospital, but she and her newborn child were returned to the ship as soon as was possible. When the *Ariadne* was then ordered to return to Germany, three of the passengers threw themselves overboard and drowned.[16]

The Swiss, too, were closing their doors, as Dr. Heinrich Rothmund had announced at Évian. That same month, in talks with the German legation in Bern, Rothmund declared that Switzerland had "as little use for these Jews as has Germany" and warned that his government would soon take measures to avoid being "swamped" by fleeing Austrian Jews. It is thought that Rothmund was one of the drivers behind the German decision, in October 1938, to invalidate the passports of German Jews, requiring that they be reissued with a red *J* stamped across the identity page and with the addition of the name "Sara" for women and "Israel" for men. The cruel logic was that this would make it easier to identify fugitive Jews at the frontiers. Rothmund had thereby made it significantly harder for German Jewry to escape Hitler's Reich. Little wonder, perhaps, that he would earn himself a reputation as an anti-Semite.[17]

Other countries followed suit. That same autumn, the Polish Ministry of the Interior—presumably anticipating an influx of the estimated seventy thousand Polish Jews then living in Germany—decreed that, henceforth, restrictions would be placed on the automatic right of return of Polish citizens living abroad. In response, a few days before the decree was to come into effect, the German police launched a long-prepared operation to deport Polish Jews, some twelve thousand of whom were systematically arrested all over Germany, taken to collection centers, and then transported in sealed trains to the Polish frontier. Reluctant to allow them to enter, the Polish border authorities directed them to an unused barracks at Zbąszyń, where they would linger in a legal no-man's-land until their fate was decided. One Red Cross nurse recalled thousands of refugees living in desperate circumstances, "crowded together in pigsties . . . the old, the sick and children herded together in the most inhuman conditions." Some, she said, even tried to escape back into Germany.[18]

One of the families thus affected was that of seventeen-year-old Herschel Grynszpan, who was living illegally in Paris at the time but heard news of his family's tribulations via a postcard he received in early November. Frustrated and desperate, he tried in vain to send money but was stymied by an intransigent uncle. He then decided to avenge himself on the cause of his distress. He bought a revolver and a box of bullets, went to the German embassy on the Rue de Lille, and asked to see an official. Ushered into the office of legation secretary Ernst vom Rath, he pulled out the gun and—with a cry of "*Sale Boche!*"—opened fire, hitting Rath twice in the abdomen, fatally injuring him. He then sat down and calmly waited to be apprehended. In his pocket was a postcard, addressed to his parents, in which he asked for forgiveness and declared that "the whole world" should hear of their suffering.[19]

What the whole world heard, however, was Nazi outrage. In the two days that it took Rath to die from a ruptured pancreas, German propagandists ramped up the hyperbole. In this they were aided by the fact that Rath died on November 9, the most darkly symbolic day in German history: the anniversary of the collapse of the German empire in 1918 and of Hitler's failed Beer Hall Putsch of 1923, when fifteen Nazi putschists (and an unfortunate waiter) had been gunned down by the Bavarian police. Consequently, it was easy for Propaganda Minister Joseph Goebbels to depict Rath as yet another Nazi martyr, a victim of Jewish perfidy. His diary entry on the subject dripped with cynicism: "In the afternoon the death of the German diplomat Rath is announced. That's good." Rath's death would be exploited to whip up a popular fury against the Jews and ramp up the anti-Semitic persecution. Within hours, a brutal pogrom was launched, targeting German Jews, Jewish-owned businesses, and synagogues, which, though intended to appear spontaneous, was minutely orchestrated by the Brownshirts of the *Sturmabteilung* (SA) and Heinrich Himmler's praetorian guard, the *Schützstaffeln* (SS).[20]

The result was the *Kristallnacht* (the Night of Broken Glass), an orgy of organized violence in which Jewish shops were looted, synagogues were burned out, and, as one British report noted, "half-drunk mobs armed with crow bars and bricks began window smashing . . . mishandling Jews and placarding shops with handbills." Nearly three hundred synagogues across Germany were destroyed, Jewish cemeteries and prayer houses were desecrated, and over seven thousand Jewish businesses were ransacked. In addition, some thirty thousand Jewish men were arrested and sent to the concentration camps and at least ninety-one people were killed.[21]

In the months that followed, Jewish emigration from Germany soared, with as many as one hundred thousand Jews—a fifth of the pre-1933 total—seeking to leave the country. But the same difficulties and restrictions that were in evidence at Évian still applied, and many of the emigrants struggled to find a country that would accept them. Some of them were assisted in their flight by the Chinese consul general in Vienna, Ho Feng-Shan, who distributed visas for Shanghai to anyone who wanted one, despite the protests of his superiors. Though the validity of the documents was highly dubious—not only because Shanghai did not require visas but also because it was then under Japanese occupation, so beyond the consul general's remit—they at least enabled would-be emigrants to provide a plausible end destination, thus easing their applications for exit and transit visas. Though many Austrian Jews exploited this ruse to escape beyond China to the United States or the Philippines, some fifteen thousand would ultimately find refuge in Shanghai itself. Among the latter was Eric Goldstaub, a seventeen-year-old Viennese Jew who had been turned away from countless consulates in 1938 before finding his way to Ho Feng-Shan, who gave him twenty visas for him and his extended family.[22]

Most Austrian Jews sought out the traditional, legal routes, which meant lengthy applications and months of waiting as part of the quotas permitted for entry into the United States and elsewhere. Even then, however, there were difficulties. As one refugee recalled:

> I needed permission to leave Austria. For this I had to provide evidence that I was a Jew, that I was a legal resident in Vienna and had no criminal record. I had to obtain proof that I did not owe any taxes and was not liable for military service. For each of these documents I had to queue at least three times at the competent authority, first to obtain the application form, then to submit it duly filled in and finally collecting the approved document—if it were ready. At each office, I was one of hundreds standing for hours in kilometre-long queues.[23]

For some, the bureaucratic procedures required were positively Kafkaesque. Twenty-three-year-old Eric Lucas left his home in Aachen soon after *Kristallnacht* and came to Britain, where he tried to find a way to bring his parents to safety. In the spring of 1939, he was still scouring London's embassies to find somewhere that was willing to give them a visa. As he recalled in his later memoir, it was a trying business. Lacking passports, his parents were unable to apply for foreign visas, yet the German authorities insisted that they could only apply for a passport if they already had a visa. Hope, Lucas wrote, slowly faded. He would never see his parents again.[24]

Understandably, some sought to game the system. In May 1939, the liner *St. Louis* set sail from Hamburg bound for Cuba, carrying nearly a thousand passengers, most of them German Jews. In their desperation to leave Hitler's Germany, most of those aboard had taken US immigration quota numbers for 1940 or 1941 and intended to spend the intervening time in Cuba, for which purpose they had purchased landing permits from the Cuban embassy in Berlin. Crossing the Atlantic and enjoying the luxuries that the *St. Louis* had to offer, they were blissfully unaware that the Cuban government, fearful of a Jewish influx, had issued a new decree that effectively nullified their permits. Only when the *St. Louis* was prevented from docking in the harbor at Havana on the morning of May 27 did the grim reality of their predicament begin to dawn. The mood on board, one of the refugees recalled, "was one of desperation."[25]

What followed was an ignoble squabble, in which the Cuban government stubbornly resisted efforts by the Americans and others to persuade them to do what they themselves would not countenance: let the refugees in. An appeal from the passengers to President Roosevelt went unanswered. Argentina, Paraguay, Brazil, Colombia, Uruguay, and Chile all refused to step in. The Canadians were no more accommodating; their minister of justice stated that he was "emphatically opposed" to allowing any of the refugees entry. Even an offer by a Jewish aid agency to pay the Cuban government half a million dollars to allow the passengers to disembark was rejected.[26]

The *St. Louis*, meanwhile, steamed up and down the Florida coast, shadowed by US Coast Guard vessels. The passengers were within sight of the safety of the shoreline yet increasingly despairing that they would ever be permitted to set foot upon it. Finally, on June 7, following an unequivocal refusal from the US State Department to allow the passengers to disembark, the *St. Louis* turned for home. In a deal brokered by the American Jewish Joint Distribution Committee, the vessel would dock at Antwerp and its unfortunate passengers would be shared between France, Holland, Belgium, and the United Kingdom. Many of them would not survive the Holocaust.[27]

IT IS EASY TO BE CRITICAL OF THOSE WHO REFUSED TO assist Jewish refugees in the prewar years. With the benefit of hindsight, their actions appear heartless and cruel, an expression of the same prejudicial impulses that lay at the root of the crisis. It cannot be denied, for instance, that there was a degree of anti-Jewish sentiment behind the refusals—latent perhaps, and certainly not of the virulent strain espoused by the Nazi regime, but anti-Semitism nonetheless. Jews were seen all too often as undesirable, potentially disruptive elements, ideally someone else's problem.

It is certainly true that anti-Semitism was not just a German disease. In the maelstrom of its fraught post-1918 politics, and under the tutelage of the Nazis, Germany had certainly plumbed new depths of the oldest prejudice and had metastasized it with murderous intent and a malevolent veneer of pseudoscience. But it is important to note that anti-Semitism was, in some form at least, almost universal. Historically, anti-Jewish prejudice was a constant, motivated variously and serially by religious doctrine, xenophobia, fear of economic competition, and exclusive ideas of nationalism.

From the late nineteenth century, the competing pressures of migration and growing national sentiment spurred a renewed spike, with anti-Semitism emerging not only as a constant feature of right-wing—and especially radical right-wing—thought, but also as a prejudice that enjoyed a degree of social respectability, especially among the elites.

Central Europe was grievously afflicted. Indeed, given that Poland and Hungary contained some of the largest per capita Jewish populations, it was perhaps inevitable that tensions there would be heightened. Both countries saw widespread popular anti-Semitism, which was legitimized by prominent nationalist politicians such as Gyula Gömbös, Hungarian prime minister from 1932 until his death in 1936, and Roman Dmowski, leader of the Polish National Democratic Party who was a prominent advocate of Jewish emigration from Poland. Though neither country espoused the sort of exterminatory racism that would soon become state policy in Hitler's Germany, both would practice sporadic official discrimination in the 1920s and '30s, most obviously in the form of a numerus clausus, which limited Jewish access to higher education.[28]

Western societies were often little better. In France, the Dreyfus Case of the 1890s became a salient example of the seismic social and political effects that such tensions could generate. By the 1930s, the rise of Action Française, whose virulent brand of nationalism and anti-communism contained many overtly anti-Semitic sentiments, showed that those tensions were far from quelled. Indeed, in 1936, France's Jewish socialist leader Leon Blum would be dragged from his car and almost beaten to death by members of an Action Française splinter group.

Britain, too, had seen popular anti-Semitism rise alongside Jewish immigration over the preceding decades, culminating in the emergence of Oswald Mosley's British Union of Fascists. For those who eschewed the overt thuggery of Mosley, there was the more genteel prejudice of the pro-German groups The Link or the Right Club, which advocated an end to "Jewish control" and numbered the Duke of Westminster and William Joyce—the later "Lord Haw-Haw"—among its supporters. Neither was the United States immune to infection. There, the lynching in 1915 of a Jewish man, Leo Frank, who had been convicted of murder was both an expression of and a spur to a growing anti-Semitic sentiment. This bigotry would find its voice not only through the revived Ku Klux Klan and the overtly pro-Nazi German American Bund but also via the more "polite" prejudice of the restrictions placed on Jewish admissions to the country's senior universities.

Yet, there was more to the collective reluctance to help Jewish refugees than just anti-Semitism; economic and social concerns also played a part. Given that German emigration policy forbade departing Jews from taking any wealth they had with them, the vast majority of those who were able to leave would have little to their names, making them much less attractive to their would-be hosts. Unsurprisingly, hardheaded realpolitik calculated that the expected burdens on sometimes fragile economies and societies made large-scale immigration of impoverished Jews undesirable.

In addition, there was a political imperative, a concern that aiding Jewish emigration from Germany could be perceived as assisting the Nazi regime in carrying out its nefarious plans. Up until 1938, Nazi policy had broadly been to "encourage" Jewish emigration through harassment, marginalization, petty persecution, and policies aimed simply at denying Jews a livelihood. In this way, the Nazi regime expected, with some justification, that Germany's Jewish population would leave of its own accord. In some instances, the link was made very explicit: when Jews were sent to the concentration camps in the aftermath of *Kristall-nacht*, for instance, they were told that they would be released if they started emigration proceedings. In such circumstances, it is perhaps easy to see how the delegates at Évian or the Cuban officials dealing with the *St. Louis* might have concluded that facilitating that emigration, however justified it might have been on humanitarian grounds, was essentially doing the Nazis' dirty work for them.[29]

Of course, those dealing with the thorny question of Jewish emigration in 1938 and 1939 could not have imagined that Hitler's Germany would soon seek to exterminate European Jewry. They did not know what horrors were coming. Nonetheless, in the months and years that were to follow, these diplomats and bureaucrats would be tested anew. The vast majority of them would be found wanting.

2

THE BLOOD-SOAKED EARTH

By THE MIDDLE OF SEPTEMBER 1939, THE PEOPLE OF Przemyśl were nervous. The handsome old city, on the banks of the river San in southern Poland, was no stranger to hardship. In its long history, it had weathered storms of Mongols, Ruthenes, Hungarians, and warlike Swedes, and during the First World War it had endured one of the most brutal sieges of the time before falling to Russian forces, with over one hundred thousand casualties. Nonetheless, the new threat it faced must have seemed especially worrisome.

At first, the German invasion of Poland, which had begun at dawn on September 1, would have appeared rather distant; after all, Przemyśl lay more than 250 kilometers (155 miles) to the east of the German frontier. However, the Wehrmacht advance was so swift and Luftwaffe air attacks so far-reaching that the distance was quickly bridged. Already on September 8, the city was bombed by the Germans for the first time, causing widespread damage and spurring a partial evacuation of the civilian administration. By that time, refugees fleeing the invasion further west were already streaming into the city, bringing with them horrific stories of the race war that the Wehrmacht had brought, telling

of the casual brutality and wanton killings of civilians and prisoners of war alike. They would have spoken, perhaps, of the events
at Częstochowa the week before, where as many as one hundred
Jews were massacred, purportedly in retaliation for the killing of
three German officers in an ambush outside the city, or of what
had happened at Wołoskowola, where two hundred Jews were
forced into a school building, which was then set alight. Hearing
these bloody stories, Przemyśl's twenty thousand Jews, fully one-
third of the population, must have wondered darkly what would
become of them.[1]

Any hope that they might be spared similar treatment was
quashed when German forces finally entered the city on September 15. The persecution of Przemyśl's Jewish population began
immediately—ranging from casual violence to the public humiliation of cutting the beards or ringlets of the Orthodox—as had
become routine over the previous two weeks of conflict. In time,
the soldiers returned with more venal motives, ransacking Jewish
businesses and homes before loading their loot onto Wehrmacht
trucks and carrying it away.[2]

Things soon got worse. Over the following few days, the
Germans began rounding up Jews, particularly members of the
intelligentsia, such as doctors, lawyers, and teachers. Eight units
of *Einsatzgruppen*—task forces of SS and policemen charged with
"pacifying" the areas behind the front line—had followed German
forces into Poland and had cut a bloody swath through Polish
society, targeting those who were considered politically or racially
damaging to German interests. In Poland's far south, it was units
of *Einsatzgruppe I* that had followed on the heels of the Fourteenth Army and now arrived in the area of Przemyśl. They had
already committed a number of atrocities on their way east, not
only to fulfill their supposed remit of "combating Polish banditry"
but also to carry out a de facto ethnic cleansing, creating such
terror that their imminent arrival would often spur Polish Jews to
flee eastward.[3]

Przemyśl, earmarked as being on the new frontier between the German and Soviet zones of occupation, was the culmination of their murderous rampage. The Jews of the city were rounded up piecemeal, some on the pretense of being required for a work detail, others simply picked up off the street. Some of them were then forced to perform gymnastics in the open, publicly tormented by their captors before being marched at gunpoint toward the city's outlying villages. One eyewitness recalled seeing a group of around one hundred Jews being forced to run along the road. Stripped half naked, with their hands tied behind their backs, they were forced to chant "Jews are pigs!" by their accompanying guards. When one of them fell, he would be pistol-whipped or kicked until he got back to his feet. The men's faces, the witness recalled, were "distorted with pain," while Polish bystanders crossed themselves in terror.[4]

One group of Jews was force marched to the cemetery in the village of Pikulice. Before the Jews could realize their predicament, a heavy machine gun was unveiled, which quickly opened fire, sweeping back and forth, unleashing what an eyewitness described as "a scene from Dante's hell." As German officers walked among the dead and dying, delivering the coup de grâce to those still breathing, another batch of unfortunates was brought to the site and dispatched in the same way, then another, then another. "All the men driven through the streets in the morning lay there, dead," the witness recalled.

The corpses were lying on their backs or sides in the most contorted positions, some on top of others, with their arms outstretched, their heads shattered by the bullets. Here were pools of blood; there the earth was rust coloured with blood; the grass glistened with blood; blood was drying on the corpses. Women with bloodied hands were hunting through the pile of bodies for their fathers, husbands, sons. A sickish sweet smell pervaded the air.[5]

It is thought that as many as six hundred Jews were murdered in the villages around Przemyśl over three days, making it the largest single massacre of Jews during the September campaign of 1939. The victims were buried in three mass graves that were each 200 meters (656 feet) long.[6]

To some extent, the Przemyśl massacre conformed to the pattern that had already been set during the campaign. It is notable that the war diary of the commander of the German Fourteenth Army, under whose control the city fell, reported such attacks against the civilian population only as "lapses in discipline." In fact, since the very first day of the German invasion, Polish Jews and Gentiles alike had been treated with exceptional, wanton cruelty by the Germans, targeted for executions, reprisals, rapes, and atrocities. Indeed, it has been estimated that, during the five-week military campaign alone, the Germans carried out more than six hundred massacres against Polish POWs and civilian populations.[7]

But while a brutal pattern had already been established, the action at Przemyśl nonetheless marked a definite departure and an escalation of violence. For this was no reprisal, no collective punishment for German lives lost in combat—however disingenuous that excuse might have been. Neither could it be explained by the weasel phrase "fog of war," its victims thereby dismissed as so much collateral damage from the exigencies of the wider conflict. Rather, the massacre at Przemyśl marked a malignant novelty; it represented the systematic slaughter of an entire community, which the perpetrators considered to be less than entirely human. It was a dark portent of even darker days to come.

SUCH HORRORS WOULD CONTINUE BEYOND THE END OF formal hostilities, which occurred with the surrender of Polish forces at the Battle of Kock on October 6. A week earlier, German and Soviet representatives had met in Moscow to divide up the spoils. The resulting Boundary and Friendship Treaty of

September 28, 1939, drew a line of partition between the German and Soviet areas of occupation, which neatly split Poland between them. On the German side of the line, the former Polish lands were divided into two parts: the northern and western districts were annexed directly to the Reich, while the southern and central areas were established as a nominally separate entity—the so-called General Government. The latter, which included both Warsaw and Kraków, was entirely dependent on the whim of Berlin and was run by Hitler's confidante and former lawyer Hans Frank, who would rule his fiefdom with an iron hand.

Life for Jews and Poles in the two German-occupied areas was hard. Both were relegated to the lowest ranks of society, where they were reduced to the status of a despised underclass, fit for little else but exploitation and persecution. Yet, while Poles were treated as racially inferior by the Germans, Jews were seen as barely human at all, regarded, essentially, as vermin. Subjected to myriad new regulations introduced by the Germans, Jews were required to wear an armband with the Star of David on the right arm and were forbidden to travel by train, hold large denominations of cash, collect rent, or manage their own real estate. Jewish bank accounts were frozen. Their businesses were "Aryanized," subjected to a forced sale to a non-Jewish purchaser at less than market value. Their property was subject to confiscation, looting, and, as often as not, daylight robbery. "Every day our apartment is visited by German soldiers who, under various pretexts, rob us of our possessions," the schoolgirl Mary Berg noted in her diary. On the streets, Jews were forced to step off the pavement to make space for Germans or risk being beaten up. The young, especially young women, lived in constant fear of being kidnapped and abused. Elderly Jews, meanwhile, were routinely forced to shave off their beards, and rabbis were ordered to sweep the streets. As one diarist wrote: "The days passed, filled with persecution, humiliation and hideous torments. No one felt safe day or night."[8]

Unsurprisingly, the weeks after the close of hostilities saw huge swaths of the Polish population on the move in search of safety. Many Jews, particularly those in the areas that had been annexed directly to the Reich, fled across the new Soviet frontier in the hope that life in the Soviet zone would be better than in the German-occupied area. It could be a perilous journey. In one example, a group of fugitive Jews was handed over to German troops by their guide while they were en route to the Soviet frontier. They were lined up against a wall and numbered one to eleven. The soldiers then shot all of those who had been given odd numbers. "My mother and I had even numbers . . . and we were let go," recalled one survivor.[9]

Elsewhere, the Germans actively "assisted" the refugees in their flight, deporting Jewish communities en masse—including the entire Jewish populations of the towns of Pułtusk and Łańcut—to the Soviet zone. As one eyewitness noted, such deportations were carried out with extreme brutality.

> We arrived at the river San on the third day of our exile. What happened there is difficult to describe. On the bank of the river, Gestapo-men were waiting and driving people into a boat, or rather a raft of two unbalanced boards, from which women and children fell into the river. We saw floating corpses everywhere; near the bank women stood in the water, holding their children above their heads and crying for help, to which the Gestapo-men answered by shooting.[10]

Those who reached the border found that their tribulations were only just beginning. For their part, the Soviets could be wholly unsympathetic, and their border guards were under orders to turn back all those—the vast majority—who did not possess the correct paperwork. In one instance, a standoff ensued when Soviet troops attempted to force a group of one thousand Jewish refugees back across the border. The official comment on the incident from Berlin tartly summarized that "the expulsion of the Jews did not proceed as smoothly as had been expected." Even those who made it across the frontier risked a lengthy interrogation if they were caught by the Soviet secret police, the NKVD. This was the fate of the Dreksler family that autumn. Polish Jews from Wierzbnik, near Radom, they had entered the Soviet zone without being apprehended but were stopped in Łuck (now Lutsk, Ukraine), where they were asked to fill out a questionnaire, including the question of where they ultimately intended to settle. Their answer of Palestine so irritated their interrogating officer that he sent the family to a work camp at Archangel in the Soviet far north. For them, as for so many others, it was the beginning of a long and bloody odyssey.[11]

At the same time, the Germans carried out mass deportations of Jews from the annexed areas of northern and western Poland into the General Government, which was regarded by its masters in Berlin as something of a racial dumping ground. One notable destination was Nisko, 200 kilometers (124 miles) southeast of Warsaw on the river San, a rural area of around 1,000 square kilometers (386 square miles) that had been conceived by SS chief Heinrich Himmler and his deputy Reinhard Heydrich as a Jewish "reservation" into which those unwanted populations could be expelled. Already in the winter of 1939–1940 Nisko was home to tens of thousands of Jews from Pomerania, Moravia, and Vienna, all of whom had been sent there by zealous local Nazi officials who were keen to curry favor with their superiors by making their fiefdoms *judenrein*, "free of Jews." Polish Jews arriving at Nisko that winter described a place of utter desolation, with no infrastructure, insufficient accommodation, and little protection from the elements. Welcoming the refugees, Adolf Eichmann, the SS officer in charge of the resettlement operation, did little to ease their misgivings: "There are no apartments and no houses. If you build your homes you will have a roof over your head. There is no water. The wells throughout the region are poisoned: cholera, dysentery and typhus prevail. If you start digging wells, you will have water." In total, nearly one hundred thousand Jews were transported to the Nisko "reservation." What they experienced there over the following months would be little more than extermination by neglect.[12]

Yet, for all these horrors, it was non-Jewish Poles, who, initially at least, came to feel the brutal nature of German rule most keenly, with murders of Christian Poles outnumbering those of their Jewish compatriots in those opening months by four to one, as casual violence swiftly became commonplace. The American vice-consul in Warsaw, Thaddeus Chylinski, kept a record of the sufferings of the Polish people. The "bloody reign" of the Gestapo, he recalled, began in mid-October 1939, with a "high-pressure terror campaign" to remove the leadership of the nation and beat the remainder into submission. "There appears to be no logical explanation for the arrests," he wrote in his later report. "Roundups, executions, confiscation of property and homes, as well as humiliations in various forms, kept the population in a state of fear and mental torture." One of the earliest victims of the German occupation was Elżbieta Zahorska, a twenty-four-year-old Warsaw University student who was executed by firing squad in early November 1939 for tearing down propaganda posters that blamed Britain for Poland's predicament. Refusing a blindfold, she wanted to look her killers in the eye.[13]

It was effectively open season on Polish civilians. This fact was demonstrated most vividly at Wawer, near Warsaw, at Christmas 1939. On the evening of December 26, two German officers were shot and killed in a bar in the town while trying to arrest two local petty criminals, Marian Prasuła and Stanisław Dąbek. After the assailants made their escape, the German authorities decided on a "pacification action," rounding up more than one hundred men from Wawer and the neighboring suburb of Anin, who were dragged from their homes or picked up on the streets and brought to the office of the local German military commander, where they were arraigned before a kangaroo court. The judges did not seek to ascertain the circumstances of the crime; Prasuła and Dąbek were already known to them. Rather, they merely asked the names and ages of the men, confirmed that they were Polish, and confiscated and destroyed their papers. The prisoners were then made to line up in the snow, where they had to endure not only the cold but also the kicks and abuse of the German soldiers. At around five o'clock the following morning, a Wehrmacht major delivered the verdict of the "investigation": to prevent any recurrence of the crime, those detained were to be executed, although in a gesture of clemency every tenth man would be spared. With that, the men were led in batches of a dozen to the town square, where they were lined up and machine-gunned. In total, 114 men were murdered; the youngest of them was only fifteen. In addition, Antoni Bartoszek—the proprietor of the bar where the German officers had been killed, who had called on the gendarmerie for assistance—was hanged above the front door of his property, *pour encourager les autres*. It was a brutal application of the principle of collective responsibility. As one of the German officers was heard to explain: "Polish people killed them. Polish people will answer for it."[14]

In addition to such brutal repressions and reprisals, all of those considered in any way inimical to Berlin's interests—landowners, politicians, lawyers, judges, priests, teachers, and doctors—were targeted. As Hans Frank confided to his lieutenants, the Polish elite was to be "liquidated," on the order of Hitler himself, so that the Polish nation would not reemerge. The result was a series of "actions" in which intellectuals and prominent individuals—many of them listed in the *Sonderfahndungsbuch*, a "special investigation book" produced by the Gestapo headquarters in Berlin—were rounded up, incarcerated, and then disappeared.[15]

There were some infamous examples. The academic staff of the Jagiellonian University in Kraków was called to a meeting with the new Gestapo chief in the city, *SS-Obersturmbannführer*

Bruno Müller, in early November 1939, supposedly to discuss the German plans for higher education. When they arrived, the doors of the hall were locked behind them and they were told that, as a source of anti-German attitudes, they were to be arrested forthwith. In all, 172 professors and fellows from one of the oldest and most prestigious universities in central Europe were sent to the Sachsenhausen concentration camp, where many of them would perish.[16]

Perversely, a spell in a concentration camp would have been perceived as a merciful sentence by the majority of the Polish victims of such actions. Most of them were simply shot out of hand by their German captors, in forests, town squares, or prison courtyards. Executions in the woods at Palmiry, to the northwest of Warsaw, for instance, began that December and would continue into the summer of 1941, with victims brought to the site in trucks, blindfolded, and then led into the forest to face their end amid the freshly dug pits. Most prominent among the estimated 1,700 Poles and Jews murdered at Palmiry were the former speaker of the Polish parliament and deputy president Maciej Rataj and the athlete Janusz Kusociński, who had won a gold medal at the Los Angeles Olympics in 1932. Both of them were murdered in June 1940. In total, it has been estimated that German efforts to exterminate the Polish elites in 1939 and 1940—known collectively as the *Intelligenzaktion*—would account for some hundred thousand lives.[17]

While both Poles and Jews found themselves victims of the Germans' targeted executions, as well as their random reprisal actions, Jews had to contend with the additional peril of being confined to ghettos. In fact, the ghettoization policy was itself an expression of failure. The Nisko "reservation" and the wild local deportations that had accompanied it had scarcely resolved the Jewish "problem." They had merely created a deadly chaos on the territorial fringes of the General Government while demonstrating that further large-scale deportations were—for the time being at least—impractical. Ghettoization, then, represented a temporary solution to a self-inflicted problem. Based upon an order from Reinhard Heydrich of September 21, 1939, the policy was simple: Jews were to be concentrated in sealed districts of the major towns and cities, so that they could be better exploited economically in the short term and then more easily deported when a decision about their fate was made. Accordingly, the first ghetto was established in Piotrków Trybunalski, south of Łódź, late in 1939, with Jews being forced into it in January 1940. Eventually, that ghetto would contain some twenty-eight thousand souls. The only Jews of the city who were legally permitted to remain outside the ghetto were the family of one Jakub Witorz, who had Turkish citizenship, and that of an Egyptian named Kem. Even at this early stage of the German persecution of the Jews, it was clear that possession of a foreign passport could be a lifesaver.[18]

Through 1940 and beyond, nearly three hundred ghettos were set up across occupied Poland. Among the most significant were those in Łódź, Warsaw, Będzin, Kraków, and Lublin. The establishment of the Łódź ghetto was decreed on February 8, 1940, with German inhabitants ordered to vacate the area designated for Jewish settlement and Jews ordered to move in. Boundaries were delineated and barriers built. A Jewish Council was established under an "elder"—sixty-two-year-old former insurance salesman Chaim Rumkowski—to deal with health, finance, housing, and registration. The provision of food was expected to be paid for by the surrender and sale of the valuables that the Germans assumed the Jews would take with them, although only a fraction of the foodstuffs required would ever be delivered.

Mary Berg recalled hearing about the creation of the Łódź ghetto from a friend, who described it as "a massacre." Jews had been ordered to assemble with only fifty pounds of luggage, she reported in her diary, while extensive house searches were conducted in which the sick were dragged from their beds and those discovered to be hiding were chased out into the street and shot.

For those who opted to comply with the order, the day was scarcely easier. "The quarter of Łódź which has been turned into the ghetto," Berg wrote, "is one of the poorest and oldest sections of the city; it is composed mostly of small wooden houses without electricity or plumbing. . . . It has room for only a few tens of thousands, but the Germans have crowded three hundred thousand Jews into it."[19]

This would be the dark reality for the vast majority of Polish Jews. Consigned to the filthiest and most inhospitable areas, in overcrowded accommodation, with insufficient supplies of food, and at the whim of their new German masters, they hoped for the best and awaited their fate.

THE DEPREDATIONS OF HITLER'S WEHRMACHT AND SS IN Poland in 1939 were not the only hardship and terror that the Polish people had to endure that winter. Stalin's Soviet Union—Hitler's ally in all but name—also played a nefarious role. Invading Poland from the east at dawn on September 17, more than a fortnight after the German attack, the Red Army had hoped to avoid the opprobrium provoked by Hitler's invasion by casting their action as a humanitarian intervention, claiming that they were bringing "protection" to the Belarusian and Ukrainian minorities imperiled by the supposedly imminent collapse of the Polish state. Despite the propagandistic gloss, however, the Red Army's invasion differed little from its German counterpart, with some five hundred thousand combat troops supported by nearly five thousand tanks, five thousand armored vehicles, and two thousand aircraft advancing with the express instruction to destroy Polish forces in a "lightning strike." Polish border guards and reserves, already reeling from the German invasion in the west and lacking the wherewithal to resist a full-scale Red Army invasion, generally fell back in confusion, with individual units fighting a brave but futile rearguard action.[20]

After the military confrontation had come to an end and formal Polish resistance had been quelled, the Soviets began reshaping society in their zone of occupation. At first, it was hoped that a spontaneous "revolutionary justice" would prevail, and Red Army officers made impromptu speeches to the ordinary population, imploring them to rise up against their class oppressors. Hastily formed "red militias," often composed of released criminals, channeled popular discontent in the direction of the Polish state, the landlords, the nobility, and the church. Countless properties were duly ransacked, and any officials or noblemen who got in the way ran the risk of being lynched. In one instance, a local landowner was tied to a post and two strips of skin were cut from his body. His wounds were then dressed with salt and he was made to watch while his family was executed.[21]

Following this settling of scores, the Soviet administration embarked on a spurious exercise in democracy. A month after the Red Army's invasion, rigged elections were held, with compulsory voting and a closed list of candidates, for new "National Assemblies" in the two annexed territories, which were now designated Western Belarus and Western Ukraine. The rationale behind the elections was quite simple: they were an attempt to adorn the Soviet conquest and occupation of eastern Poland with the illusion of democratic legitimacy, thereby giving foreign communists and fellow travelers something to defend in the face of any public scrutiny. More than that, the Soviets were working from the Kremlin psyops playbook, forcing subject populations to vote in blatantly rigged elections as a method of demoralizing them, ensuring their complicity, and undermining potential resistance. With those political and psychological goals achieved, the new assemblies duly petitioned the Supreme Soviet in Moscow with the request that they be permitted to join the Soviet Union, which—of course—was granted. The two regions were then annexed to the existing Soviet republics of Ukraine and Belarus, respectively, and the newly elected "National Assemblies" promptly dissolved themselves, their territories seamlessly absorbed into the USSR.

At the same time, a wave of arrests targeted the remaining class enemies, as well as all those who might obstruct the imposition of Soviet rule or be deemed in any way anti-Soviet. The net was thrown very wide, encompassing political opponents, aristocrats, businessmen, and intellectuals, as well as representatives of the old Polish administration—from army officers and policemen to border guards and foresters. The reasons given for their arrest varied enormously, ranging from petty crime to anti-Soviet conspiracy. Most, however, were not even told why they were detained. To the Soviet mind, it was clear that class, profession, or background alone made them a legitimate target for repression.

Many of those arrested were destined to languish in jail, but the Soviet authorities also made liberal use of the traditional practice of deportation, sending countless thousands, including whole families, to an uncertain fate in the less-hospitable regions of the Soviet Union, predominantly Kazakhstan and the depths of Siberia. Roused in the early morning by Soviet soldiers, deportees were usually given just minutes to pack their essentials before being taken to the railheads and the waiting cattle wagons. Conditions on the trains were horrific; each one was supplied with only a small stove and a hole in the floorboards to serve as a latrine. One deportee recalled that no food or water was provided for the entire journey east, which could last weeks, although buckets of snow were handed to the deportees, which they would melt on the stove to sustain themselves. At each stop along the way, the dead were unloaded—mainly the old and the very young—to be stacked alongside the tracks.[22]

It is estimated that as many as one million former Polish citizens were deported east by the Soviets in 1939 and 1940. And, given that the criteria for repression and deportation were strictly class-political, Polish Jews were not exempt. Indeed, the third large-scale deportation from eastern Poland, which took place in June 1940, is thought to have been composed of around 60 percent Polish Jews. Their crime, for the most part, was to have applied to leave the Soviet zone of occupation.[23]

A few months earlier, in the spring of 1940, in a striking example of German-Soviet collaboration, a Gestapo commission had begun touring the Soviet zone, collecting applications from those who wished to settle in German-occupied areas, including ethnic Germans, Polish refugees seeking to return home, and—perhaps surprisingly—Polish Jews who, having fled east at the outbreak of war and tasted life in the Soviet Union, preferred to take their chances on the German side of the new frontier. Nikita Khrushchev, who would later become the Soviet leader after the death of Stalin, described in his memoir the "long lines" outside the repatriation commission. "When I looked closer," he wrote, "I was shocked to see that most of the people in line were members of the Jewish population. They were bribing the Gestapo agents to let them leave as soon as possible to return to their original homes." German officials were no less incredulous and were naturally unwilling to grant Jews the right of return at a time when the Nazi regime was just beginning to grapple with the "Jewish problem." On one occasion, an astonished German officer turned to the assembled throng. "Jews! Where are you going?" he asked. "Don't you realize that we will kill you?" Their applications duly rejected by the Germans, such unfortunates would be handed back to the NKVD and branded as "anti-Soviet elements." They would soon be earmarked for deportation to Siberia.[24]

Both occupying powers, therefore, quickly began to remake their respective zones of occupation in their own hideous image. Where the Germans sifted and sorted their newly subject Polish populations according to the perverse theories of Nazi pseudo-science—with Jews and Poles alike consigned to the lowest rungs of an imagined racial hierarchy—so the Soviets sorted their populations according to the no less dubious ideas of Marxism, applying crude class criteria to decide who would be favored and who would face the full wrath of the Soviet state. Whereas the Germans expropriated Poles and Aryanized Jewish businesses, the Soviet zone saw private property abolished and all businesses nationalized. In both zones, to be a member of the intelligentsia or of the former ruling class became a life-threatening condition, with suspect individuals rounded up to be interrogated and neutralized. Participation in past actions—such as having fought in the Polish-Soviet War of 1920 or the Wielkopolska Uprising against German rule in 1919—could lead to retrospective arrest as an anti-Soviet or anti-German element. In both zones, Polish populations were viewed at best as suspect, at worst as totally expendable. Little wonder, perhaps, that so many Poles—Jews and non-Jews alike—were looking for an escape.

WITH THE COUNTRY THUS PARTITIONED BY ITS NEIGH-bors once again, Poland's government fled into exile. Already on September 6, the Polish supreme commander, Edward Śmigły-Rydz, had ordered a general withdrawal to the east bank of the Vistula, followed by an evacuation of the high command to Brest (Brześć), 200 kilometers (124 miles) east of Warsaw. After that, Poland's senior political and military authorities were largely powerless, retreating southeast toward the comparative safety of the Romanian frontier. The Soviet invasion of September 17 proved to be the final straw. That day, Śmigły-Rydz gave the order to evacuate across the border into Romania. He was so crushed by events that he contemplated suicide. "The road to Romania led over a bridge," an eyewitness recalled. "Ministry after ministry and embassy after embassy were called out over a megaphone to cross the little border bridge, heading into Romania. This sad parade of vehicles included a group of trucks belonging to the Bank of Poland and carrying the Polish gold reserves to safety. I was in absolute awe as I watched this long and sad parade."[25]

Some days later, shortly before Warsaw capitulated to the Germans, an instruction from Śmigły-Rydz was delivered to the Polish defenders still in the capital. It was an elaborate exercise, which involved a courier stealing an airplane in Romania and sewing a piece of silk bearing the message into the lining of his uniform before being flown into the besieged city under fire. The order—which would serve as the foundation of the Polish underground resistance—was no futile, romantic gesture. It drew on Poland's long, painful history of foreign occupation and was nurtured by a folk memory of resistance that had been buried for barely a generation. Entrusted to General Michał Karaszewicz-Tokarzewski (who had taken the underground pseudonym "Torwid"), it demanded that a core of Polish officers establish resistance cells, which would gather intelligence, secrete weapons and ammunition, and prepare communications and forgery operations to fight the German occupation while remaining loyal to the government-in-exile. The resulting SZP, *Służba Zwycięstwu Polski*, or Service for Poland's Victory—later renamed as the ZWZ, *Związek Walki Zbrojnej*, or Union of Armed Struggle—provided the germ of what would become the largest and most thoroughgoing resistance movement in wartime Europe.[26]

After the surrender of Warsaw, the focus shifted to the establishment of a functioning government-in-exile. At the end of September, the president of the Polish Republic, Ignacy Mościcki, who had been interned in the town of Bicaz in northeastern Romania, resigned his office, citing his inability to effectively execute his role from captivity. Following the procedures laid down in the Polish constitution, he transferred power to a group of politicians around General Władysław Sikorski who had already fled to Paris. There, a candidate for the presidency was found in Władysław Raczkiewicz, an eminent lawyer and former speaker of the Polish Senate, who—crucially—was acceptable to supporters of the prewar regime, the opposition, and the French. After taking the oath of office in the Polish embassy in Paris, Raczkiewicz promptly appointed Sikorski as his prime minister, at the head of what was, in effect, a government of national unity with representatives drawn from all the main opposition parties, representing a clean break with the prewar ruling regime. Sikorski's government-in-exile would embody the legal continuation of Polish sovereignty, maintaining diplomatic relations with Poland's international allies and serving as the supreme authority for the growing Polish underground resistance movement.

Poland, then, was not dead yet, but it was certainly on life support. And though the establishment of the government-in-exile and Polish underground might appear to have been straightforward, both were fraught with complications caused by Poland's conspiratorial traditions and contemporary political tensions. For one thing, Sikorski's appointment was anything but uncontroversial and was opposed by many of those who still supported the prewar regime. One estimate even suggested that only a quarter of Sikorski's generals actually supported him. At the same time, the birth of the Polish underground was by no means easy. The rich Polish tradition of resistance to foreign occupation was a boon, of course, but it led to a plethora of resistance groupings, representing each of the political parties as well as countless other splinters, many of which were hostile to one another. It would take until the spring of 1942 for the majority of them to be united under the banner of the *Armia Krajowa*, or Home Army.[27]

Moreover, given the perilous environment in which all Poles found themselves, whether in the German or Soviet zones of occupation, trying to organize active resistance was often akin to signing one's own death warrant. Both the Gestapo and NKVD quickly infiltrated many such groups, and arrest was almost inevitable. As the captured underground courier Jan Karski recalled, Gestapo interrogation could be bestial. Back in his cell and reflecting with "humiliation and impotent rage" on his last beating, running his tongue across his broken teeth, feeling his bloodied, distorted face, Karski was so desperate that he attempted suicide, slicing a stolen razor blade into his wrists.[28]

NKVD interrogations were even more brutally efficient. In the Soviet zone of occupation, by the early months of 1940 the cadres of the nascent ZWZ had been thoroughly compromised, and their nominal leader, Colonel Emil Macieliński, had become an NKVD informant. The Soviets were much more accomplished at infiltrating and suppressing insurrection than the Gestapo ever was, in particular targeting foresters and gamekeepers to deny the resistance any foothold in the countryside. According to a leading historian of the period, the Polish underground "never had a chance" against the NKVD.[29]

With all the difficulties they had establishing themselves, it was essential for the Polish underground to maintain contact with the government-in-exile in France and, later, after that country's defeat in June 1940, in London. To this end, radio contact would become key, but in the early days of the occupation it had been slow to establish, so diplomatic communication was sent to outposts in Budapest, Bucharest, and Kaunas, from where couriers carried the correspondence to occupied Warsaw. In some instances, those couriers were also used for direct communication with the government-in-exile, even if it took several weeks of perilous travel. One of the most famous was Jan Karski, whose mission west in February 1940 to Paris and Angers, France, where the Polish government-in-exile was based, provided Sikorski's ministers with vital information on the dark fate being endured by their countrymen back in Poland. Karski, a twenty-five-year-old former artillery officer, had only recently been inducted into the underground and, thanks to his language skills and photographic memory, had been given the task of courier. In only his second such mission, he was sent to France, which meant he had to hike across the Tatra Mountains, then travel by train via Budapest, Venice, and Milan to Paris before going on to Angers. Though he had not been sent specifically to report on conditions in occupied Poland, such was the thirst for information in exile government circles that he was supplied with a stenographer and asked to provide all the information he could recall. The result was the first of Karski's "reports," which must have made unsettling reading for his political masters.[30]

He began by outlining the overall situation in the country: the repressions endured, the mentality of the German occupiers, and the role played by ethnic Germans. Essentially, it was open season, he explained. "If someone dares to speak Polish out loud on the street, he can be instantly slapped, bothered, or beaten up. Same goes for not getting out of a German's way, for not showing appropriate courtesy." Poles were being resettled from the occupied territories, he said, and were given only two hours to pack their belongings before being deported in inhuman conditions. Karski painted a grim picture of a nation close to its breaking point. The Germans "want to destroy the Polish spirit," he said. "Poles are unbelievably depressed, fearful, and despairing. There is an incredible degree of hatred toward the Germans. The common people believe that the Antichrist has descended on earth . . . that the stakes are the life or death of the entire Nation."

Yet it was his assessment of the plight of Polish Jews, and of Polish-Jewish relations, that would have alarmed the government-in-exile most. In the Soviet zone of occupation, he told them, there were considerable tensions, arising primarily from the perception among non-Jewish Poles that their Jewish neighbors had welcomed the Soviet invasion as a liberation, or—worse—that they "direct the work" of the Soviet secret police. In consequence, he warned, Poles are "bitter and disappointed" in relation to the Jews, regarding them as "devoted to the Bolsheviks." Ominously, he concluded that the Poles were waiting for the opportunity for revenge, a "repayment in blood."

For Jews in the German zone, the outlook was little rosier. There, Karski explained, Jews were subject to harsher treatment at the hands of the Germans than their non-Jewish neighbors were; they were "outside of the law, outside of the protection of the authorities. Officially, they are intended . . . for destruction or removal." More worryingly, Karski noted that the lack of legal protection for Jews risked inducing non-Jewish Poles to become complicit in their expropriation and persecution. The Jewish question, he warned, "is a quite dangerous tool in the hands of the Germans," as it could "create something akin to a narrow bridge upon which the Germans and a large portion of Polish society are finding agreement." The antidote to that development, he said, was "to endeavor to create something along the lines of a common front . . . an understanding that in the end both peoples are being unjustly persecuted by the same enemy." However, he lamented that "such an understanding does not exist among the broad masses of the Polish populace."[31]

Karski's stark appraisal would doubtless have struck a chord, chiming with the thoughts and discussions, then ongoing in Polish émigré circles and beyond, about where the prewar republic had fallen short and what any future Poland should look like. By its very nature and composition, of course, Sikorski's exile government represented a rejection of the prewar regime—the semi-authoritarian patronage state that had collapsed the previous autumn—but significant questions remained. Sikorski had started well, issuing a declaration of principles late in 1939, in which he announced that the sole purpose of his government was "the rebirth of a great and sovereign Poland that will be equally just for all its citizens." Soon after, he had publicly promised Poland's national minorities "justice, free national and cultural development, and the protection of the law." But some voices were demanding more, including an unequivocal repudiation of the discriminatory nationality policies of the prewar regime and an explicit declaration of Jewish rights, seeing the Jewish issue as a fundamental test of the exile government's professed democratic ideals. It remained to be seen how well Sikorski could navigate these difficult waters, reconciling such demands with the various shades of political opinion within his government, as well as maintaining the sometimes grudging sympathy that Poland enjoyed in the international arena.[32]

Though Karski's words would doubtless have been discomfiting to the Polish ministers in Angers—not least his comments about Polish-Jewish relations—his presence there would have been regarded as a minor victory for one émigré in particular, a former minister without portfolio in the exile government named Aleksander Ładoś. Ładoś had served in a number of significant diplomatic posts through the 1920s and '30s. He had been the secretary of the Polish delegation at the peace negotiations that had led to the Treaty of Riga with the Soviets in 1921 and had then headed the eastern Europe department of the Polish Ministry of Foreign Affairs. A diplomatic career followed, with postings as envoy to Riga in 1926 and the following year to Munich, as consul general, before domestic Polish politics derailed his diplomatic ambitions. Ładoś's support for the People's Party (*Stronnistwo Ludowe*, or SL) and his opposition to the regime of Józef Piłsudski made his position in the foreign service untenable, and he was dismissed in 1931.[33]

Now rather portly and prematurely white-haired, looking older than his fifty years, Ładoś—like many of his fellows among the military and political class—had escaped from Poland via Romania in September 1939 and had found his way to Paris. There, he made contact once again with General Sikorski, an old ally from the political opposition. With Sikorski's elevation to prime minister, Ładoś was appointed as minister without portfolio, with special responsibility for setting up clandestine channels of communication with Poland—the very same channels that Karski had now used in his mission to the west.[34]

By the time of Karski's arrival, however, Ładoś had already stepped down from his position. His appointment in Sikorski's first exile government had been partly based on his membership in the Polish People's Party; government posts were divided between the major political parties, and as the senior representative of the SL in France in October 1939, Ładoś had gotten the nod. However, by the New Year, other, more senior figures had arrived in the west, and so he was obliged to stand aside in favor of Stanisław Kot, a prominent SL politician who was appointed as minister of the interior. Consequently, it was Kot who asked Karski to record his thoughts on the situation in Poland when the latter arrived in Angers in February 1940.[35]

All this left Ładoś at something of a loose end, and, because he was a loyal supporter of Sikorski, a new role was sought for him. At the time, the government-in-exile was concerned that its representatives would not be recognized, especially by neutral states. Given that countries such as Sweden, Turkey, and Switzerland would potentially play an important role in the government's communications with Poland, Sikorski was keen to have capable and politically reliable ambassadors in those locations. Initially, then, it was planned that Ładoś would become the ambassador in Ankara, but when the idea was blocked by the Turkish government, a vacancy presented itself in Switzerland, where the incumbent had been compromised by a spying scandal.[36]

So it was that Aleksander Ładoś was appointed as Polish envoy to Switzerland, arriving in Bern at the end of April 1940. A member of the embassy staff, Stanisław Nahlik, remembered that the new arrival was very different from his predecessor, Tytus Komarnicki. Whereas Komarnicki had been diminutive and "neurotic," he recalled, Ładoś was "phlegmatic" and "of imposing height and corpulence." While Komarnicki had been constantly on the move, "running around the building," Ładoś hardly left his office. And while Komarnicki had micromanaged every aspect of his ambassadorship, Ładoś was never seen in his office before eleven o'clock and spent "a significant portion of the day in the horizontal position." Nonetheless, for all the differences—and peculiarities—of style, Nahlik was soon full of admiration for his new boss. Ładoś, he noted, had an "excellent work ethic," never acted on impulse, and wrote "quickly, efficiently and legibly . . . in beautiful flowing Polish."[37]

For all his linguistic talents, however, Ładoś faced a considerable struggle to gain the official recognition of the Swiss authorities. Switzerland was in a profoundly difficult situation in 1940. Its traditional neutrality, aided by the remote fastness of its mountainous interior, was threatened now as never before, especially when the fall of France that summer left it as a lone island of democracy in a totalitarian sea. Thus imperiled—as much by simple geography as by the pan-German ambitions of the Nazis—the Swiss reaction was twofold. The first was a show of strength: reservists were called up and positions in the so-called national redoubt in the heart of the country were reinforced. The clear intention was to make any German foray into Switzerland as costly in time, men, and matériel as was humanly possible. As the commander in chief of the Swiss army, General Henri Guisan, told his officers that summer, Switzerland would never surrender. They would "continue fighting in their positions until they had no ammunition left," and if they ran out of ammunition, they would use their bayonets. "As long as a man has one shell left or is able to use his hand weapon," Guisan said, "he shall not surrender."[38]

Alongside that bellicose defiance, Switzerland adopted a conciliatory tone to avoid provoking its German neighbor unnecessarily. And it was in this spirit that Ładoś found his appointment complicated by the wider political situation. Like the Turkish government, the Swiss were wary of inciting the wrath of the Germans by recognizing a representative of a state that—according to Berlin—had ceased to exist. Moreover, though the Swiss could justify maintaining their recognition of an existing ambassador, they balked at accepting a new appointee, especially a former minister in the exile government. German protests were duly forthcoming. The German envoy to Bern, Otto Carl Köcher, complained that any Swiss recognition of the "Polish pseudo-government" would draw "an appropriate reaction." His superior, German foreign minister Joachim von Ribbentrop, summoned the Swiss ambassador in Berlin to warn him that recognizing the appointment of Ładoś would be interpreted by Germany as "an unfriendly act," adding that the Führer himself had been "extremely indignant" about the matter.[39]

In such circumstances, a compromise clearly had to be found. The Swiss foreign minister, Marcel Pilet-Golaz, reassured Berlin that he would take the German view into account and offered Ładoś the position of "chargé d'affaires ad interim"—the usual title for a deputy temporarily acting in place of an absent head of mission—along with the assurance that he would still be able to enjoy the full scope of diplomatic rights and privileges and that he would be formally accredited in due course. The Polish government-in-exile accepted the proposal, and, on May 31, 1940, Aleksander Ładoś took up his post at the Polish mission in Bern.[40]

Ładoś was joining a diplomatic staff that had already been pared to the bone by the demands of the war, with many personnel having left to join the Polish forces that were forming in France. Only ten members of the staff remained. One of the most interesting among them was Captain Szczęsny Chojnacki, nominally military attaché but in reality the senior Polish intelligence officer in the Swiss capital. He would be a highly significant player in the Allied intelligence network as it developed in Switzerland, and his "Darek" spy ring—and particularly his connection to the prolific Polish spy Halina Szymańska—would later provide a vital link between the OSS (Office of Strategic Services, a forerunner of the CIA) under Allen Dulles and the oppositional circle within the German military intelligence organization, the *Abwehr*, led by Admiral Wilhelm Canaris.

Away from the sensitive world of high-level espionage, Ładoś's new colleagues were mostly members of the legation's staff. Most significant among them were First Secretary Stefan Ryniewicz and Vice-Consul Konstanty Rokicki. Ładoś's deputy, Ryniewicz, a tall, easygoing thirty-six-year-old from southeastern Poland, had worked at the embassy in Bern in the early 1930s and had spent a period in the embassy in Riga before returning to Switzerland at the end of 1938 as first secretary. Regarded as an extremely capable civil servant, Ryniewicz was also a committed Polish patriot, who—as a teenager—had hidden guns for Polish forces in their clashes with Ukrainians in his native Tarnopol. Rokicki, meanwhile, was a thirty-nine-year-old Varsovian who had served in the Polish cavalry during the Polish-Soviet War before entering the diplomatic corps in 1931. After service in Minsk and Cairo in the mid-1930s, he had served, alongside Ryniewicz, in the Polish mission in Riga, where the latter acted as best man at his wedding. It is likely that it was Ryniewicz who engineered Rokicki's transfer to Bern in 1939.

In the constrained circumstances of 1940, then, it was Konstanty Rokicki who became the de facto head of the consular section, located on Thunstrasse, where he was responsible for—among other things—handling passport applications, especially of refugee Jews. In this, he was assisted by a number of nondiplomatic local staff, most notably Juliusz Kühl, a slim, rather bookish Polish Jew who had lived in Bern since arriving to study economics there in 1929. It would be Kühl who would provide vital contact to numerous Jewish organizations in trying to assist the refugees.[41]

Yet, as ambassador—even unofficially—it was Ładoś who held the overall responsibility, and in this he would be guided by his own instincts and experiences. For one thing, he was positively predisposed toward Poland's Jewish populations. As a member of the centrist People's Party, he eschewed many of the more overtly nationalistic positions of his fellow Poles. But more than that, his own recent experience had taught him much about mutual tolerance and respect. During his flight from Warsaw to the Romanian frontier in September 1939, he had twice been assisted by ordinary Jews acting out of simple human kindness. Jews were often accused of "deep self-interest," Ładoś would later write, but these experiences had taught him "to see things differently."[42]

More importantly—and significantly in light of his later actions—like many Poles of his generation, Ładoś appears to have had a somewhat relaxed attitude to officialdom. Growing up before the First World War in a country that was partitioned between Russia, Germany, and Austria-Hungary, he would have been well aware of the idea of *konspiracja*, a term describing an outward conformity and obedience to authority that could hide a host of underhand or subversive activities. Indeed, in this regard he had form. As a young man, he had been arrested by the Austrian authorities for pro-Polish agitation and sentenced to internal exile, away from the Slavic provinces of the empire. Settling in the Tyrol, he had then borrowed the papers of a Russian friend in order to apply for a passport, and in this way had escaped into Switzerland. Similarly, his escape from Romania to France the previous autumn had been facilitated by the use of an "unofficial passport," produced as a favor by a local bureaucrat.[43]

It remained to be seen what qualities and experiences Ładoś would bring to his ambassadorship, of course, but one might reasonably conclude from such episodes that he was not a man overly burdened with respect for the legal sanctity of official documents.

3

"IN A SHORT TIME, IT WILL BE TOO LATE"

In the summer of 1940, as France was fighting for its life against the German blitzkrieg, another takeover—no less hostile—was taking place on Europe's eastern fringe, almost unnoticed by the world's media. For more than six months, the three Baltic states—Estonia, Latvia, and Lithuania—had endured a de facto military occupation by Stalin's Soviet Union. Secretly consigned to the Soviet sphere of influence by the Nazi-Soviet Pact of the previous August, these countries had been browbeaten into accepting Red Army garrisons, which—at seventy thousand men in total—exceeded the combined standing armies of the three host nations. One by one, they had sent their senior politicians to Moscow to negotiate less onerous terms, but to no avail. As the Lithuanian delegation noted with resignation, arguing with the Kremlin was akin to "throwing peas against a wall."[1]

Now, with France entering its death throes, Stalin decided to translate that military stranglehold into political control. In early June, his minions began to complain about sundry unspecified "irregularities" occurring in the Baltic states: political chicanery, secret alliances, kidnappings, or encouraging Red Army soldiers to desert. As before, senior politicians trooped to Moscow to refute such charges as best they could, but they found that they could make little headway against the tsunami of confected outrage delivered by Stalin's foreign minister, Vyacheslav Molotov. Lithuania was first to feel his ire. Its prime minister, Antanas Merkys, was forced to sit through a tirade of demands and accusations before, finally, Molotov's feigned patience was exhausted. Then, on the evening of June 14, Merkys was presented with an ultimatum. Just as German troops were entering Paris, Molotov delivered the coup de grâce, demanding the appointment of a Soviet-friendly cabinet, an end to the "hostile activities" of the Lithuanian government, and the entry of yet more Red Army troops. The fulfillment of these demands, Molotov warned, was an "elementary condition." In the days that followed, similar ultimatums were delivered to the Latvian and Estonian governments. Baltic independence, which had blossomed for a generation after the First World War, was being extinguished.[2]

Over the next few weeks, events moved with dizzying speed. Soviet "representatives" were sent to the Baltic states to oversee their transformation; provisional "people's governments" were formed, including left-wing journalists and compliant placemen. At the same time, a wave of arrests targeted the broad swaths of society that Moscow considered to be in any way anti-Soviet. Within a month, new elections were held with a Kremlin-approved list of candidates, widespread voter intimidation, and outright fraud; in one Lithuanian electoral precinct, turnout reached a remarkable 122 percent. A week or so later, the resulting "people's parliaments" declared the establishment of Soviet power and petitioned Moscow to be admitted to the USSR as Soviet socialist republics, requests that were granted by the Supreme Soviet in early August. Lithuania joined the USSR on August 3, Latvia on the fifth, Estonia the day after. From the Kremlin's perspective, it had been a textbook operation. Within less than two months, three sovereign states had been threatened, intimidated, occupied, and incorporated into the USSR, with barely a shot being fired.[3]

With political control came social control. As the American consul in Kaunas, Owen Norem, wrote to Washington that summer: "The Sovietization process is being intensified. . . . Estate owners, former leaders, and wealthy people are receiving attention. Arrests are being made consistently and so silently, usually under cover of night, that a veritable pall has descended over the country." The Lithuanian president, Antanas Smetona, fled to Germany, wading across a stream into East Prussia to escape Soviet troops. His prime minister—Antanas Merkys, who had attempted to negotiate with Molotov—was arrested and sent to a prison in the Russian interior; five of his ten-member cabinet were not so fortunate and would be murdered by the firing squads of Stalin's NKVD.[4]

The rapid pace—and brutal nature—of Sovietization no doubt came as a great shock to the populations of the Baltic states, especially those who had something to lose from the imposition of communism. But one group of people was especially discomfited: Lithuania's refugee Jews. Lithuania had taken in large numbers of Poles, especially Polish Jews, who had fled northward following the German and Soviet invasions of Poland the previous autumn. As Polish resistance to the invaders had been finally quelled that October, most Polish military and administrative personnel had escaped southeastward, across the narrow frontier with Romania, one of Poland's few comparatively friendly neighbors. A second escape route, however, had been northeast into Lithuania, which, though not especially friendly—diplomatic relations between the two countries had been grudgingly restored only in 1938—was at least easier to reach, being half the distance from Warsaw than the Romanian border.

Many Polish Jews took Soviet proclamations of tolerance and equality at face value and simply fled east in 1939, but some—especially the Orthodox among them—were wary of throwing themselves on the mercy of Stalin and his godless Soviet Union. Instead, they headed north, into Lithuania, from where they hoped to find onward passage or perhaps see out the war. Now, the Soviet occupation and annexation of Lithuania upset those plans. For them, the prospect of becoming Soviet citizens in the summer of 1940 was scarcely more appealing than it had been the previous autumn, and so many started to look for an exit.

That summer, a desperate scramble began among Polish refugees in Lithuania to get their paperwork in order. The priority, for those whose papers had expired or had been lost in their flight the previous year, was to find replacements. To assist in meeting this need, the Polish mission in Bern sent at least four hundred blank Polish passports to the British consulate in Kaunas, which represented Polish interests in Lithuania following the closure of the Polish embassy the previous autumn. The British consul there, Sir Thomas Preston, had been consul in Ekaterinburg at the time of the murder of the Russian imperial family there, in July 1918, so was sympathetic to those wishing to escape the Soviet Union. Consequently, he was willing to bend the rules, issuing not only the Polish passports but also over a thousand British travel documents to refugee Jews, enabling them to find a way out to Sweden or Palestine.[5]

In time, however, another exit route presented itself. The previous autumn, the Japanese empire had appointed a consul to Kaunas for the first time, a thirty-nine-year-old diplomat named Chiune Sugihara. As a Russian expert within the Japanese diplomatic service, Sugihara had converted to Orthodoxy, married a Russian woman, and served in the Manchurian foreign office in Harbin. During the 1930s, it is thought that he had collaborated with Polish military intelligence on the so-called Promethean project—a scheme that sought to undermine the Soviet Union by fanning the flames of nationalist sentiment among its subject nationalities. When Sugihara was sent to Kaunas, his primary remit was that of determining the intentions of the German military in nearby Poland and East Prussia, trying to ascertain whether—and when—Hitler intended to attack the USSR. In that task, it seems,

Sugihara's collaboration with the Poles continued. His primary contact, Michał Rybikowski, a Polish intelligence officer posing as a Russian named Peter Ivanov, was running an Allied spy ring out of the Japanese embassy in Stockholm. Through him, Sugihara would come to employ two additional Polish military intelligence officers—Captain Alfons Jakubianiec and Lieutenant Leszek Daszkiewicz—who would travel across the eastern Baltic using Manchurian passports supplied by Sugihara, gathering information that Rybikowski would pass to the government-in-exile in London and Sugihara would pass on to Tokyo.[6]

According to Daszkiewicz, the idea of using an exit route for Polish refugees via Japan was already being discussed in April 1940. In the weeks that followed, the idea would crystallize further. That summer, a young Dutch Jew in Lithuania by the name of Nathan Gutwirth contacted the Dutch consul in Kaunas, Jan Zwartendijk, to ask if—with Holland now under German occupation—he could apply for a visa for the Dutch colony of Curaçao, in the hope that he could use it as a stepping stone to the United States. Unsure, Zwartendijk contacted his superior, the Dutch ambassador in Riga, who duly informed him that entry into Curaçao did not require a visa at all. With that realization, a viable exit route began to take shape. If Curaçao could be cited as a destination, and Japan could be given as a transit country, then refugees could apply to the Soviet authorities to permit them to leave.[7]

Soon, word of the scheme spread through the Jewish refugee community in Lithuania, spurred not least by the Zionist Dr. Zorach Warhaftig, who advised the teachers and students of a number of rabbinical schools, or yeshivas, that the Japan-Curaçao route was a valid possibility for escape. In due course, Zwartendijk and Sugihara found themselves inundated with Jews seeking their assistance. As Sugihara would later recall: "Outside the consulate . . . I saw a large crowd of Polish refugees behind the fences. . . . There were not only male refugees, among them were women, old people and children. They all seemed very tired and exhausted. I did not know whether they had any place to sleep in those days, maybe they just slept in the station or on the street."[8]

As an intelligence officer, Sugihara was unaccustomed to such attention and was a little unfamiliar with the mundane world of visa procedures, so he cabled Tokyo to ask for advice. He was told that he was not to issue transit visas to any traveler not holding a confirmed end visa with a guaranteed exit from Japan. Given that Curaçao could be interpreted as a final destination, he concluded that, though Tokyo would not appreciate his actions, there was sufficient leeway within that instruction to allow him to indulge his humanitarian instincts and issue the necessary transit visas. In any case, he noted, it was "completely useless" to continue to discuss the matter with Tokyo.[9]

Just as Sugihara was turning a deaf ear to his superiors, another diplomatic exchange was underway that would be crucial to the enterprise. On July 25, Stalin's representative in Lithuania, Vladimir Dekanozov, wrote to Moscow outlining the refugee crisis then developing in Vilnius and Kaunas and recommending that the transit of those wishing to leave through the USSR should be permitted. It was rather un-Soviet in its generosity, but Stalin nonetheless approved the suggestion on July 29. Thereafter, the authorities would not impede the transit of Jewish refugees, en route to Curaçao, through Soviet territory. Sugihara was thereby free to issue his visas in the reasonable hope that their recipients would be able to leave the USSR.[10]

By the last week of July, then, a veritable cottage industry had sprung up in the leafy streets of Kaunas, with hundreds of Jewish refugees—the vast majority of them Polish—desperately collecting the necessary paperwork to escape Soviet-controlled Lithuania. First, they would visit Zwartendijk to get a "Curaçao visa"—in reality an official stamp stating, in French, that the Dutch territory did not require a visa for entry—of which Zwartendijk and his staff issued 2,400 in eight days. Then they would proceed to the Japanese consulate to obtain a Japanese transit visa from Sugihara. One eyewitness recalled her experience:

There were a lot of people waiting in line at the Japanese Consulate. Everyone had a story, everyone was trying to get somewhere, but most people did not have a definite destination and did not have money. [Sugihara] asked us where our parents were, and we replied that our father was not living and our mother had no papers. After we told him, he looked very sympathetic, he looked like such a kind man. He nodded his head, and stamped our passport. We were terribly frightened of all authority figures, and we were very nervous and scared the whole time we were there. We kept on saying "thank you," "thank you" in Polish, and he raised his hand to let us know it was ok and smiled at us. We were crying and shaking when we left his office.[11]

Sugihara worked tirelessly. On July 27, he issued forty visas; a section of each had to be handwritten in Japanese calligraphy. The following day, he issued 119; the day after that, 257. He eventually had to ask Zwartendijk to slow down his production of the Curaçao visas because he couldn't keep up. But he continued issuing his visas, even after Zwartendijk had been forced by the Soviets to close the Dutch consulate and after the Japanese consulate itself was shut down. There are reports that he was still issuing visas even as he left Kaunas on September 1, distributing stamped, blank documents from the window as his train departed for Berlin. In total, Sugihara would issue at least 2,139 official transit visas. The number issued unofficially is not known.[12]

Of course, even for those who benefited from Sugihara's largesse, their concerns were not yet at an end. There was still Soviet bureaucracy to be endured and negotiated, and it was not always an easy process, despite the laissez-passer advocated by Dekanozov and agreed to by Stalin. One Polish diplomatic report of January

1941 stated that Polish refugees wanting to apply for a visa to leave the USSR were required to pay a substantial fee in US dollars, in spite of the fact that the possession of foreign currency was explicitly prohibited by Soviet law. Even if they negotiated that Kafkaesque trap, the refugees still faced a lengthy journey across the Soviet Union, most usually on the Trans-Siberian Railway, followed by a passage across the Sea of Japan from Vladivostok to the port city of Tsuruga, throughout which they were always at the mercy of overzealous and often capricious Communist officialdom. At Vladivostok, for instance, refugees could be stripped of any obvious valuables by Soviet border guards, who issued a receipt, stating that the items could be reclaimed when the refugees returned to the USSR. For those who were destitute and planning a new life in exile, it was a bitter blow.[13]

Others found that, despite their best efforts, they had the wrong documentation. While Soviet bureaucracy was willing—theoretically at least—to issue exit visas to citizens of Lithuania, it stopped short of allowing Soviet citizens to leave the country. With Polish identity documents no longer recognized, therefore, the individual's adopted citizenship could determine his or her fate. There were other pitfalls. A group of seventy-two Jewish refugees was denied entry to Japan in March 1941 because they had not obtained the necessary Curaçao visa prior to getting a Japanese transit visa from Sugihara. Sent back to Vladivostok, the group was then confined to their ship for a few days, under suspicion by the NKVD of being Japanese spies. Finally returned across the Sea of Japan, they were relieved to find that their entry into Tsuruga had been cleared and the necessary Curaçao visas for their onward journey had been secured. As one of them recalled, arriving in the Japanese port was like "heaven."[14]

On another occasion, some thirty refugees arrived in Tsuruga with visas that had been forged, most likely after Sugihara's consulate had been closed down and he was issuing blank documents to anyone who wanted one. This was not in itself unusual, but these visas were patently substandard—all thirty had been issued in the name of "Jakub Goldberg"—so their bearers were, again, sent back whence they had come. Yet, without Soviet entry visas, they were denied reentry into the USSR and so were doomed to sail to and fro in the Sea of Japan, in legal limbo, until they were finally given permission to land in Japan, on the condition that they would leave the country within three weeks.[15]

OF COURSE, THE DIFFICULTIES ENDURED BY SUGIHARA'S refugees—even those with badly forged documentation—paled into insignificance when compared to the plight of those Jews they left behind. Across German-occupied Poland, the process of ghettoization proceeded apace, with new ghettos being established that summer across the region, from Aleksandrów to Żyrardów. Though it is often assumed that a policy of ghettoization was being implemented by the German administration in Poland, there is little evidence of a coherent set of principles and procedures, beyond the immediate desire to segregate Jews in discrete, urban areas, so as to better control and exploit them. As one contemporary commentator noted: "It is a mistake to think that the conqueror excels in logic and orderliness. We see quite the opposite of this. Everything that is done by those who carry out his exalted will bears the imprint of confusion and illogic. The Nazis are consistent and systematic only with regard to the central concepts behind their actions . . . the concept of complete extermination and destruction."[16]

In consequence, ghettoization took a number of forms. One was the ghetto at Będzin, in the newly expanded Reich province of Upper Silesia. Located in the industrial conurbation around Katowice and Chorzów, Będzin—renamed Bendsburg by the Germans—had been home to a large and vibrant Jewish community before the war. Jews made up over 60 percent of the total population of around forty thousand. The Polish defeat in 1939 had brought the usual atrocities: the town's synagogue was burned down by the Germans and a number of massacres of prominent Polish and Jewish individuals had followed. But annexation to the Reich had brought Będzin under the jurisdiction of the gauleiter of Silesia, Fritz Bracht, who preferred "his" Jews to be exploited as a labor resource, rather than being confined to a ghetto. Hence, the "ghetto" in Będzin—as well as that in nearby Sosnowiec—was open and unfenced, though these were the only two locations in Upper Silesia in which Jews were permitted to live.[17]

The key figure in the exploitation of Będzin's Jews was Moshe Merin, a thirty-five-year-old local man who emerged as elder of the Jewish Council, primarily due to his ability to speak German and complete lack of scruples. According to one contemporary, Merin was a chancer who had been "pretty much on the decline" prior to the war, having divorced and racked up gambling debts, before emerging as the self-appointed "king" of Będzin's Jews. The Jewish Council, or *Judenrat*, of which he was head, was a parody of self-government: an organization that appeared to be responsible for religious and social matters but was in truth merely a conduit for the transmission and execution of German orders. The Jewish Council leaders, who were often the least suitable for this onerous task, were trapped in a murderous relationship with their German masters, as both arch-collaborators and victims. Like Chaim Rumkowski in Łódź, Merin believed that the Jewish community could only save itself if it could be made indispensable to the German war effort. Survival, then, in Merin's variant of the Faustian pact, was to be achieved through absolute obedience and collaboration, an attitude that temporarily earned Merin the benevolence of his German masters, as demonstrated by the "royal reception" he received on a visit to Warsaw.[18]

The world over which Moshe Merin was lord, however, was a miserable one. Though the ghetto was not enclosed, the area in which Jews were permitted to live was nonetheless strictly delineated, meaning that overcrowding quickly became endemic. One contemporary survey estimated that population density in the ghetto averaged five people per room. As Merin himself pointed out in a report to his German superiors, "The part of the town in which the Jewish inhabitants have been resettled contains houses of the oldest type, the most elementary comforts are not present in these houses, they have no water supplies, the privies and rubbish bins are often in a condition beyond words."[19]

As if that were not enough, the ghetto was geared, first and foremost, toward economic exploitation, and the vast majority of its inhabitants were sent out to work, often in poor conditions, facing privation, prejudice, and arbitrary violence on a daily basis. One of Będzin's inhabitants recalled that they lived in a state of siege: "No one was allowed to leave or enter the town without the permission from the SS, and the parameters of my life were more restricted still. I walked to the factory and I walked home. From time to time I'd go . . . to pick over the slag heaps on the edge of town looking for coal pieces good enough to burn. There were police and guards everywhere."[20]

Documents—for identification or exemption—assumed vital importance, especially the "certificates of employment," which each worker had to possess, and which permitted them to travel to and from their place of work. Financial exploitation was constant: Jews were obliged to pay a *Kopfsteuer* (per-capita tax), as well as monthly taxes (dependent upon their financial status), state taxes, and an annual community tax. Better-off individuals were often forced to make additional "tributes," and the community as a whole was forced to hand over quantities of gold and silver, often as restitution for some imagined offense. Nonpayment of any of these demands invited punishment, which could range from the forced billeting of poor individuals in a nonpayer's apartment to being sent to a concentration camp. Będzin's Jews were entirely dependent on their wits, their good fortune, and their documentation.[21]

Of course, despite their hardships, the inhabitants of the Będzin ghetto were not yet walled in, which could not be said of the largest of the ghettos in occupied Poland: Warsaw. The German plans for the former Polish capital were nothing if not ambitious. As elsewhere, Jews bore the brunt of the early legislation. Mobilized as forced labor, their bank accounts frozen, forbidden from using public transport, and obliged to wear a white armband, they were exposed to the full hostility of Nazi race law. Yet, in the early spring of 1940, a planning document was presented to the city's German authorities that would impact the lives of all Varsovians. The "Pabst Plan" was presented to Hans Frank, the governor-general of the occupied Polish territories, on February 6. It foresaw the reduction of the former Polish capital to the status of a provincial town; a city with a population of more than 1.3 million would be systematically razed and reborn as the German *Warschau*, a regional center with a population of around one hundred thousand German settlers and officials, in which only the Old Town would escape the radical redevelopment. With barely one-twentieth of the area of the city slated for survival under the plan, this meant that all of its inhabitants were scheduled, in one way or another, to disappear.[22]

One possible destination for those surplus populations emerged in the summer of 1940: Madagascar. The idea of using the island as a Jewish reservation had originated with the German anti-Semitic theorist Paul de Lagarde in the late nineteenth century, before being briefly revived by both Zionists and British anti-Semites in the 1920s. In 1937, the idea was investigated once again, this time by the Polish government, which sent a joint Polish-Jewish commission to the island to examine the possibilities, before concluding that Madagascar's tropical climate was not suitable to sustain a large population.[23]

By this time, of course, the Madagascar idea had long been part of Nazi thinking, with a number of senior figures, including Joachim von Ribbentrop and Hermann Göring, making favorable reference to the prospect, naturally unconcerned by the climatic difficulties that it presented. Indeed, at the time of the Évian

Conference in 1938, Nazi ideologue Alfred Rosenberg stated in a newspaper article that Madagascar was his favored "solution" to the Jewish refugee problem. Nonetheless, given that it required French cooperation, the idea fell from favor, until, in the summer of 1940, two things happened to revive its fortunes. Firstly, France's defeat appeared to place all French colonial territories at least nominally at Berlin's disposal. Secondly, the preliminary planning that had been done landed on the desk of Reinhard Heydrich, Himmler's deputy in the SS and the man with overall responsibility for what had become known as "the Jewish question."[24]

Heydrich set to the task with his customary dynamism, warning off his rivals and delegating much of the real work to his trusted lieutenant Adolf Eichmann. Already in July, memoranda were drawn up to show how Jewish communities under German control could be prepared for deportation overseas. The following month, another document crystallized Heydrich's plans: a million Jews were to be deported to Madagascar each year for the next four years. The plan didn't bother to sugarcoat the realities. It was foreseen that the new inhabitants would swiftly die off due to disease and the primitive conditions, and while they lived they would serve as hostages, to ensure the good behavior of their "racial comrades" in the United States. Most tellingly, perhaps, Philipp Bouhler—the head of the "T4" program, the involuntary euthanasia of the disabled and incurably sick, through which some 250,000 individuals had already been murdered—was nominated to supervise the operation. Madagascar was to be a ghetto in all but name.[25]

The Madagascar Plan caused quite a stir in Germany. Goebbels was uncharacteristically laconic in his diary on July 26, but he nonetheless noted approvingly that "all the Jews are going to be deported to Madagascar," adding that it was to become a German protectorate. Hitler, too, was enthusiastic, and shared the news with Benito Mussolini and Hans Frank, telling the latter—who was worried about the influx—that deportations of German Jews to the General Government would be halted as a result. At the time, some local Nazi leaders were so impatient to be rid of "their" Jews that they even organized their own deportations, sending thousands to Vichy France with only a day's notice.[26]

There was similar excitement—albeit for different reasons—among German and Polish Jews. Those in Germany, most of whom were yet to witness the true murderous nature of the Nazi regime, were initially horrified, and a group of senior Jewish leaders appealed to the pope for support in protesting against the idea. The diarist Victor Klemperer noted the resigned reaction of a friend to the rumor, sighing that "now . . . we'll all be packed off to Madagascar." Jewish reaction in occupied Poland was rather different. The elder of the Warsaw Jewish Council, Adam Czerniaków, was told about the plan by an SS officer, who declared that "the war would be over in a month and we would all leave for Madagascar." "In this way," Czerniaków noted in his diary, "the Zionist dream is to come true." Whatever reservations he still had, the halting of ghetto building that summer must have served to stoke the hope that a change for the better was perhaps in the offing.[27]

In the end, the Madagascar idea died a natural death, killed off by military necessity and British stubbornness. Just as it had become a possibility with the German defeat of France in the summer of 1940, so it became an impossibility with the failure to defeat Britain that autumn. With Britain still in the war, and the Royal Navy still (however nominally) in control of the world's sea-lanes, the Germans could scarcely spare the ships required for the deportation of millions of Jews to a distant island, even if they cared little for the deportees' well-being. After a summer of frenetic activity, then, the Madagascar Plan was finally abandoned. As one historian has written, "Once again, the alluring vision of quick and total solution to the Jewish question cast its magic spell, only once again to disappoint." Any further solutions would likely have to be found nearer to home.[28]

Already in August 1940, while the planning for the Madagascar idea was still in full flow, the construction of ghettos in Poland had resumed. In Warsaw, a brick wall three meters (ten feet) high, topped with barbed wire and shards of glass, began to be erected around much of the districts of Muranów, Powązki, and Nowolipki in the northwest of the city. The resulting ghetto was divided into two sections: a larger area to the north and a smaller section to the south, with the dividing line along Chłodna Street, which could not be ceded to the ghetto as it was an important east-west thoroughfare. Access between the two sections was possible through a gate, and later across a footbridge spanning the road. Once the boundaries of the ghetto were delineated, Jews were ordered to move in, while non-Jews were told to leave, precipitating a chaos of migration, with "handcarts and wagons moving in all directions and everyone afraid the gendarmes might confiscate their belongings." The establishment of the ghetto was formally announced by Hans Frank on October 16, 1940; it was sealed off the following month. Some four hundred thousand people—about 30 percent of Warsaw's population—were confined to a space that took up less than 3 percent of the former Polish capital.[29]

As elsewhere, the German authorities preferred others to do their dirty work, so they dragooned the Warsaw Jewish Council to act as their proxy. On November 4, all of its twenty-four members were summoned to a meeting with the Gestapo, along with another twenty-four "alternates," people picked up at random on the streets outside. The council members were told that they had three days to organize the collective move into the ghetto or else the twenty-four alternates would be shot. In the heated meeting that followed, those who tried to convince the council to refuse to carry out the order found little support. Most were not just afraid for the lives of the hostages but feared that if they didn't comply then the Germans would force the city's Jews into the ghetto themselves with their now-customary violence.[30]

Within the ghetto, there was panic, with gruesome rumors spreading about German intentions. For many, it was an existential shock. There was a spate of suicides. Diarist Chaim Kaplan lamented that, "we are [now] segregated and separated from the world and the fullness thereof, driven out of the society of the human race." Some attempted to see the establishment of the ghetto as a positive development, as it meant that Jews were now beyond the reach of their persecutors. But for most, their primary concerns were more immediate: How would they find food or accommodation? As there were still islands of comparative wealth in the ghetto in the early months of its existence, some could at first subsist by bartering their possessions for food, in the hope that their tribulations would soon be at an end. Decent accommodation could also be found, initially at least, if one had the wherewithal to pay for it. For the majority, though, overcrowding quickly became endemic, with numerous families often occupying a single apartment and sanitary conditions deteriorating rapidly. In this respect, the Łódź ghetto provided a shocking example. There, over 160,000 people were crammed into an area of 1.6 square miles in the poorest area of the city—on average 5.8 persons per room—in which barely seven hundred of the nearly thirty-two thousand apartments had running water. People lived in such close proximity to one another that the basic conventions of privacy and hygiene could no longer be observed. Little wonder, then, that disease was soon rife, and the suicide rate quickly rose.[31]

Warsaw's statistics were scarcely better. For most in the ghetto, the everyday reality was filth, poverty, and gnawing hunger. With an official food ration of only eight hundred calories per day—mainly from bread, potatoes, and fats—a good deal of energy and time was consumed finding additional sustenance, whether through barter or contraband. Smuggling, indeed, quickly became common, with money and valuables going out and provisions coming in, all carried by an army of smugglers—from children sneaking through the sewers to large gangs, which bribed the ghetto guards and smuggled in bulk. Before long, food became a universal obsession: the only subject of conversation, as people discussed which foodstuff could be obtained where, how it could best be prepared, and who needed to be bribed to get it. As one Warsaw diarist wrote: "My belly talks, shouts . . . and drives me mad."[32]

For others, especially children, begging became a way of life, and beggars quickly thronged the streets of the ghetto. As Władysław Szpilman recalled, they were ubiquitous and not at all shy about harassing passersby. "Merely getting from the tram stop to the nearest shop was not easy," he wrote. "Dozens of beggars lay in wait for this brief moment of encounter with a prosperous citizen, mobbing him by pulling at his clothes, barring his way, begging, weeping, shouting, threatening." Giving them money, however, was ill-advised, Szpilman believed, as it would only "bring more and more wretched figures streaming up from all sides, and the good Samaritan would find himself besieged, hemmed in by ragged apparitions spraying him with tubercular saliva, by children covered with oozing sores."[33]

Some of the beggars were less confrontational. Rubinstein—nicknamed the "mad jester"—was a philosopher-fool who would wear garish outfits and coin slogans and bon mots, many of which went to the heart of the ghetto experience. His most famous motto was "Alle glaych, arum on reikh"—all are equal, poor and rich—which soon came to appear darkly prophetic. Another poignant example, that of a family of beggars arrived from Łódź, shows how the brutal conditions in the ghetto contributed to the sort of "natural wastage" that its German masters would have applauded:

> At first, they numbered eight people. Their entire belongings consisted of two baby strollers. The father pushed three children in one, while the mother kept two others on top of the second. They rolled the strollers along the curb and sang old Yiddish

songs. They had beautiful voices. He sang and she sang, accompanied by six children's descants. After a while there were only four voices; then there were three, then one stroller disappeared, along with the family's shoes and what was left of their outer garments. Finally only two people and one stroller remained. The father pushed while the mother lay in the stroller, singing to accompany her husband. She was thirty-nine years old, but looked one hundred. Together they sang the same songs and were given the same pennies as they had received the year before.[34]

Most ghetto inhabitants had to work, and many found employment in the huge number of workshops and factories that sprang up across the ghetto, mostly producing wares or textiles for the German war effort. In time, the ghetto would be transformed into a vast labor camp, with "unproductive elements"—children, the elderly, and the disabled—being the first to be deported to an unknown fate. Understandably, perhaps, the idea emerged among Jews that the key to survival was work. This belief, based on the rational projection that the Germans would not kill "productive elements," was highly seductive. Yet it would soon prove entirely illusory.[35]

In the meantime, life went on. Cafés and soup kitchens opened; theatrical troupes formed; there were music-hall recitals. One singer—Marysia Ajzensztadt—was dubbed "the Nightingale of the Ghetto." In this way, a strange new normality developed. People clung onto life, but it was a very constrained existence, a world in which one's daily travails could only be wished away for so long. As Władysław Szpilman noted, a sense of melancholy was all-pervasive: "You could go to a restaurant or a café. You met friends there, and nothing seemed to prevent you from creating as pleasant an atmosphere as in a restaurant or café anywhere else. However, the moment inevitably came when one of your friends would let slip a remark." At that moment, the "perfect illusion" evaporated.[36]

In truth, Jews in the Warsaw ghetto were captives, of course, entirely at the mercy of the Germans and subject to ever-narrowing restrictions on their lives. Already forced to wear an armband with the Star of David, by November 1940 their property and employment rights had already been revoked, and they were also banned from owning radios and telephones and traveling on public transport. Mail in the ghetto was also circumscribed, with any outgoing communications subject to censorship and Gestapo approval, while incoming parcels were generally confiscated.[37]

This dependent, subordinate status had been made brutally clear to the Jewish Council at the outset. Working essentially at gunpoint, its members were under no illusion about being merely cat's-paws, the sullen executors of German policy. Adam Czerniaków, the council's elder, a stout former engineer, was a man of good intentions who—unlike his contemporaries in Łódź and Będzin—had assumed his post motivated by an honest desire to protect his people from the worst excesses of the Germans. Yet, goodwill was not enough, and Czerniaków quickly found himself assailed from all sides. According to diarist Mary Berg, he soon appeared to be "a broken man," crushed by the futility of his duties. "I have never seen him smile," she wrote, "but this is quite natural considering his heavy responsibilities. To have to deal with the Germans every day, and, at the same time, to bear with the complaints and reproaches of a starving, embittered and distrustful population—such a task is certainly not enviable. I am not surprised he is always so gloomy."[38]

As part of the veneer of autonomy, the council had its own organizations for maintaining order. The first was the *Jüdischer Ordnungsdienst*, or ghetto police, an unarmed group of Jewish policemen—numbering around 2,500 in Warsaw—who guarded the gates of the ghetto, directed traffic, and attempted to suppress the endemic smuggling. Though they would be criticized by posterity for their cruelty, they were, in truth, merely a fig leaf for the brute reality of German control. Indeed, they were often treated by the Germans with open contempt. On one occasion, a group of ghetto policemen found themselves caught in an SS roundup, in which they were "beaten with rubber truncheons, relieved of [their] caps and service number badges, and . . . brutally shoved into the ranks of a passing column of inmates." Recounting the event, one of the victims was surprised that his insistence to his captors that he was, in fact, a ghetto policeman, had a counterproductive effect, bringing about "a fresh series of beatings with a rubber truncheon."[39]

Perhaps the most poignant example of the tragic role played by the ghetto police is that of Calel Perechodnik, a ghetto policeman from the town of Otwock, southeast of Warsaw, who joined the force in the spring of 1941 in an attempt to improve living conditions for himself, his wife, and his baby daughter. In his searing memoir, which he wrote shortly before his suicide in 1944, Perechodnik was perhaps too forgiving of himself for his role as ghetto policeman, dismissively noting that he merely collected taxes and distributed bread. But there was one salient event for which he couldn't forgive himself. He had been promised by the Germans that ghetto policemen and their families would be exempt from the deportations that resulted from the liquidation of the Otwock ghetto in August 1942. It was a promise that was not kept. In the roundup of Otwock's Jews, Perechodnik had to watch as his wife, Anka, and daughter, Aluszka, were deported to their deaths in Treblinka. "All has been lost," he wrote. "May God have mercy on me." Though he recognized the criminal barbarity of the Germans, he now berated himself for his "recklessness" in believing that, by collaborating, he could save himself and his family. In a letter written to his dead wife, he tried to explain his thinking: "I was a fatalist. I thought that whatever had to be would be.

But I never imagined that you would perish and I would remain alive." The title of his memoir, hastily written while in hiding in Warsaw in 1943, was *Am I a Murderer?*[40]

Much more significant than the ghetto police was Warsaw's Bureau for Combating Bribery and Speculation, generally known as *Trzynastka*, or "the Thirteen," after its address on Leszno Street. Founded late in 1940 by Abraham Gancwajch, the Thirteen was essentially a front for the Gestapo and, in that way, wielded some considerable power, not least as it operated its own prison. Its members—known colloquially as "gamekeepers" for their green-trimmed caps—were supposed to combat smuggling, but increasingly they sought to infiltrate the ghetto's nascent resistance cells, thereby slipping ever closer to outright collaboration. Significantly, Gancwajch did not need to answer to Czerniaków and the council; he reported instead directly to the SS. The diarist and later ghetto historian Emanuel Ringelblum noted darkly in his journal the saying that those who joined "the Thirteen" could never leave.[41]

For those living in the ghetto, with its semblance of order, it was perhaps possible to adapt to the new normality. But, in crucial respects, ghetto life was not normal. For one thing, the German authorities were entirely above the pseudo-legal system they had created. When they ventured into the ghetto, SS men or Gestapo officers would routinely ignore any instructions from the ghetto police. Holding the monopoly on power and lethal force, they could act with complete impunity. As one diarist noted, incursions into the ghetto were not unusual: truckloads of SS men could appear at any time to snatch a suspect, beat up passersby, or enact some petty humiliation. In one incident, a small group of Germans appeared and began to loot a Jewish shop. As they left, one of them turned and fired his pistol into the crowd that had gathered to watch, killing an eleven-year-old child. He then calmly climbed back into the car and drove away. It was a terrible yet highly symbolic act.

Jews might have their cafés and their music halls and their police-men in the ghetto, but they had no rights at all.[42]

The point was demonstrated not only by casual brutality but also by more subtle means. The very definition of a Jew, for in-stance, could be astonishingly vague. It was, of course, an article of Nazi faith that the definition was not merely religious but rather had to be racial—or pseudo-racial—yet that raised the intractable problem of how to empirically identify the Jewish "race." Within the Reich, that problem was solved by the gentle art of genealogy, with the Nuremberg Laws of 1935 declaring that a Jew was any-one descended from at least three grandparents who were Jewish, or two grandparents if the individual concerned was a member of the Jewish religious community. Despite the obvious circular argument employed, resulting confusions could usually be cleared up thanks to the availability of local parish records.[43]

In occupied Poland, however, the problems of identifying who was a Jew and who wasn't proved to be more trying. Of course, Polish Jewry—especially its unassimilated, Orthodox compo-nent—conformed much more closely to the Nazi stereotypes attributed to the Jews. In large measure, therefore, the question of who was a Jew was relatively swiftly and easily resolved by Ger-man forces. Nonetheless, some legal framework was considered necessary, and soon after the invasion German administrators began to wrestle with the problem, initially applying simple re-ligious criteria, sometimes with the less-than-entirely-clarifying rider that "a Jew should be defined as a person born to Jewish parents." Attempts at further clarification followed, most draw-ing on religious affiliation and Jewish parentage but—lacking sufficient genealogical underpinning—relying at least in part on self-certification or the simple authority of the official concerned, all of which rather echoed the quip from Vienna's anti-Semitic mayor, Karl Lueger, from forty years earlier: "I decide who is a Jew." Unsurprisingly, perhaps, Himmler would before long put a stop to all such efforts at legal clarification, demanding that "no

decree concerning the definition of 'a Jew' should be published."
Such "stupid commitments," he explained, "only tie our hands."[44]

Despite this evident vagueness about racial definitions, German authorities in occupied Poland nonetheless exhibited a mania for documentation. Everyone living under German occupation had to have the right paperwork in order to exist. In this, Jews, too, were not exempt. Failure to provide the correct papers—on demand—was to risk death. Yet, Poland did not have the same bureaucratic traditions as Germany, and possessing official identification had not previously been mandatory for Poles. As one scholar has written: "Hundreds of thousands of citizens of the Republic of Poland, of all sorts of nationalities and faiths, especially inhabitants of villages and small towns, successfully went about their social and economic lives without any documents confirming their personal identity." This relaxed attitude naturally posed a problem for the incoming German authorities, and in the first instance, prewar passports, ID cards, or birth certificates were accepted, before the so-called *palcówka* identity document was introduced by the Germans in November 1939, which was required to be carried at all times by all former Polish citizens.[45]

In such circumstances, it is perhaps unsurprising that a vibrant market quickly developed in occupied Poland for false identity papers: the birth and baptismal certificates of the deceased and, of course, foreign passports. Nonetheless, despite the ingenuity and brilliance of the forgers, Polish Jews faced a specific predicament. Under the Polish Republic, they had endured many hardships and no small measure of popular anti-Semitism, but they had enjoyed civic and legal protection, not least under the March Constitution of 1921. By late 1939, however, Poland had ceased to exist and Polish law had been declared null and void. Thereafter—though they were required to be identified like everyone else—Jews were effectively stripped of the fundamental rights as citizens that they had previously enjoyed. The General Government did not deign to grant them any civic or legal rights and even decreed, early in 1941, that Jews in the territory were beyond the legal protection of the state. As Jan Karski had noted in his first report to the Polish government-in-exile the previous year, Jews existed only at the whim of their new German masters. The example that Karski gave was highly instructive. He described the Gestapo response to a complaint by a Jewish shopkeeper who had been robbed in Warsaw. The officer explained the lack of any reaction to the crime by saying, "Anything can be taken away from a Jew, for anything Jews possess has in fact been obtained by way of legalized robbery." He went on to state that "anyone who so wishes may kill a Jew—and our law will not condemn him for it."[46]

To make matters worse, by the time most of the ghettos were established, late in 1940, Poles and Jews alike had endured more than a year of persecution, marginalization, and impoverishment, much of it with the intention of exacerbating existing antagonisms and so preventing the emergence of any feeling of solidarity between the two groups. To this end, there were some notable direct actions. In Łódź, for instance, the Germans destroyed a synagogue and blamed it on the Poles; they then destroyed a church and blamed it on the Jews. Beyond that, much of the effort was led by propaganda, such as the common Nazi trope that the Jews spread disease. This, indeed, was the primary public rationale given by the German authorities for the establishment of the ghettos: the Jews were being isolated to protect the wider population from infection. As one inhabitant of the Warsaw ghetto recalled, German propaganda sought to drive a wedge between the Poles and the Jews to prevent any possible collaboration. "Walls were covered with posters depicting the Jews as repulsive and dangerous criminals or as vampires sucking Polish blood. Special free films were shown that demeaned and ridiculed Jews. Public lectures were held asserting that Jews were immune to typhus but functioned as carriers of the disease and could pass it on to Aryans." He concluded that it was "no wonder that so many

Poles . . . began to curse the Jews." In this way, the already strained relations between Polish Jews and their non-Jewish neighbors were soured further, making any sense of fellow feeling or mutual support across the ghetto walls that much harder to achieve. By the time they entered the ghettos, therefore, the Jews were already very much alone.[47]

Far from being a refuge from German tyranny, as some more optimistic Jews had initially thought, the ghettos represented the very opposite: a place in which Polish Jews—stripped of their rights and possessions, of their political representation, and of their support networks—could be sacrificed to whatever diabolical scheme Berlin could imagine.

EVENTS IN OCCUPIED POLAND WERE NOT OCCURRING IN A vacuum, however. They were being watched and reported on by the domestic representatives of the Polish government-in-exile: the nascent Polish underground forces of the ZWZ (the Union of Armed Struggle), successor to the SZP. Though its primary rationale was the preparation of military resistance against the German and Soviet occupiers, in the early months of the war the ZWZ also busied itself with intelligence gathering, commissioning reports on all aspects of Polish life under occupation and passing them on to their superiors in France and later in London. Another source of information for the government-in-exile was the underground newspaper *Biuletyn Informacyjny*, or *Information Bulletin*, a weekly produced clandestinely in Warsaw that, remarkably, boasted an unbroken production run through the war, from its foundation in November 1939 to the liberation from German rule in January 1945.

Given that it was initially ethnic Poles who bore the brunt of Germany's organized repression—as witnessed at Wawer, Fordon, Palmiry, and countless other massacre and execution sites—it was at first their predicament, rather than that specifically of Polish Jews, that formed the core of the ZWZ's intelligence reports.

However, as the German persecution of Jews in occupied Poland began to get into gear, so the focus of the information supplied to the government-in-exile began to shift. It was via this route, for instance, that news of the brutality, daily humiliations, and arbitrary violence experienced by Polish Jews at German hands first found its way westward. The establishment of the Łódź ghetto was reported by the *Biuletyn Informacyjny*, though scant details of its operation were then available, and in the autumn of 1940, the creation of the ghetto in Warsaw was duly communicated to London. In an editorial on November 28, 1940, the *Biuletyn Informacyjny* described the "gigantic crime" that was in progress. "In this manner," it said, "the Hitlerites' insane plan to enclose 410,000 people into a tiny isolated area, completely devoid of free space and greenery, has been achieved." Those people, it went on, "have been condemned to the inevitable consequences of epidemics and slow death from hunger."[48]

Such information demanded a response, and the result was a gradual shift in the focus of the government-in-exile's activities. From the outset, the exile government encompassed many of the opinions of ordinary Poles, including, in some cases, anti-Jewish prejudice, despite Sikorski's desire for his administration to distance itself from the prewar regime. Consequently, there were some who still saw the solution to Poland's "Jewish question" as the encouragement of emigration following the conclusion of hostilities, whether to Palestine or, as some suggested, to the Soviet Black Sea coast.[49]

However, by the summer of 1940, the dawning awareness of Germany's murderous intentions toward Polish Jewry caused all but the most hard-hearted to reevaluate their positions. It was no longer enough to postpone the issue of what should be done with Poland's Jews to an indeterminate future date. If the government-in-exile could do anything to help them, it had to be done now. In addition, having fled from Angers to London with the fall of France, the government had to bear in mind wider political considerations. Exposed to the sometimes chill winds of Western public opinion, Sikorski's government found that it would be well-advised to burnish its liberal democratic credentials and actively repudiate the prejudicial minority policies of the prewar regime. The result, in early November 1940, was the so-called Stańczyk declaration, a statement delivered by Sikorski's labor minister, Jan Stańczyk, at the symposium of the World Jewish Congress in London. Stańczyk announced his government's new position: denouncing all those in prewar Poland who had "allowed themselves to be seduced . . . by totalitarianism, racism and anti-Semitism" and reaffirming a new opposition to all antidemocratic political ideas. Most significantly, perhaps, he spoke on the future of Polish Jewry, which, he said, would be granted rights and duties in a future, liberated Poland, with the freedom to "develop their culture, religion and folkways without hindrance." It was very much a statement of intent, a commitment to adopt best practices regarding minority policies after Poland's liberation. As such, it was of little immediate benefit to those Jews who were then suffering in German ghettos on Polish soil, but it was at least a start.[50]

While the Stańczyk declaration was still being discussed in London, some Polish diplomats were already engaged in assisting Jewish refugees. Aleksander Ładoś, newly arrived in Bern, was one of them. That summer, in addition to dealing with the large numbers of refugee Polish Jews already present on Swiss territory, he was presented with a large-scale humanitarian crisis. In mid-June 1940, some thirteen thousand men of the Polish Second Rifle Division crossed the Swiss frontier, along with elements of the French Forty-Fifth Corps, and laid down their weapons. The division had been formed earlier that year from émigrés and army personnel who had escaped from Poland's defeat in September 1939 and had been charged with the defense of Belfort in Alsace, eastern France. However, with the wider French collapse in May 1940, the division was left exposed, and so, under its redoubtable commander Brigadier General Bronisław Prugar-Ketling, it executed a fighting withdrawal toward the Swiss frontier. As one of its number recalled, it was "a moving island of Polish defence, in a sea of French chaos."[51]

Once arrived on Swiss soil, the first problem the Polish soldiers faced was the Swiss intention to deport them to France, arguing that, as part of a French corps, the Second Rifle Division should be sent back alongside surrendered French forces. Mindful of the fate that could befall Polish troops, especially those of Jewish origin, at German hands and keen that they might, at some point, be able to rejoin the fight, Ładoś and his staff at the Bern embassy argued that Polish forces in the west were still subject to the orders of the Polish government-in-exile and so should be interned in Switzerland, rather than deported to an unknown fate as prisoners of war. After much patient negotiation with the Swiss authorities, this principle was finally acknowledged, and the Poles were permitted to remain in internment camps in Switzerland.[52]

Once the prospect of deportation had abated, the next problem was what to do with the internees. To this end, Ładoś would secure for Polish soldiers the possibility to work in Switzerland and to resume their education, with secondary, vocational, and technical courses being established within the camps, all under the motto "Learning for Poland, Working for Switzerland." Ładoś also went out of his way to cater to the needs of the many Polish Jews interned among them, ensuring that they were supplied with religious necessities and that Jewish holidays were recognized. It appears that he also sought to defuse the latent anti-Semitism in the internment camps by sending his special greetings to the Jewish soldiers and reminding all of the internees about the suffering of the Jews at the hands of their common enemy. In his later memoir, Ładoś recalled his pleasure at receiving a note of thanks "for the fatherly care and kindness shown to Polish soldiers of the Jewish faith." While it would be the ambassador who took the plaudits, it was his employee, Juliusz Kühl, who acted as the primary intermediary, visiting the camps and addressing the everyday concerns of the prisoners.[53]

Meanwhile, Ładoś and Kühl assisted the large number of Polish citizens who managed to enter Switzerland in those months after the German and Soviet invasions, the majority of whom were Jewish. In cooperation with the government-in-exile, the mission in Bern provided material, moral, and financial aid to refugee Poles, including setting up a hostel, helping them to enroll in Swiss universities, and providing passports to those who had lost their papers en route. As such activities rapidly exhausted the funds of the Polish mission in Bern, Ładoś was increasingly forced to look elsewhere for financial support, not only to the government-in-exile in London but also to local aid organizations. In the process, Kühl became the contact point for those Swiss welfare agencies that concerned themselves with Jewish matters, forging connections that would prove vital in the months and years to come.[54]

Elsewhere, there were other Polish officials who felt that they needed to act. The Polish consul in Marseilles, Jan Małęczyński, played an important role in that perilous autumn of 1940 in supplying visas and passports, among others, to fugitive Jews. Małęczyński was a part of the network set up by the American journalist Varian Fry to assist fugitives and escaped British servicemen who were fleeing from occupied France. Fry's "rat-line" across the Pyrenees is thought to have assisted as many as two thousand people in escaping from German-occupied France, including the novelist Heinrich Mann and the political philosopher Hannah Arendt. Arendt's experiences at this time as a stateless Jew, at the mercy of a faceless, malign bureaucracy, would be one of the most formative of her life.[55]

In Istanbul, meanwhile, the Polish consul there, Wojciech Rychlewicz, was wrestling with the influx of Polish refugees— both Jews and non-Jews—who were making their way into Turkey in 1940. Already in August of that year, he found it necessary to petition both the Foreign Ministry of the government-in-exile in London and Polish émigré organizations in the United States for additional funds to assist in meeting the subsistence costs of hundreds of Poles, most of whom were en route to Palestine and elsewhere. "Our current funds," he warned, "will last no longer than October."[56]

In due course, Rychlewicz would find that official and legal responses were insufficient for dealing with the influx. He began issuing certificates of religious affiliation to Jewish refugees, falsely attesting that the bearers were Catholics. In this task, he enlisted the help of a Polish Catholic priest, Antoni Wojdas—pastor of an ethnic Polish village in Turkey called Polonezköy—who forged baptismal certificates for the new arrivals, showing them to have been baptized in Poland many years before. Armed with these forgeries, the refugees—many of whom had escaped from the German and Soviet invasions of Poland the previous autumn—were not only able to apply for visas to Brazil, the United States, and British-mandated Palestine but also were able to stay in Turkey, which otherwise limited Jewish residency to only two hundred individuals per month. Rychlewicz was concerned that their names should not be too obviously Jewish, thereby risking discovery, but the list of those he helped still contained a host of Jewish names: from Epsztejn and Rozenbaum to Szwarcbart and Perlberger.

Among the 330 individuals known to have been assisted by Rychlewicz was Ellen Meth, a seventeen-year-old from Rzeszów who had fled with her family, first to Lwów (now L'viv in Ukraine) and then to Istanbul, arriving in the summer of 1940. Safe on the shores of the Bosporus, the family members briefly enjoyed the sights but were preoccupied with securing both their own onward journey and getting Ellen's grandmother, who had been unable to travel with them, out of Soviet-occupied Lwów. "We spent our days going from consulate to consulate, waiting in endless lines just to get a visa application or to speak to some official without ever getting any encouragement; no country seemed to be inclined to offer us refuge. We applied for entry visas to countries we never even heard of." Finally, by chance, they ran into an acquaintance from Rzeszów, who told them that Brazil was offering ten thousand visas to Catholic Poles and that false baptismal certificates might be sourced from the Polish consulate. Duly "reclassified" as Catholics by Rychlewicz, the family was able to successfully apply for visas to Brazil. Ellen's grandmother, sadly, was not so fortunate. Despite the family's desperate efforts, they were unable to secure the necessary papers for her to leave the Soviet zone of occupation, so she remained in Lwów and would in due course be murdered in Auschwitz. Later in life, Ellen would speculate over the motive of "the Polish consul," noting that she knew "for a fact" that no money changed hands. It was, she concluded, simply "an act of decency."[57]

There was also Polish involvement at the other end of the Sugihara escape line. In Tokyo, the Polish ambassador, Tadeusz Romer, played a vital role in smoothing the passage of the refugees and in many cases providing succor and accommodation for them while they were on Japanese territory. Already in August 1940, as the first of Sugihara's refugees arrived in Tsuruga, Romer established the Polish Committee to Aid War Victims, with the aim—as he explained to the government-in-exile in London—of providing arriving refugees with information, loans, housing, translation services, and so on.[58]

As in Istanbul, the most pressing need was for documentation and funds, and in both areas Romer led the relief effort. Given that Sugihara's visas were valid for only ten days—scarcely enough time for the new arrivals to find their feet, let alone arrange their onward travel—Romer successfully requested that the Japanese authorities extend the period of validity to three weeks. He also petitioned the British, Australian, and Canadian representatives in Japan to raise their issue quotas for visas, stressing the urgency of the situation and expressing the hope that the goodwill toward Poland, as a fellow combatant nation, might extend to the granting of extraordinary "visas of sojourn" to Polish refugees for the duration of the war.[59]

One of those saved by a Sugihara visa was Oskar Schenker, a former judge from Kraków who had fled to Lithuania when the Germans invaded Poland in September 1939. He paid effusive tribute to Romer in an article published the following year, declaring that the ambassador "set the example himself" with his dedication to and "fatherly affection" for the refugees. "He often worked tirelessly well into the night. In all this he exhibited such balance, such understanding, that anyone who came in contact with him was impressed by his deep and thorough approach to the problems he was faced with." After the tribulations of the previous year, Schenker recalled his arrival in Japan in October 1940 with unbridled gratitude as a return to something like normality. "I was lucky to be one of the first," he wrote.

> I must admit that I could not contain the emotion that accompanied me when, after a year of wandering and uncertainty about the next day, I was finally able to step on to the threshold of the Polish Embassy. The white eagle at the gates to the building, the Polish language, spoken loudly and openly, the uniform of our Defence Attaché . . . all this made such an impression on me, that for a moment during the first audience with His Excellency Tadeusz Romer, the Ambassador of Poland, I could not utter a single word.[60]

Poland's diplomats still had an important role to play in upholding civilized standards in a world that appeared to be rapidly abandoning them. And, at the other end of the Eurasian continent, some of their fellows were soon to demonstrate that they were of similar mind.

IN THE EARLY MONTHS OF 1941, LEO WEINGORT, A TWENTY-one-year-old Jew in the former Polish city of Lwów, was looking for a way out. Originally from Bielsko-Biała in Upper Silesia, he had fled the town in September 1939, first to Łódź, then to Warsaw, then to Lwów after the Soviet invasion of September 17, mindful perhaps that—as a Jew of military age—he might be particularly targeted by the occupying Germans. At first, Weingort was content in Lwów, but the restrictions and privations of Soviet rule soon began to grate. Already in the spring of 1940, he wrote to his brother Saul—a rabbi who was living in Montreux, Switzerland, at the time—stating that he was looking to escape, perhaps via Lithuania or Latvia. "In spite of the nice weather," he wrote, "it is always cold here." It was almost certainly a coded criticism of the restrictions that the Soviet authorities were imposing. As Sugihara had discovered in Kaunas, there were many Polish Jews who—while grateful that they had not found themselves in the German-occupied areas of Poland—were nonetheless profoundly unenthusiastic about living under Soviet rule for the long term. As one of their number would write in his diary a few months later:

> What we are most afraid of is that they'll never let us leave here. The border of the Soviet Union is worse than the Great Wall of China. Alienated from the West, from our own country, from a bourgeois, democratic, western culture, we are afraid that we will never return to our own folk, to our homes, to our European culture. This fear of a lifetime spent in a Bolshevik paradise is what troubles us most.[61]

Leo Weingort probably shared these concerns, but he also feared for his parents and sister, who had fled to Warsaw in the autumn of 1939 and so were dealing with the more immediately perilous conditions of the German occupation. In August 1940, he wrote to his brother again, worried that no good news was coming out of Warsaw. "I reproach myself for having left Mama and Papa," he wrote. "I am beside myself because I cannot help them. . . . Please make every effort to arrange to have them come to you."[62]

Saul had left Poland only weeks before the outbreak of war to take up a position teaching in a yeshiva in Montreux. In the months that followed, he had received numerous letters from his brother and other family members, in which they asked, with mounting desperation, if he could source passports or visas for them to ease their escape—a task that had been made considerably more difficult by the German decision, in October 1940, to forbid Jewish emigration from the territory of the General Government. From then on, Jews in German-occupied Poland were effectively trapped.[63]

Leo, too, was faced with increasing restrictions. The first wave of deportations from the Soviet zone of occupation had been carried out in February 1940, targeting mainly former officials of the Polish state but nonetheless alarming many by its scale, with more than 150,000 being deported to the collective farms and gulag camps of the Soviet interior. More significantly, Leo had heard that Polish passports would no longer be recognized by Soviet officials, thus making his own hoped-for escape all the more complex. In response, he wrote to his brother, stating that, if he were to get out of the Soviet Union, he would need a passport for another country, "possibly South America."[64]

Saul duly made inquiries at the Polish embassy in Bern, where he had already made contact with the legation's representative for Jewish affairs, Juliusz Kühl. He was told that Latin American passports could indeed be sourced for Polish citizens, but—as in the example of Chiune Sugihara—they could only be used for the trip across and out of the Soviet Union. Once the refugees were in Japan, Kühl added, new papers would have to be sought from the Polish embassy there, and the Latin American papers would have to be returned to Bern. Throughout, Saul Weingort recalled,

Kühl was rather unenthusiastic, stressing that he could give no guarantees that the ruse would work and cautioning that he had only heard that others had tried.[65]

Despite the warning, Saul considered it worth the attempt, so asked about the next steps. He was told to return with a photograph of his brother, along with essentials such as his date and place of birth. The cost, he was told, would be one thousand Swiss francs, which would go to a local notary named Rudolf Hügli, who would supply the passport. By the time another letter arrived from his brother that spring, the situation had already deteriorated. Writing from Kaunas now, Leo stressed that it was difficult to write from Lwów, presumably because of Soviet censorship or surveillance, and he asked again for his brother's assistance, adding, "Think of me, for in a short time it will be too late." Saul redoubled his efforts, borrowed the necessary money from his fiancée, and returned to Kühl with the required details and a photograph. Soon after, he received a Paraguayan passport in his brother's name, which he forwarded to Leo. Accompanying it was a letter, addressed to Leo, from Rudolf Hügli, asking for confirmation of receipt by telegram and advising him that he would need to apply for a Japanese transit visa upon arrival in Kobe. It closed by wishing him a good trip.[66]

The first of the "Paraguayan passports" was thereby issued. It had come into existence largely through serendipity—through the example set by a Japanese consul in distant Lithuania, through a letter from Soviet-occupied Lwów to a rabbi brother in Montreux, through the willingness of Polish diplomats to assist the needy, and through the pious dishonesty of a Swiss honorary consul. It was a modest start to one of the most remarkable rescue operations of the Holocaust.

4

A CRIME WITHOUT A NAME

SHORTLY BEFORE DAWN ON SUNDAY, JUNE 22, 1941, GERMAN forces advanced across the "boundary of peace" that had divided them from their Soviet allies. The attack that followed—launched by over three million men, along a 1,300 kilometer (800 mile) front from the Baltic to the Black Sea—was prefaced by an air assault and an artillery bombardment of unprecedented ferocity. It was the start of the largest invasion, and the bloodiest campaign, in the history of warfare, and it would turn many of the assumptions and allegiances of the previous twenty-two months on their heads.

Aleksander Ładoś was not surprised by the attack. He had never been convinced that the Nazi-Soviet relationship would last; he thought that it defied "historical logic." Consequently, in the weeks before the invasion, he had prophesied that Hitler was about to turn on his erstwhile ally. Departing from Bern for a few days earlier in June, he had told the British ambassador, David Kelly, that before he returned Germany would have attacked the USSR. Kelly replied that the available intelligence suggested the opposite, and that the German-Soviet relationship appeared to be thriving. Two weeks later, Kelly sent Ładoś a telegram stating simply, "*Vous aviez raison*"—"You were right."[1]

Elsewhere, the German attack provoked surprise, consternation, even relief. Winston Churchill, waking to the news at his residence at Chequers in Buckinghamshire, gave a "smile of satisfaction." In Berlin, meanwhile, Goebbels broadcast to the nation that day, reading Hitler's words in which he damned the "Jewish Anglo-Saxon warmongers" and placed Germany's fate, once again, in the hands of its soldiers. When he had finished, he confided to his diary in pompous style about hearing "the breath of history." It was "a solemn moment," he said, after which he felt "totally free." Only Stalin, it seems, was unaware of the threat he was facing. When petitioned by his generals for permission to return fire early that morning, he had refused, telling them that the attack was only a provocation and that they should avoid any unnecessary escalation. It would take him a few hours to realize the seriousness of his predicament.[2]

Some of Europe's Jews were also rather blind to the new reality that Operation Barbarossa appeared to presage. In Warsaw, Władysław Szpilman allowed himself to believe that Germany was now bound to lose the war. Mary Berg was similarly enthused, writing in her diary about the outbreak of German-Soviet hostilities: "Who could have hoped it would come so soon!" Yet, although such instincts might have been correct in the long term, in the short term, Jews would find themselves under more brutal pressure than before, as Nazi Germany's exterminatory impulses began to find more coherent and determined expression. From the very start of the Barbarossa campaign, Jews in the border areas overrun by German troops were routinely maltreated or massacred. In Gargždai, for instance, east of Memel (now Klaipėda, Lithuania), some six hundred Jews were rounded up by German gendarmes in the days after the invasion; four hundred of them would be murdered after being forced to dig a mass grave. They were condemned on the spurious charge of "crimes against the Wehrmacht."[3]

Similar scenes ensued across the border regions. At Białystok, German troops carried out a pogrom, chasing Jews through the narrow streets and throwing hand grenades into the cellars of the Jewish quarter. Jews were pulled from their homes, put up against the walls, and shot. Others were driven to the city's domed Great Synagogue, where they were locked inside before the building was set on fire. Those who tried to escape were machine-gunned and their bodies were hurled back into the flames. Some two thousand Jews are thought to have been killed there that day. At a conservative estimate, as many as forty thousand Jews were killed by German forces in Poland alone in the first three weeks of the new war. By the end of October, as many as half a million Jews are thought to have been murdered across the region.[4]

One of the worst examples of this wanton killing occurred in the eastern Polish city of Lwów, where a mixed population of Poles, Jews, and Ukrainians had already endured two years of brutal Soviet occupation. It made for an especially volatile atmosphere, with Ukrainian nationalists now keen to win German favor by fostering anti-Semitic violence, while many Poles were ready to avenge themselves for the humiliations and privations they had suffered under Soviet rule. Already prior to the arrival of the Germans in the last week of June 1941, Jews in the city—their numbers swollen to more than 150,000 by refugees from the provinces—had been terrified of what was to come. "We have to be ready for the worst" one of them wrote, "and accept everything we are faced with with stoicism." What followed would exceed even their worst nightmares.[5]

As the Germans arrived on the morning of June 30, Ukrainian militias were already roaming the streets of the city, targeting Jews. They had been well primed as to what was expected by their new German masters, and the stereotype of "Jewish Bolshevism" had already gained widespread credence. As the section of society most enthusiastic about the arrival of the Soviets in 1939, Polish Jews were popularly perceived as being among the primary beneficiaries and supporters of the Communist system. So, when that system was abruptly removed with the withdrawal of the Red Army and the Soviet administration a week earlier, it had been the Jews who had borne the brunt of the impulse for revenge. As a contemporary leaflet warned them: "You welcomed Stalin with flowers. We will lay your heads at Hitler's feet."[6]

That desire for revenge, however misplaced, was made all the more urgent by the discovery of thousands of decomposing bodies of former prisoners of the Soviets, who had been murdered by the NKVD prior to the withdrawal and were littering the cells and courtyards of Lwów's three prisons. The city's Jews were now rounded up for the grisly task of exhuming and cleaning the bodies of the murdered prisoners prior to their reburial. It would not take long for the Jews to be subjected to much more brutal treatment.[7]

The following day, July 1, these actions degenerated into a full-scale pogrom, with Jews dragged from their homes and forced to scrub the streets by hand or pick up manure. Jews were abused and beaten. Women were chased by a baying mob. Some were raped. One young Jewish woman, who had her hair publicly cut off and was chased naked down the street, committed suicide. Predictably, perhaps, much of the killing centered on the city's prisons, especially the Brygidki prison, where many of the victims of the Soviets had been discovered. There, those Jews dragooned for the grisly task of exhuming the victims of the Soviets often found they were simply digging their own graves. Once the exhumations were complete, they would routinely be lined up and shot. One man was spared only when the execution squad was dismissed by a German officer, who said, "Enough for today," after forty-seven Jews had been executed; he was the next in line. Another eyewitness watched helplessly as his father, a rabbi, was beaten to death with an iron bar by an "elegantly dressed" Ukrainian. As one survivor noted, "I didn't believe people could do this to people. I've never seen atrocities like it." According to official German sources, some five thousand Jews were murdered during those few days in Lwów, while an additional three thousand were executed by the Germans in the municipal stadium.[8]

One of those who survived the horrors in the city was Leo Weingort, who had received his Paraguayan passport via his brother in Switzerland earlier that year but had hesitated to leave, as he wanted to secure passports for his family and fiancée as well. When Leo managed to write to his brother again that autumn, after what must have felt like an agonizing period of silence, he suggested that the passport had already saved his life. Writing in code to evade the censors, he told his brother, "I have the results and it is useful. I would like it for our parents and Rose." He closed—en clair—in a plaintive tone: "I hope we will survive and the sun will shine again."[9]

FAR FROM THE KILLING FIELDS OF CENTRAL EUROPE, THE Polish government-in-exile was initially enthusiastic about the turn of events that Barbarossa signified. Surely, they reasoned, a public falling-out between the two criminal regimes that had invaded and occupied Poland would mark an important step on the road to eventual liberation. In a memo to Prime Minister Sikorski on the day of the German invasion, General Kazimierz Sosnkowski was unequivocally optimistic, stating that Barbarossa could be "highly advantageous" for the Polish cause.[10]

While such prognostications were perhaps understandable from the safe distance of London, events on the ground in occupied Poland presented a much less rosy view. Once the spontaneous massacres and inflamed passions of vengeance had subsided, the targeting of Jews by the Germans didn't abate; rather, it accelerated. Very soon after the front line had passed through, the active "cleansing" of populations began, utilizing the same tactics that had been deployed in the "decapitation" of Polish society after September 1939: systematic executions carried out by the *Einsatzgruppen* of the SS and their collaborators.

The *Einsatzgruppen* would reach their bloody apogee in 1942, but already in the summer and autumn of 1941 they began to cut a murderous swath through the Jewish communities of eastern Poland and the western USSR. There was nothing spontaneous about their work. It had been thoroughly prepared by the German political and military hierarchy, building on previous operations in Poland, and was perfectly aligned with Nazi ideology. In January 1941, the head of the SS, Heinrich Himmler, had given voice to the Hitler regime's intention to reduce the population of the USSR by some thirty million through the wholesale extermination of those considered racially worthless. By May, Reinhard Heydrich, Himmler's deputy, had passed on to the SS leadership cadre the order to kill all Soviet Jews in the coming conflict.[11]

The *Einsatzgruppen* took to their task with murderous alacrity all along the new eastern front, from Riga to Odessa. Their methods were simple; Jews were routinely rounded up in the areas behind the front lines and shot, en masse. In the few weeks that followed the invasion, every town or city with a Jewish population witnessed atrocities and massacres, in some cases many times over. Over three thousand Jews were killed in the area of Tauragė in Lithuania; 332 were shot at Vitebsk, 510 in Brest-Litovsk, over 1,000 in Minsk, and at least 5,000 in Vilnius. Further south, it was the same: two thousand were killed in Lutsk in Ukraine, six hundred in Zhytomyr. In Vinnytsia, the initial SS roundup—for the purposes of "registration"—produced a "less than satisfactory result," so those Jews who had already been captured were sent back to their homes with the instruction to bring more of "their kind" back with them the following day. They complied, and more than six hundred Jews were duly murdered. Tens of thousands of Jews were killed that summer by German forces.[12]

As the *Einsatzgruppen* were getting into their grisly stride, two events in the autumn of 1941 demonstrated German thinking on the legal issues surrounding mass killing and foreshadowed what was to come in the streamlining of that process. In early August, the Germans received some fourteen thousand Jews from refugee camps in Hungary who, crucially, did not have Hungarian citizenship. While Hungary would endeavor to protect its own Jews from the worst effects of its collaboration with the Third Reich, it had little inclination to protect those Polish or Slovak Jews who had found themselves on Hungarian territory, and so shipped them to the northeastern frontier and handed them over to the Germans. Lacking the legal protection conferred by citizenship, then, those Jews found themselves completely at the mercy of German forces and were deported in cramped freight cars to a temporary camp outside the Ukrainian city of Kamianets-Podilskyi. At the end of August, the decision was then made to "relocate" the Jews of that city, along with the stateless new arrivals, with the result that over twenty-three thousand Jews—men, women, and children—were force marched about sixteen kilometers (ten miles) to an area littered with craters from the recent fighting. There, over three days, they were systematically slaughtered by the men of the *Einsatzgruppen*, with the shell holes serving as mass graves.[13]

If the massacre at Kamianets-Podilskyi showed the German tactic of exploiting the lawless space created by their aggression to carry out mass killings, so events at Auschwitz concentration camp that autumn demonstrated the direction in which Germany's methods of killing were headed. Already in the summer of 1941, the disadvantages of mass shooting were clearly in evidence. Not only were such killings far too public—with rumors passing down to the civilian population, as well as photographs being illegally taken by those present—but there were also concerns about the psychological effect that this method had upon the killers. On witnessing a small-scale *Einsatzgruppen* massacre that summer near Minsk, Himmler himself was shaken. As an eyewitness recalled, "He couldn't stand still. His face was white as cheese, his eyes went wild and with each burst of gunfire he looked at the ground." With many members of the *Einsatzgruppen* finding solace in alcohol, discipline inevitably deteriorated. One unit commander, *SS-Gruppenführer* Erich von dem Bach-Zelewski, even began to worry about what sort of men the killing actions were creating: "Either neurotics or savages!"[14]

It is not surprising then that numerous efforts were made in the months that followed to streamline and depersonalize the killing process. While using explosives proved too messy and unreliable, poison gas appeared to show some potential. In trials at Sachsenhausen concentration camp that autumn, forty Soviet prisoners of war were killed after they were packed into the sealed rear compartment of a specially adapted box van, into which the vehicle's exhaust gasses were redirected. It was a method that had first been used in the killing of Polish psychiatric patients in January 1940, but the successful trial, along with the new urgency of finding alternative killing methods, meant that an order was now placed with a Berlin coach builder for thirty similar conversions. Those vehicles would be sent to Chełmno extermination camp, west of Warsaw, where gassing operations began in December 1941.

At the same time as the gas vans were being tested, experiments were already underway at Auschwitz, using the industrial, cyanide-based fumigant Zyklon B. The first attempt was not an overwhelming success. A group of Soviet and Polish prisoners was placed into a sealed cellar of Block 11, the punishment block, but—after being exposed to an insufficient amount of Zyklon B—some of them were still alive the following morning. When subsequent tests rectified the problems and were shown to kill prisoners swiftly and consistently, the commandant of Auschwitz, Rudolf Höss, informed his superiors of the success. All that was required now was the construction of purpose-built killing facilities, which the camp at nearby Auschwitz-Birkenau would soon provide.[15]

The extermination and concentration camp at Birkenau was begun in October 1941, initially as an overflow for the concentration camp at Auschwitz, a short distance away. It was intended, at first, as a labor camp, to exploit some of the hundreds of thousands of Soviet POWs who had fallen into German hands following the invasion of the Soviet Union that summer. Constructed over the winter of 1941–1942, the camp was huge, spreading over some 175 hectares (423 acres), almost twenty times the area of Auschwitz I. Within that, some three hundred buildings were constructed, mostly wooden stable blocks, which—though designed for fifty-two horses each—were made to accommodate upward of five hundred human beings, giving an initial projected capacity of 150,000. With no sanitary facilities, conditions in Birkenau were brutal from the outset. Of the ten thousand Soviet POWs who were brought in to construct the camp in October 1941, fewer than a thousand were still alive five months later, when the camp became operational. It would become the largest killing site in the Third Reich's archipelago of death.[16]

By the time that Auschwitz-Birkenau was open for business, the Germans had already begun the mass deportation of Jews. The processes that had previously been practiced piecemeal—such as in the murderous chaos of the Nisko plan—were put into more concerted action in the autumn of 1941, when the initial success of the invasion of the USSR appeared to show that the time was ripe for the next phase of ethnic cleansing. The Jewish populations of some of Germany's biggest cities were the first to be targeted. In October and November 1941, twenty deportation trains—or "transports," each carrying an average of one thousand people—left Vienna, Prague, Berlin, Frankfurt, Hamburg, and Cologne, bound for the ghetto at Łódź. On those outward journeys, at least, conditions were relatively civilized: third-class passenger carriages were used, with bench seats, and the threat of force—though implied—was rarely made explicit. Often, the German authorities encouraged Jewish community organizations to assist the process, providing food parcels and a modicum of emotional and logistical support. Crucially, the entire operation had the veneer of normality and legality. Each deportee would have received their deportation notice some days earlier, instructing them when and where to present themselves. They were given a precise list of what they were permitted to take with them and what they had to surrender to the authorities. All baggage was to be labeled with the transport number and the name and address of its owner. And, for those thinking of defying the deportation order, the notice carried on its front page the various paragraphs of German law upon which the deportation was based. To defy the order was to commit a criminal offense. Consequently, the mood among the deportees was generally one of bewilderment rather than fear. There were exceptions, of course—and suicides were not uncommon—but the vast majority packed their possessions, wondered about where they would be sent, and said their goodbyes.[17]

If the veneer of civility was successfully maintained during the journey, arrival in the ghetto at Łódź delivered a brutal dose of reality. The overcrowding and squalor of the ghetto was overwhelming, and the new arrivals reacted with visceral disgust. "They shouted, they were indignant," one ghetto chronicler wrote, adding that the new arrivals only exacerbated the existing difficulties, paralyzing the ghetto's meager transport system, reducing the rationing allocations, forcing up prices, and spurring the black market. Amid the horrors, one positive result of the influx of Jews from Germany and Austria was a degree of cultural enrichment in the ghetto, with an increase in concerts and public performances. Those of pianist Leopold Birkenfeld, newly arrived that autumn from Vienna, were described as "a feast for the ghetto's music lovers." It was understandable, perhaps, that ghetto inhabitants took such pleasures while they could. That year the death toll was rising inexorably, with dysentery and typhus commonplace, exacerbated by the Germans' efforts to prevent the removal of fecal waste. Within weeks of their arrival, the new deportees experienced a death rate that far outstripped that of established residents, with the elderly succumbing to heart disease and tuberculosis, while some younger individuals found refuge from their torments in suicide.[18]

After the "success" of the deportations to Łódź, the Germans repeated the exercise that winter, with an additional thirty-two thousand Reich Jews being dispatched to three new destinations: the former capital of the Belarusian Soviet Republic, Minsk; the former Lithuanian capital, Kaunas; and the former Latvian capital, Riga. As before, that veneer of civility, which had been paper-thin at best, swiftly slipped. The threat of force was now more manifest, and Gestapo men routinely rifled through the possessions of waiting deportees, looking for alcohol, jewelry, or anything else worth stealing. The journey, too, lacked even the most rudimentary comforts, with third-class carriages often being replaced by goods wagons, especially for those who were disabled or bedridden. It was not unusual for frail or elderly deportees to perish during what could be a five-day journey.[19]

Faced with such existential challenges, the majority of deportees would not have noticed that, with their deportation, they had become nonpersons. Already stripped of their Reich citizenship by the Nuremberg Laws of 1935, they had then been obliged to surrender all birth, marriage, and death certificates, as well as any financial papers and savings books, when they had registered for their "evacuation." Permitted to keep only their passports, if they had them, they were probably unaware that their remaining political and civil rights, such as they were, were automatically forfeited at the moment of their departure from the German Reich. With that, their remaining assets and property passed— after the deduction of any outstanding debts and the costs of their deportation—automatically to the German state. Consequently, those who arrived from Germany into the ghettos of Kaunas, Minsk, or Riga had no legal rights at all. They might still try to brandish their German passports, but they were nonpersons, citizens of nowhere. They now inhabited an extralegal space in which there was no obstacle or impediment—beyond the logistical—to their further deportation or extermination. It was for this reason that false papers and forged passports would often become essential for deported Jews if they were to survive. As the historian Timothy Snyder has written, "False documents were a step back toward the world of recognition by the state . . . a piece of paper that permitted a return to a zone where some kind of law functioned."[20]

At the time, of course, few Jewish deportees would have perceived the perilous implications of their sudden statelessness, and, for all of them, arrival at their destination brought more immediate concerns. Kaunas, Minsk, and Riga already had ghettos, where the local Jewish populations had been corralled, starved, and terrorized for much of the previous six months since the arrival of German forces, and conditions were predictably horrific. One of the new arrivals, Heinz Bernhardt from Berlin, discovered that the shabby collection of buildings to which he was billeted in the Minsk ghetto was strangely deserted. He swiftly divined what had happened: "It looked as if a pogrom had taken place there. Pillow feathers everywhere. Hanukkah lamps and candlesticks lying around in every corner." He was right. To make room for the new arrivals, the ghetto's former residents had been taken out by the SS and shot. By way of confirmation, Bernhardt was shown a heap of refuse, "with parts of human bodies sticking out."[21]

Overcrowding also plagued the Łódź ghetto, and in January 1942, the German authorities ordered a resettlement action, affecting some ten thousand people. The ghetto administration decided to select "undesirable elements"—prisoners, the elderly, and those incapable of work—for the transport, declaring that only those who surrendered themselves voluntarily would be permitted to take the allocated 12.5 kilograms (27.5 pounds) of luggage with them. Take-up was meager. Life in the ghetto was certainly hard, but nobody wanted to be sent to an unknown fate. There was widespread fear, and the postmen who delivered the deportation notices became known as *Malchamoves*, or "angels of death." One of them recalled that the recipients would often burst into tears, as rumors were already going around that deportees would be exterminated. The rumors were grimly accurate. What awaited the deportees from Łódź was the extermination camp at Chełmno and the gas vans of the SS. The vast majority of them would be murdered upon arrival.[22]

An eyewitness recorded the progress of the killing. Szlamek Winer, a thirty-year-old Jew from Izbica, arrived at Chełmno as a prisoner in early January 1942 and was then sent out to the nearby Rzuchowski forest to labor as a gravedigger. He described how the trucks arrived at the site, parking close to the graveside. The drivers got out, leaving the engine running, as "screams, desperate sobbing and banging" could be heard from inside. After around fifteen minutes, the driver returned to his cab and shone a flashlight through a window into the back of the truck. If he was content that his human cargo was all dead, he would switch off the engine and give the order for the vehicle to be cleared. With a billow of exhaust fumes, the doors were opened and the gravediggers began to unload the mass of bodies inside. Winer recalled that "they lay, tangled up, in the filth of their own excrement, looking as if they had just lain down to sleep, their cheeks a natural colour without any pallor. The bodies still warm."[23]

After throwing the bodies into the pits, the gravediggers would then clean the truck, sweeping out the filth with their own shirts. An hour later, another vehicle would arrive, and they would repeat the process. For some, the horror was compounded by personal loss; one of the men recognized the corpse of his fourteen-year-old son as he was being thrown into the pit. All of them were aware that theirs was only a temporary reprieve. Given that they evidently knew too much, it was normal for the men of the grave-digging detail to be shot at the end of each day. As one of them said to Winer on his arrival at the site, "We are dead, but you must try to get out of this hell." Winer did precisely that. On January 19, he absconded and made his way to Warsaw.[24]

The day after Winer's escape, a meeting in an elegant villa in the suburbs of Berlin showed the direction in which Nazi thinking on the Jews was evolving. At Wannsee on January 20, Reinhard Heydrich, Himmler's deputy in the SS, convened a meeting of thirteen senior civil servants from across the German government and Nazi Party administration to discuss what had come to be known as the "Final Solution of the Jewish Question." There, in refined surroundings, he explained how the previous policy of encouraging emigration had run into difficulties with the outbreak of the war, and he informed his guests that a new policy would henceforth take its place: that of the "evacuation" of European Jews "to the east." This phrase was, of course, a euphemism for murder, and Heydrich helpfully went on to explain that the new policy consisted of working deported Jews to death through hard labor, after which any surviving remnant would be "handled accordingly." This action, however, was only to be a temporary solution, he said, adding that "practical experiences"—a reference perhaps to the experiments carried out in Auschwitz—were being gathered that would be of "great significance" to the "imminent" Final Solution. In the meantime, Europe would be "combed from west to east" for an estimated eleven million Jews, Heydrich said, who would be deported eastward into the ghettos prior to their being transported further "to the east." The wording was necessarily vague and euphemistic, but, as Heydrich's guests were well aware, what their host was outlining was the wholesale extermination of European Jewry.[25]

A month later, on February 27, 1942, the arrival at Auschwitz of the chief of construction of the SS, Hans Kammler, heralded significant changes. For some time, the SS had been carrying out the so-called 14f13 program, a sifting of the concentration camps to identify and exterminate those prisoners who were unable to work. In the early phase, those thus identified had been gassed in the sanitoriums that had earlier been used for the T4 euthanasia program, which had targeted those Germans suffering from hereditary diseases and disabilities. Now, though the successful experiments with Zyklon B provided a new possibility, Auschwitz I was found to be ill-suited as a killing site, because using the makeshift gas chamber and crematorium in the camp necessitated the temporary suspension of all normal routines, so as to preserve a modicum of secrecy. As Kammler recognized, if the killings were to continue on a large scale, a bespoke extermination site would be required.

At the same time, the camp at nearby Birkenau—by now largely complete—was looking for a purpose. Having been established to hold Soviet POWs, it stood mostly empty, as the majority of Red Army prisoners had either been taken directly to the Reich for forced labor or else had been left to die in makeshift, open-air prison compounds close to the front line. Following Kammler's arrival, therefore, Birkenau would begin its career as an extermination camp. Kammler approved plans for the construction of a large new crematorium in Birkenau and oversaw the conversion of the so-called red house, an existing brick building on the site, into a gas chamber. In this curiously organic way, the deliberations of Nazi mandarins in Berlin meshed perfectly with the practical realities on the ground, and a camp once intended to hold Soviet POWs was set on the path to become the primary killing site in the genocide against the Jews.[26]

Soon after, on March 20, 1942, Birkenau received its first prisoners. A small transport of elderly Polish Jews from Upper Silesia was brought straight to the red house, where they were murdered, and their bodies were buried in a nearby meadow. Three days earlier, the extermination camp at Bełżec—near Lublin,

270 kilometers (168 miles) to the northeast—had also commenced operations when a transport of Jews from Galicia was murdered using exhaust gasses from a stationary tank engine.

The unfortunates being deported to these sites rarely had much inkling of what awaited them. There was a natural unwillingness to embark on a journey into the unknown, of course, so the German authorities assuaged their concerns by providing a mendacious, rosy narrative of life in the "labor camps." In mid-April 1942, an SS officer posing as the commander of one of the destination camps appeared in the Łódź ghetto, where he gave precious—and entirely fictitious—information on the condition of those already deported. They were in a large camp named Warthebrücken, he explained, which was home to around one hundred thousand Jews. The barracks there were in "perfectly decent order," food supply was "exemplary," and those fit to work were employed repairing roads and carrying out agricultural tasks. It all sounded so attractive that some Jews who had previously succeeded in having their names removed from the deportation lists now volunteered to be deported, in the hope that the earlier they could establish themselves in the new camp, the better it would be for them. The deception was so successful that a ghetto chronicler reported that "the menace of deportation has ceased to be as terrible as it was before."[27]

It did not take long for the mask to slip. When the time came for them to board their trains in early May, deportees were dismayed to be ordered to step back and drop all of the baggage, bedrolls, and packages that they had with them and leave them on the platform. They were permitted to board only in what they were wearing. When those personal effects were then gathered up and carted away, through the ghetto, to storehouses, the sight "cast a chill" over those who remained. The sense of foreboding was such that, in the days that followed, there was a spate of suicide attempts among those scheduled for deportation. As one eyewitness recalled, the new arrivals, once so elegant and refined, had now been reduced to "ghosts, skeletons . . . ragged and impoverished," who were not even permitted to embark on their onward journey with so much as a knapsack. The grim premonitions that they had had upon their arrival in the ghetto, he lamented, "had proven all too true."[28]

JUST AS GERMAN POLICY TOWARD THE JEWS EVOLVED IN the period after the invasion of the USSR, so knowledge of the deportations and the first killings—though piecemeal—began to spread to the outside world. More significantly, word of the new horrors was not slow to arrive in Western capitals. Already in September 1941, the intelligence reports of the Polish underground spoke of the mass killing of Jews, noting that the Germans

> wrap the slaughter in mystery, apparently taking the Jews away in an unknown direction. The local population, forced to dig graves and bury corpses, relates with details the results of this "resettlement." . . . In Lithuania almost all Jews have already been murdered . . . in Niemenczyn 600 Jews . . . in Ejszyszki 200, in Troki more than 1000. Of 70,000 Jews who were in the ghettos of Vilna [Vilnius] only 40,000 remain.[29]

Another report spoke of the conditions in the Warsaw ghetto, where "most people are starving in the literal sense of the word. More and more emaciated corpses are seen on the streets swollen from hunger. Typhus and dysentery are rife." Aleksander Ładoś, too, attempted to alert London to the growing mass murder of the Jews in occupied Poland. In November 1941, he told the British minister to Switzerland, David Kelly, that some 1.5 million Jews who had been living in eastern Poland had "simply disappeared. . . . Nobody knows how or where."[30]

That autumn, underground intelligence reports informed the government-in-exile in London not only of the Babi Yar massacre outside Kyiv—which had taken place late in September and had cost some thirty-three thousand lives—but also of the decree issued by Governor-General Hans Frank authorizing the death penalty for those Poles who dared to assist Jews in any way. This decree, unique in German-occupied Europe, was no idle threat. When, in April 1943, the Germans discovered eleven members of the Wajntraub family sheltered in a specially built bunker on Henryk Olszewski's property in the village of Skórnice, south of Warsaw, they wasted no time in punishing the miscreants. While the Wajntraub family was murdered in the bunker with grenades, Henryk and his stepson Leon were taken away to an unknown fate. The remaining seven members of the Olszewski family, including three children under five, were all killed in their own house, which was then burned to the ground.[31]

The Olszewski family would be posthumously named among the over seven thousand Polish Holocaust rescuers. Of the Righteous Among the Nations, Poland has the largest contingent by nationality. The Olszewskis' bravery, and that of other such families, was remarkable, but there was another side to the story that was beginning to emerge. Already at the start of the war, concerns had been raised in the government-in-exile about the persistence of anti-Semitic attitudes among the Polish population, attitudes that were often exacerbated by the realities of occupation: whether the "divide and rule" and active fostering of anti-Semitism practiced by the Germans or the consequences of the brutal Soviet occupation, which left many angry and embittered at the perceived collusion between local Jews and Soviet Communists.[32]

By the middle of 1941, then, such attitudes—stoked by German propaganda—had not abated; on the contrary, they were proving remarkably durable. As a report to the government-in-exile in London explained, though the Polish population categorically disapproved of the Germans' treatment of the Jews, "it would nonetheless be a grave error to suppose that anti-Semitism among the Poles is a thing of the past." Most worryingly, perhaps, reports from the Polish Home Army that summer expressed concerns about the participation of local populations in pogroms against Jews in eastern Poland, as some appeared to have viewed the German attack on the Soviet Union as an opportunity to avenge themselves on their Jewish neighbors. For the government-in-exile, which was seeking to position itself favorably in the new constellation of its allies, such reports were a painful reminder that relations between Gentiles and Jews in occupied Poland were under more strain than ever before. For all the laudable optimism that Sikorski's government showed in its declarations on the Jewish question, it was clear that it was an argument that would splutter on for some time yet.[33]

While Polish leaders wrestled with the question of what to do with the information they were receiving, Britain's cryptographers, too, were gaining at least partial knowledge of what was going on in the ghettos and camps of eastern Europe. Bletchley Park had been decoding a proportion of German Order Police transmissions since September 1939 and—despite some setbacks—had collated sufficient reports of the mass executions of Jews that it was able to pass the material on to the British government with a degree of confidence in the larger picture that was being presented. Consequently, in a radio broadcast on August 24, 1941, Churchill spoke of "a crime without a name" being committed behind the lines on the eastern front. "Since the Mongol invasions of Europe in the Sixteenth Century [sic]," he said, "there has never been methodical, merciless butchery on such a scale."[34]

As those partial details mounted up, the Polish underground began to join the dots, and by the end of that year, its intelligence reports were already writing of "the removal of Jews from Europe" and their "complete elimination." "Jews in the east are being systematically murdered," one report noted. Though the hideous reality appeared to be staring them in the face, the only unknown, according to underground intelligence, was the precise method being employed. "It is not yet clear," a report from December 1941 concluded, "how the Germans will rid Europe of Jews: expulsion or murder." It would not be long before any lingering doubt was removed.[35]

At the same time that governments in the western half of Europe were trying to decipher the true, horrific nature of events taking place in the eastern half, Jews in the very eye of the Nazi storm were beginning to look for a way out. One of them was Gutta Eisenzweig, a twenty-four-year-old living in Warsaw. Born to a middle-class Jewish family in 1917, Gutta had grown up in an Orthodox, Yiddish-speaking household and attended Warsaw University, graduating in the spring of 1939. The arrival of the Germans that autumn made it immediately clear to her that the occupation would involve a "more than or-dinary" cruelty. Confinement to the ghetto in 1940 hit especially hard. "We had entered hell," she recalled. "We had lost our belief in humanity."[36]

In such circumstances, comfort lay in preserving a semblance of normality, and Gutta contributed to that by starting a school for girls within the ghetto, as well as by writing for the ghetto newspaper, the *Gazeta Żydowska*. In addition, some succor was provided from the outside, in the form of parcels containing food and medicines that were sent from the Jewish aid agencies abroad. In Gutta's case, she had a useful foreign contact in Mr. Eli Sternbuch, a Jew from St. Gallen in Switzerland, who—through mutual friends—had been introduced to her before the war and had become a suitor. By chance, Sternbuch, along with his brother Yitzchak and his sister-in-law Recha, was already closely involved in providing aid for Jews. The formidable Recha had helped to smuggle fugitive Jews out of Nazi-occupied Austria in 1938, and all three were now engaged in sending food parcels and medical supplies into occupied Warsaw.[37]

By the autumn of 1941, numerous organizations and indi-viduals were already involved in supplying vital aid to the ghettos in occupied Poland, especially the largest, such as Warsaw, Łódź, and Będzin. Alongside individuals such the Sternbuchs, there was Alfred Szwarcbaum, who had escaped from Będzin with his family in 1940 and established himself as a one-man aid operation working out of Lausanne, where he concentrated on raising funds and distributing essentials to those in need. Saul Weingort was also stepping up his activities. Though he had started out sending packages only to his relatives in Poland—and had procured that Paraguayan passport for his brother Leo the previous spring—he began to expand his aid work, dispatching packages to a broader circle of contacts in Warsaw, Vienna, Tarnów, Łódź, and elsewhere, often responding to direct requests from strangers.[38]

In addition, a number of aid agencies were also active, including the American Jewish Joint Distribution Committee, commonly known as the Joint, which was involved in fundraising for Jewish causes; the World Jewish Congress and its relief agency RELICO; the Orthodox Agudath Israel; and the *Hilfsaktion für notleidende Juden in Polen* (Support Action for the Suffering Jews of Poland), which operated out of Zürich. The quantities supplied were considerable. The accounts of the latter for 1941 revealed that foodstuffs worth some twenty-two thousand Swiss francs—including consignments of sardines, chocolate, rice, and coffee—were sent to Warsaw, Będzin, and Kraków. Gutta Eisenzweig recalled that "thousands of packages" were received in Warsaw from Agudath Israel, every one of which was "inestimably precious" to the ghetto's inhabitants, restoring hope and the will to live.[39]

What was common to many of the Jewish aid agencies was that they operated out of Switzerland, exploiting that country's location, its neutrality, and its political status as an island of democracy in Axis-controlled Europe. And it would be through these aid networks that the last two members of the Ładoś Group—Abraham Silberschein and Chaim Eiss—fell into place. It would be an exaggeration to imagine the group as a tight-knit conspiratorial cell, cooperating closely in the production of fraudulent passports; rather, it should be seen as a somewhat looser organization in which collaboration as well as independent action was possible. Its core consisted of six members—Silberschein and Eiss alongside Aleksander Ładoś, Stefan Ryniewicz, Konstanty Rokicki, and Juliusz Kühl—all of whom were fully apprised of the passport operation, while others on the fringes were not.[40]

As we have seen, the diplomatic members of the group—Ładoś himself, along with his colleagues Ryniewicz, Rokicki, and Kühl—were all in place by the summer of 1940. Yet, although the group had already collaborated in the production of a Paraguayan passport for Leo Weingort earlier that year and for Henryk and Maria Goldberger in May 1940 (the earliest documented example), it seems they had not yet considered expanding their operation beyond the meeting of a few special requests. That began to change in the late summer of 1941.[41]

One of the catalysts for that shift was the case of the French socialist politician Pierre Mendès-France, who arrived in Switzerland that autumn. Mendès-France had been arrested by Vichy French authorities in Morocco in the summer of 1940 and charged with desertion—despite the fact that he had advocated a continuation of the fight against German occupation. Tried in the summer of 1941, he was sentenced to six years imprisonment by a military tribunal but managed to escape during a routine hospital appointment. Using crudely forged identity documents, he fled to Switzerland, ferried across Lake Geneva by well-wishers, with the intention of traveling to London to join Charles de Gaulle's Free French. However, though now safe on Swiss soil, for onward international travel he needed a better passport, so he turned for assistance to the Jewish aid agency RELICO and its director, Abraham Silberschein.[42]

Silberschein was himself a refugee. Born in Lwów, he had trained as a lawyer and had served as a member of the Polish parliament in the mid-1920s before devoting his energies to advocating the Zionist cause. It was in this context that he had first come to Geneva, in August 1939, to attend the Zionist Congress, only for his return to be prevented by the outbreak of war. Forced to remain in Switzerland, Silberschein duly established RELICO—shorthand for the Relief Committee for Jewish War Victims—and set about assisting Polish Jews living under German occupation. That winter he had been part of the entourage of the Polish composer Jan Paderewski, along with other Polish diplomats, which had participated in a League of Nations session to discuss the destruction of Poland, so he was already acquainted with the Polish diplomatic staff in Bern. Now, the arrival of Mendès-France in the autumn of 1941 strengthened that connection further, as it would be via this channel that Mendès-France was provided with a Polish passport in the name of "Jan Lemberg," as well as a Cuban visa for his onward journey, all of which enabled him to travel to Portugal and on to London.[43]

Amusingly, Mendès-France's escape was almost derailed by his own vanity. The passport that was provided to him by the Polish mission gave the bearer's age as forty-six, twelve years older than the French politician actually was. Taking umbrage, Mendès-France is said to have spilled ink over the passport—accidently or not—thereby making it unusable. When a replacement was provided, it was explained to him that the Swiss had an agreement with the Vichy regime, whereby a sealed train staffed with Swiss personnel was permitted to travel once a week unhindered and unchecked through Vichy territory to the Spanish frontier, on condition that it did not contain men of military age—that is, between seventeen and forty-five. Hence the insistence that "Jan Lemberg" had to be forty-six years old. With that, Mendès-France—prematurely aged—traveled to freedom.[44]

After Silberschein, the last addition to the group was Chaim Eiss, the representative in Switzerland of the Orthodox Jewish aid agency Agudath Israel. Like Silberschein, Eiss had been born in Poland, but he had moved to Switzerland in 1900 at the age of twenty-four and worked as a merchant in Zürich. Increasingly active in Jewish circles, he then cofounded Agudath Israel in 1912 and, during the First World War, established an aid network for Jewish refugees. By the time that war broke out again in 1939, therefore, Eiss was well-placed to serve as a conduit for aid, funds, and information between the Jewish Orthodox communities of occupied Poland and the outside world. And that is what brought him into contact with the circle around Aleksander Ładoś.[45]

The precise moment at which the provision of aid morphed into the supply of forged passports is rather unclear, but it is worth remembering that it was a step that—for Orthodox Jews at least—would not have been taken lightly. Providing aid or ritual necessities was one thing, but to involve oneself in the forging of passports was quite another, and crucially it broke the Talmudic instruction that "the law of the land is the law." Yet, as the predicament faced by Jews in occupied Poland grew more acute in the autumn of 1941, and as word of it leaked out, the threat to Jewish lives was evidently considered real and immediate enough that instructions to obey Gentile law could legitimately be overridden.

Once those religious and moral obstacles had been overcome, there just remained the practical difficulty of extending assistance effectively. Thankfully, there were precedents. Gutta Eisenzweig recalled that Eli Sternbuch was inspired to request a Paraguayan passport for her after hearing about the example of Isaac Domb, a Warsaw Jew who had obtained a Swiss passport and thereby secured a modicum of protection from Nazi persecution. It is, of course, also possible that Sternbuch heard from Saul Weingort about the passport provided for his brother Leo. Either way, connections were made between Sternbuch and Juliusz Kühl at the Polish legation in Bern, and through the latter to Rudolf Hügli, the Paraguayan honorary consul. In November 1941, a "package" duly arrived for Gutta Eisenzweig in the Warsaw ghetto containing a Paraguayan passport. These documents—the Polish passport supplied to Pierre Mendès-France and the Paraguayan one for Eisenzweig—would not only save both of their lives but would pull together the various individuals who made up the Ładoś group.[46]

As the primary supplier of blank passports, Rudolf Hügli played a crucial role in the operation, though his motivations are rather more opaque. A sixty-nine-year-old notary and a native of Bern, Hügli was something of a character in the Swiss capital. He already had a successful career as a diplomat behind him and had been responsible for establishing both a golf club and a tennis club in the city, where he and his wife hosted a popular annual ball. Most importantly, since 1931 he had served as honorary consul for the Republic of Paraguay, with responsibility for much of central Switzerland, including the cantons of Bern, Lucerne, Unterwalden, and Ticino. It was in this capacity that he was able to issue passports.[47]

Hügli's role in the passport scheme, though lucrative, was not the result of simple avarice; it was more complex than that. For one thing, he met a pressing need. Ładoś urgently needed a fresh supply of passports, having exhausted the small stock of blank Polish documents that he had inherited at the embassy, and he had been advised by the Polish Foreign Ministry in London to find an independent source. Hügli suggested himself for that role, most likely because he had already been involved with issuing "unofficial" Paraguayan visas during the refugee crisis that had followed the Austrian Anschluss in 1938. Then, as he would explain to the Swiss police years later, he had been inundated with Jews requesting papers to enable their relatives in Germany to escape. After some hesitation, he had agreed to issue visas, justifying his actions to himself with the argument that, in line with his Christian faith, it was morally permissible for him to break the law in trying to ease the suffering of those in need. Given that this decision was well-known to those Swiss lawyers with whom he had collaborated in 1938, it is likely that this was the reason he was approached by Juliusz Kühl, with the suggestion that he reprise his earlier "unofficial" activities. Hügli duly offered to sell the Poles thirty stamped, blank Paraguayan passports, which only needed to be filled out with the relevant information. They would be the first of many.[48]

Nonetheless, for all the moral justifications that he gave himself, it seems that Hügli was evidently troubled, initially at least, by his actions in issuing the Ładoś passports. In October 1941, he wrote to the Paraguayan ambassador in Berlin to explain his actions, seemingly hoping to preempt any accusations of malfeasance should his participation in the forgery operation be discovered. He outlined the circumstances of that summer, explaining how Polish citizens in the Soviet zone of occupation had had no chance of escape without foreign papers. He then reassured the ambassador that he had acted out of humanitarian concerns and stated that the few examples he had issued had been accompanied by the instruction—as had been given to Leo Weingort—to proceed to Kobe in Japan and apply for a Polish passport from the embassy there. "These people," he stressed, "never had the intention to travel to Paraguay."[49]

However, Hügli went on, the situation had changed with the outbreak of the German-Soviet War. Given that the exit route eastward across the Soviet Union had now been made impassable by the fighting, he explained, it was possible that refugees would try to travel via Germany to Lisbon, and so might come to the attention of the embassy in Berlin. He closed with the rather plaintive request that, should such cases be presented to the Paraguayan embassy, they should be recognized as Paraguayan citizens. Evidently concerned that he might be discovered, he also wrote that day to two of the recipients of his passports—Leo Weingort and Henryk Goldberger—to ask how their planned emigration was progressing.[50]

Despite Hügli's concerns for his career, the growing peril in which Polish Jews found themselves meant that word of the passports gradually spread, not only through Swiss-Jewish circles but also far beyond. That autumn, Juliusz Kühl received a number of letters from passport "applicants." One, from a Rabbi Mund from Leysin in Switzerland, thanked Kühl in advance for his kind assistance in supplying a passport for his father in occupied Poland, enclosing a photograph of the man with his three grandchildren. Another correspondent asked about the possibility of getting papers from the Dominican Republic for a brother-in-law who had been deported from Poland by the Soviets and was now stuck in Kazakhstan. A third wrote, rather tersely, to inquire about the progress of his application, stressing the urgency of the hour and asking when he might expect a reply.[51]

Kühl had a strong personal motivation for giving his energy to such cases: he was at that time trying to find his mother. Perla Kühl had lived in Sanok in southern Poland at the start of the war but had then disappeared in the chaos that followed. As her son would discover, she first moved east to Tyrawa Wołoska in the Soviet zone of occupation. From there, it appears, she was deported by the Soviets eastward, to Djambul in Kazakhstan— possibly for the offense of "cosmopolitanism," or for her foreign connections, or for the catchall crime of "anti-Soviet activity." So it was that, by the spring of 1942, Kühl was desperately contacting anyone he thought could help locate her—including Intourist, the Soviet travel agency; the Polish diplomatic mission in Kuybyshev; and the Jewish Agency in Istanbul—so that he might help her to escape the Soviet Union.[52]

While Kühl was busy trying to find his mother, word reached Warsaw of the growing operation at whose heart he stood. As Gutta Eisenzweig recalled, "Soon, a few other people also received passports to South and Central American countries. People started asking me if I could get them such papers." Gutta wrote back to Eli Sternbuch to request additional passports for her parents. At the same time, Saul Weingort was under pressure from his mother, Mathilde, who was also in Warsaw, to supply papers for his younger sister Rose, asking him repeatedly in coded language to "make arrangements" and "send results," reminding him of the urgency of the situation. In mid-January 1942, Rose Weingort received official confirmation from Bern that she had been recognized as a Paraguayan citizen.[53]

Before long, the scheme came to the attention of Abraham Lewin, a former teacher turned ghetto diarist. In the spring of 1942, he wrote in his diary, with a few inaccuracies, of the "Wajngot" family in Warsaw who had a son living in Switzerland who had sent Uruguayan [*sic*] passports to his siblings, a "sudden acquisition of nationality" that the Germans appeared to regard as legal. According to his version of events, the South American countries concerned were willing to grant citizenship to foreigners if they bought a plot of land there. Consequently, he wrote, "In the consulates of those countries in Switzerland it has been possible to buy a passport for a large sum of money."[54]

Word of the possibility of getting hold of a Paraguayan or indeed any other foreign passport was certainly spreading that winter, therefore, but only a few were yet willing to take the plunge. The reasons for this moderate uptake can only be speculated upon. Most obviously, though conditions for Jews in the ghettos of occupied Poland were certainly extremely harsh, the shift in Nazi policy toward extermination was yet to make itself widely felt. Consequently, for many—the majority perhaps—it was still possible to hope that, despite their very evident difficulties, things would turn out all right.

Moreover, for those who even considered the possibility of escape, it would have been clear to them that it was very much a leap into the unknown. For one thing, the strains of life in the ghettos had thrown up any number of crooks and chancers eager to swindle the desperate out of their money or possessions. Gutta Eisenzweig recalled how her family, eager to get news of her father, who had traveled to Łódź and not returned, had given a diamond ring to men who promised to help, only to hear nothing more in response. Ghetto historian Emanuel Ringelblum would have recognized the problem. He wrote in his journal in May

1942 about how each new day brought "another batch of lies," sometimes blackmailers, sometimes swindlers, who "persuaded people to part with money" so that they might be removed from the deportation lists. In such circumstances, it was perhaps too easy for the wary to imagine that applying for a forged Paraguayan passport from Switzerland was just so much pie in the sky. And what guarantee did they have that the German authorities would even honor such documents? They might, for instance, have heard the rumor that the Germans had rounded up all holders of foreign passports in Lithuania after the invasion and murdered them. Given the events of the previous months and years, little would surprise Poles and Polish Jews as far as German chicanery and barbarity was concerned. Was it really possible that a forged identity document could stop those murderous impulses in their tracks?[55]

Two events in the spring and summer of 1942 served to change that narrative of suspicion and futility. The first was the German decree of April 14, which ordered all holders of American and British passports in the General Government to register with the Gestapo in anticipation of an exchange. Later, in July, those in Warsaw holding Latin American passports were called to the Pawiak prison to be informed that they would be sent to Switzerland, where they would be exchanged for German citizens. Taken together, these measures caused considerable excitement in the ghettos of occupied Poland, as it appeared that some genuine chance of rescue was finally in the offing. The Weingorts in Warsaw, newly supplied with Paraguayan papers, were especially energized and began planning weddings and hoping to meet "Uncle Hügli," their savior, in Switzerland. It was, Mathilde Weingort wrote, "like a fairy tale."[56]

Of course, it was not yet clear what would happen to those who registered. It remained to be seen whether those selected were the damned or the saved. And it was still an open question whether the papers of those newly minted Paraguayan citizens would even be recognized by the German authorities. Gutta Eisenzweig summed up the dilemma that they faced: "Should I voluntarily present myself to murderers who would have no compunctions about shooting me on the spot?" Unsure and fearful, she nonetheless decided to comply with the order and duly presented herself to the already infamous Gestapo headquarters on Aleja Szucha. There, a Gestapo official received her Paraguayan passport with a "thin, vicious smile," she recalled, as if to say, "You're not fooling anyone." But then he handed it back without comment and told her that she could leave. The passports, it seemed, had passed their first test.[57]

Another shift that summer was the ramping up of the persecution of Jews across occupied Poland. Many of the smaller ghettos began to be liquidated in the spring, with their unfortunate populations sent to swell those in the larger ghettos, such as Warsaw or Łódź, or sent directly to the death camps. The Lublin ghetto, one of the largest, was all but cleared in April, with some thirty thousand Jews being deported to the new death camp at Bełżec. Such was the brutality of the deportation, according to the account heard by Mary Berg in Warsaw, that the streets of Lublin were "drenched in blood." Łódź, meanwhile, saw an increase in "resettlement" transports to the death camp at Chełmno, with nearly twenty-five thousand "resettled" in March and a further eleven thousand in May. Warsaw, though spared deportations for the time being, was nonetheless beset with rumors of imminent "resettlements," pogroms, and German "extermination squads" that were supposedly begging for permission to rampage through the city. In addition, a program of targeted killings was underway, with some fifty-two Jews—mainly political activists—being murdered by the Germans on the night of April 18. Taken from their homes at gunpoint, most were simply executed in the street. As the rumor mill swirled with such horror stories, it gradually became clear that incarceration in the Hades of the ghettos was not the end in itself; it was merely a way station to an even more sinister destination.[58]

So it was that, by the early summer of 1942, the Jewish relief organizations in Switzerland—headed by Chaim Eiss and Abraham Silberschein—became increasingly deluged with requests for Latin American passports. That June, just as the wholesale deportation and slaughter of Polish Jews was getting underway, Chaim Eiss wrote to Juliusz Kühl at the Polish embassy in Bern, listing the various requests for passports that he had received from occupied Poland and asking, "What should I do?" Up until that point, collaboration between the various individuals and groupings trying to help Polish Jews from Switzerland had been rather sporadic and intermittent, responding to isolated requests rather than showing any genuinely systematic response. Kühl's answer to that question would signal a step change and an acceleration of the passport scheme. With that, the Ładoś Group was born.[59]

5

"THEY ARE DYING. THAT'S ALL."

ON THE FINE SPRING MORNING OF MAY 27, 1942, *SS-Obergruppenführer* Reinhard Heydrich—head of Reich security services, deputy head of the SS, and "Reich protector of Bohemia and Moravia"—was being driven from his residence at Jungfern-Breschan (Panenské Břežany) to his office in the center of Prague. Heydrich was very much the rising star of the Third Reich. He had established the *Sicherheitsdienst*, the SS security arm, and had been instrumental in the creation of the *Einsatzgruppen*, the killing squads that had already cut such a murderous swath through the Jewish and Slavic populations of central and eastern Europe. Only five months earlier, he had presided over the so-called Wannsee Conference in Berlin's outskirts, where he had awarded himself oversight of the ongoing German genocide against the Jews. If the Nazi terror apparatus had a mastermind, it was Heydrich.

Heydrich's nemesis, that morning, took the form of two agents of the SOE (the British Special Operations Executive), who had been parachuted into Bohemia almost six months before with the intention of assassinating him. The action, which was code-named Operation Anthropoid, had been authorized by the Czech government-in-exile in London, not only as revenge for Heydrich's brutal rule in the Czech lands but also to raise the profile of the Czech resistance and the exile government within the Allied camp. The two agents—the Czech Jan Kubiš and the Slovak Jozef Gabčik—had positioned themselves on a sharp bend in the road in the Prague suburb of Holešovice, where they knew Heydrich's car would have to slow down. When the black Mercedes cabriolet approached shortly after 10:30 a.m., Gabčik stepped into the road, drew a Sten gun from beneath his coat, leveled it at the slowing Mercedes, and pulled the trigger, but to no effect. The Sten—notoriously unreliable—had jammed. In that moment, as Heydrich and his SS chauffeur drew their pistols, Kubiš approached from the rear and threw a grenade, which exploded against the car's back wheel. As the smoke cleared, chaos ensued as Gabčik and Kubiš fled and Heydrich and his driver attempted to give chase. Only when Heydrich collapsed in agony a few minutes later was it clear that he had been injured. The explosion had forced a shard of shrapnel through the car seat and into his abdomen, where it had lodged in his spleen. Pale-faced with the pain and staggering back toward the car, Heydrich gasped to his driver to "get the bastard!" but the assassins had already escaped.[1]

In the days that followed, Heydrich initially responded positively to treatment under the care of Himmler's personal physician Karl Gebhardt. However, after developing septicemia, his condition swiftly deteriorated and he died on June 4. Five days later, he was given a grand state funeral, held in the Reich Chancellery in Berlin, where Himmler delivered a eulogy that was both glowing and bloodcurdling, describing Heydrich as a Nazi martyr, a man "feared by the sub-humans, hated and slandered by the Jews."[2]

Retribution was not slow to materialize. The Gestapo's pursuit of Gabčik and Kubiš had thrown up the name of Lidice—a small village northwest of Prague—as home to two families who were thought to have served as contact points for the Czech resistance.

The German response was as swift as it was brutal: On Hitler's order, Lidice was to be destroyed. The day after Heydrich's funeral, the village was surrounded by German police units and thoroughly searched, yielding two hunting rifles and a rusty revolver. Then, the women and children were rounded up and taken away to the concentration camps, while all the men over fifteen years of age were herded together and executed, their bodies thrown into a mass grave. Workers of the German Labor Service then bulldozed Lidice until nothing remained. In all, some 199 men were murdered and 195 women arrested. Of ninety-five children, only eight were considered suitable for Germanization; the remainder vanished into the concentration camp system. A similar fate was later visited upon the village of Ležáky, where a radio set linked to the resistance had been found.[3]

Meanwhile, Gabčik and Kubiš were run to ground in a Prague Orthodox church, where, on the morning of June 18, 1942, the arrival of some eight hundred SS men signaled an end to their exploits. After gamely holding off German attempts to enter the church, Kubiš was mortally wounded, while Gabčik took refuge in the crypt. Keen to take him alive, the SS pumped tear gas and then water into the catacombs, but Gabčik was under no illusions about what he would face if captured, and he and three remaining Czech resistance fighters committed suicide. German retribution did not stop there. The parish priests who had sheltered the men were sentenced to death, along with Prague's Orthodox bishop. In the days that followed, a further 230 individuals who were thought to have assisted the assassins in their flight were sent to Mauthausen concentration camp and executed. Over a thousand Czechs—excluding those killed at Lidice and Ležáky—would be sentenced to death and murdered that summer, as what was left of the Czech resistance was finally "pacified."[4]

While Heydrich's assassination unleashed a brutal retaliation against Czech resistance circles, it also prompted a further escalation of the murderous measures already being inflicted on

Europe's Jews. The logic, to the Nazi mind, was simple. Given that they saw themselves as being at war with a hydra-headed "world Jewish conspiracy," any setback suffered ultimately had to be the work of world Jewry, and so it would be Jews who would have to pay the price. As Himmler explained in a speech to senior SS officers that month, Heydrich's murder would not go unanswered. "It is our sacred obligation to avenge his death," he declared, "to take over his mission and to destroy without mercy and weakness, now more than ever, the enemies of our people." Those enemies were Europe's Jews.[5]

The lead was given by Joseph Goebbels, who, as gauleiter of Berlin, authorized the arrest and deportation of an additional five hundred of the capital's Jews even before Heydrich had died from his wounds. Any further attempt at "Jewish insurrection," he warned, would result in a further 150 Jews being arrested and shot. In addition, he noted in his diary, large numbers of "incriminated Jews" were executed in Sachsenhausen. "The more of this filth that is swept away," he wrote, "the better for the security of the Reich." Across Germany, deportations of Jews were stepped up, often now encompassing those groups that had previously been exempt, such as the elderly and decorated Great War veterans, over sixty-six thousand of whom were deported to Theresienstadt that summer. In addition, ten thousand Jews were slated to be deported from Belgium, fifteen thousand from the Netherlands, and one hundred thousand from France—all destined for Auschwitz. Nazi fury, it seemed, had finally been unleashed.[6]

Yet, it was in occupied Poland that the most grievous consequences were felt. On July 19, a month after the siege in the Prague church had reached its bloody climax, Himmler was in Lublin, where he met with the SS and Police Leader for the General Government, Friedrich-Wilhelm Krüger. The previous day, Himmler had been in Auschwitz, where he had witnessed a demonstration of Jews being killed in a gas chamber. He was evidently impressed by what he had seen. In Lublin, he would inform his underling that all Jews living in the General Government were to be killed before the end of the year, using the death camps newly established at Treblinka, Sobibór, and Bełżec. By way of honoring his illustrious murdered deputy, Himmler gave the extermination program the code name Operation Reinhard. It was to be no modest undertaking. Though the Holocaust had already been underway since the second half of 1941, primarily via the grisly efforts of the *Einsatzgruppen* and the Chełmno gas vans, it was only in the summer of 1942 that the shift to a concerted program of industrialized mass killing began. It would be brutally effective. At the time of Heydrich's death, three-quarters of all those who would be killed in the Holocaust were still alive; a year later, three-quarters of them were dead.[7]

WHILE THOSE MOMENTOUS DECISIONS WERE BEING MADE, the Jews of occupied Poland were little wiser. Of course, rumors abounded of imminent deportations, of trigger-happy murder squads, or of mysterious camps from which no one appeared to return. But most of it was merely hearsay and speculation, which—though not easily dismissed—could always be trumped by the hope that all was not yet lost. That month, the elder of the Warsaw ghetto, Adam Czerniaków, personified the Jewish predicament, simultaneously begging his German masters, in vain, for clarification about the rumors while trying to stem the growing panic that such rumors engendered. "My head is splitting," he wrote in his diary, "but I am trying not to let the smile leave my face."[8]

Czerniaków's mood would have been little improved when "foreign Jews"—including those with Latin American passports—were ordered to the Pawiak prison in Warsaw on July 17. According to one eyewitness, posters had been put up around the ghetto stating that all Jews who held foreign citizenship were to appear at the police station on Ogrodowa Street to register. Mary Berg, herself in possession of a US passport, noted that many were alarmed at what the order portended. "From all sides came remarks: 'It's a bad sign if they are being taken away,' said one. 'True, we can't expect anything good will come of it for us,' said another, and a third added, 'Now they'll finish us off.'" Gutta Eisenzweig, meanwhile, was inundated with notes and letters from ghetto inhabitants desperate for her to post things or pass on messages on their behalf to the outside world once she was free.[9]

For the fortunate sent to the Pawiak—seven hundred of them, according to Berg—they were processed in the main yard, surrounded by the looming walls of the former Tsarist prison: once a byword for the Russian oppression of the Polish nation, now synonymous with the Nazi terror. The British and American passport holders were separated from the others, and each was then called forward in alphabetical order for interrogation. Mary Berg approached the table "with shaking knees" but was duly processed and sent, "through complicated corridors," to a room where she was held with fourteen other women. Those in possession of Latin American passports, she recalled, were sent to the prison cells of what had once been the women's wing. Berg noted that they spoke neither Spanish nor Portuguese, but the Germans recognized the validity of their passports. She added presciently that "it seems that the Germans need human material for exchange against the Germans interned in the American republics." Nonetheless, she recalled that the rumors were that Latin American passport holders would simply be released "on the Aryan side"—the world beyond the ghetto wall.[10]

Conditions for the foreign passport holders within the Pawiak were spartan to say the least. Confined in cramped cells with no furniture and only straw mattresses to sleep on, they must have wondered if they had made the right decision in throwing themselves upon the mercy of the German authorities. Within a couple of days, however, any such worries would have paled in comparison to the horrors that erupted around them. On July 22, the Germans began the liquidation of the Warsaw ghetto. Adam Czerniaków was informed that "all Jews, irrespective of sex and age" would be deported to the east, and the first contingent—of six thousand people—was to be provided that very afternoon. In the event of any resistance, he was told, his wife would be the first to be shot as a hostage.[11]

After doing his best to mediate between his German masters and his Jewish flock, Czerniaków was forced to admit defeat. On the evening of July 23, as the second deportation from Warsaw was being prepared, he wrote a note to the Jewish Council in which he explained that, as the deportation order was to be applied to children as well as adults, he was not prepared to agree to it. "This fills the chalice of my bitterness," he wrote. "I cannot consciously deliver helpless children to death." Consequently, he had decided to end his life: "I am powerless. My heart breaks for grief and pity. I cannot take it any longer." He begged the Jewish Council not to interpret his suicide as an act of cowardice. Rather, he said it should "show everyone the truth" and "lead them down the right path of action." He then took cyanide.[12]

For all its potent symbolism, Czerniaków's death changed nothing. The Germans ensured that he would not be publicly commemorated; his body was taken away on a handcart to be buried at dawn, with only a few mourners permitted to attend. Meanwhile, the deportation process continued, and it was diabolically simple. Each day, SS officials provided the Jewish Council with instructions regarding the numbers of deportees required, the districts of the ghetto to be targeted, and the exemption categories to be observed, such as those employed by German firms or those in the hospital or working in public health. All others were required, when ordered, to proceed to the *Umschlagplatz*—a goods yard and storage area close to the Danzig Station to the north of the ghetto—where they would be processed and held until a train was available. Deportees were permitted to take fifteen kilograms (thirty-three pounds) of baggage with them, as well as valuables, and food for a three-day journey. Those who dared to defy the deportation order and hide in their homes or factories did so at considerable risk. SS men or German police would routinely sweep cleared buildings and city blocks, and anyone they discovered would be shot out of hand.[13]

When those who complied arrived at their designated assembly points, they were duly marched in seemingly endless columns through the streets of the ghetto toward the *Umschlagplatz*. Some of them, inevitably, were herded by their captors past the cell blocks of the Pawiak, where those with foreign passports became the unwilling witnesses to their deportation. Gutta Eisenzweig recalled that "thousands of Jews marched by our windows, flanked by SS troops, who often beat and whipped them. We would hear the crack of rifle shots a hundred times a day."[14]

Once arrived at the *Umschlagplatz*, the deportees found that their torment scarcely abated. A walled-off space open to the elements, it was carefully designed to disguise its nefarious purpose. Arriving deportees were herded through a series of walled passages, which led into an open square, some 80 meters (262 feet) by 30 meters (98 feet) wide, in which there were no facilities and no shelter. Here, each new batch of deportees was forced to wait, sometimes for days, amid the detritus and excrement of their predecessors. Władysław Szpilman described the scene:

> When we arrived, it was still quite empty. People were walking up and down, searching in vain for water. It was a hot, fine day in late summer. . . . At the edge of the compound, where one of the streets ran into it, there was an unoccupied space. Everyone was giving this spot a wide berth, never lingering there but casting glances of horror at it. Bodies lay there; the bodies of those killed yesterday for some crime or other, perhaps even for attempting to escape.

IN TIME, A CORDON of SS and police moved through the square, driving the deportees out the other end of the *Umschlagplatz*, via a large gate, to the train sidings, where they were forced into the waiting cattle trucks.[15]

Their destination—for most Warsaw Jews at least—was the death camp at Treblinka. Established that summer some one hundred kilometers (sixty-two miles) northeast of the former capital, Treblinka was the archetype of a death factory, with no facilities except those required for the swift killing and disposal of large numbers of people. Arrivals were unloaded at a railway siding deep in a forest, where they were told that they would be showered and disinfected before their onward journey. To this end, the men were separated from the women and children, and both groups were herded into barrack blocks and told to undress. After that, they were forced along a walkway, obscured from the rest of the camp by an artificial hedge, which ended at an open door to a large, low building. As the deportees shuffled in, hastened along by the curses and blows of the SS guards, it took them a moment to realize that the building was not, in fact, a shower block as they had assumed. As the door was bolted shut behind them and a truck engine clattered to life outside, some of them might have guessed that they were in a gas chamber. Death from carbon monoxide poisoning would generally take around twenty minutes.

In the early phase of its existence, the camp at Treblinka was effective but chaotic. In the first month of its operation, on average over eight thousand Jews were killed every day, over three hundred thousand in total. Yet, in such a frenzy of killing, logistical difficulties quickly developed, with bottlenecks inevitably arising either in the transports to the camp or in its internal killing operation. So many Jews had died on the long journey to the site, for instance, that their corpses, stacked on the station platform, served as a grim advertisement to new arrivals of the horrors that went on within. Similarly, the bodies of the thousands already killed were simply buried in mass graves on the site, where decomposition quickly caused the thin covering of sandy earth to heave and bubble with escaping gasses. Far from being an efficient killing factory, therefore, as one historian of the period has observed, Treblinka's operation "had the qualities of a crazed massacre."[16]

Unsurprisingly, then, back in Warsaw dark rumors quickly spread. Treblinka's sloppy operation meant that a small handful of deportees were able to sneak back to the city, bringing hideous, harrowing tales with them. Gutta Eisenzweig recalled one such individual—a "wild-eyed man"—telling her what was happening at the camp, from where he claimed to have just escaped. "They are burning Jews," he reported, demanding that she tell the world once she was free. Gutta didn't believe him. "I couldn't," she wrote. "It was too incredible." Other accounts brought little clarity. One, by a courier named Zalman Frydrych, who had followed the deportation trains to see where they went, noted that the destination camp was too small to accommodate the many thousands sent there, while further inquiries revealed that no food was being delivered to the camp and that the trains returned empty.[17]

Other accounts argued the opposite. That summer, Abraham Lewin wrote in his diary that he had heard a rumor that the deported were working in the area of Siedlce and conditions were "not bad," adding that a friend's daughter had seen a letter from one of those deported. A few weeks earlier, he had written of another letter that had supposedly arrived from Białystok, from a deported wife to her husband, telling him that the work was hard but all was well. It is not clear whether such examples were German disinformation or merely Jewish wishful thinking. The ghetto diarist Izrael Lichtensztajn demonstrated the prevalent confusion when he wondered where the deportation trains were heading. "Nobody knows!" he wrote. "Brześć, Bobrujsk, Smoleńsk. . . . These are only conjectures."[18]

Given the thin body of knowledge available to the ghetto's inhabitants, it was perhaps not surprising that the hope that the deportation was—as the Germans claimed—to a labor camp and a new life proved remarkably persistent. An exchange witnessed by

Władysław Szpilman in the *Umschlagplatz* showed the dilemma that ghetto Jews faced. In response to a man who was shouting that they were all being sent to their deaths "like sheep to the slaughter," Szpilman's father asked how he could be sure that they were going to be killed. "Well, of course I don't know for certain. How could I? Are they about to tell us?" the man replied, adding, "But you can be ninety percent sure they plan to wipe us all out!" The response from Szpilman's father was sanguine: "'Look,' he said, indicating the crowd at the *Umschlagplatz*. 'We're not heroes! We're perfectly ordinary people, which is why we prefer to risk hoping for the ten percent chance of living.'"[19]

It was this hope, perhaps, that explained the comparative lack of resistance to the deportations, with only a handful of German guards attacked and a failed attempt to assassinate the head of the Jewish police, Józef Szeryński. Nevertheless, those who remained began to make efforts to improve their chances of survival. For many, this meant attempting to find a job in one of the numerous German factories in the ghetto, given that—for the moment—employees of German firms were exempt from deportation. Abraham Lewin called it "workshop mania," as everyone tried to find work so that they would not be designated as "superfluous" and thus marked for deportation. The illusion of safety for those in work was powerful. When Adam Starkopf resolved to escape the ghetto, his neighbor tried to dissuade him, arguing that, rather than expose his wife and child to danger, he should instead concentrate on finding legitimate work. "Once I had a job [in a German factory]," he was told, "I could be certain that the Germans would not deport me." Unsurprisingly, the most prominent firms, such as uniform makers Többens and Schultz, were soon besieged by thousands of Jews pleading for work, shouting, "I have a [sewing] machine, I have a machine!"[20]

For a time, then, German industries in the ghetto boomed, multiplying—in Władysław Szpilman's words—"like mushrooms after rain." Each one attracted hundreds of would-be workers eager to get their hands on the "certificate of employment" that they thought would save them. Some of the lucky ones, Szpilman recalled, even pinned notices to their clothing giving the name and place of their employment, in the belief that this would protect them if they were caught in a roundup. Given that the wives of exempt workers were also protected from deportation, a lucrative trade in fictitious marriages also developed, in some cases between brothers and sisters, with would-be partners matchmaking not with dowries but with their prospects for escape. Sympathetic rabbis facilitated the process by providing the necessary marriage contracts without having seen the couple face-to-face.[21]

Life in the Kraków ghetto was no easier. Though it had only been established the previous year, by the summer of 1942 it was already home to around sixteen thousand Jews living in horrifically overcrowded conditions, with four families allocated to each individual apartment. The deportations began that summer, when some eleven thousand Jews were forcibly deported to the new extermination camp at Bełżec. In Kraków's case, the veneer of civility in the deportation procedure was gossamer thin, with countless arbitrary killings and other atrocities being carried out in the process. One eyewitness, Tadeusz Pankiewicz, recalled that the ghetto "boomed with gunfire" as the soldiers ran amok, shooting wildly into the crowd or into buildings, executing individual Jews, deciding life and death on a whim. He also noted the petty persecutions that were inflicted on some of the unfortunates, relating the sad tale of a blind old man being goaded and tripped by SS men, who gleefully rejoiced at the sport. "Nobody knew what amused them more, the physical pain inflicted every time he fell to the ground, or the despair experienced by his wife and son standing nearby, silent and powerless against the violence."[22]

Though the "selection" in Kraków, such as it was, was brutally haphazard, the essential principle applied by the SS—as elsewhere—was that those capable of work were to be preserved, at least temporarily. To this end, representatives of the ghetto's labor office, or *Arbeitsamt*, participated in the selection process, and a stamp in one's identity document to identify those workers who were considered vital to the war effort became an essential accoutrement. One especially amenable SS officer was often mobbed by throngs of Jews whenever he entered the ghetto, all of them desperate for him to stamp their documents. In due course, the distinction between those deemed useful and useless by the Germans would be made more explicit still, when in December 1942 the ghetto itself was divided into two parts: Ghetto A was reserved for able-bodied workers, while Ghetto B was intended to house the elderly, the sick, and those nursing young children. Naturally, Ghetto B was swiftly scheduled for liquidation. In such circumstances, it was soon imperative to find employment.[23]

One famous employer in the Kraków ghetto was Oskar Schindler's *Deutsche Emailwarenfabrik*, the German Enamelwares Factory. Schindler had come to the city in September 1939 looking for opportunities to salvage his business career, and the bankrupt, Jewish-owned enamel factory on Lipowa Street suited him perfectly. Within weeks, it was resurrected and was manufacturing mess tins and shell casings for the German army, using mainly Jewish labor from the nearby ghetto, and making Schindler a rich man in the process. Paradoxically, perhaps, it was the brutal treatment meted out to the Jews in the ghetto that would turn him from an exploiter of Jewish labor to a protector, making his factory a haven that would enable over a thousand Jews to survive the war.[24]

Łódź, too, was feverishly making itself economically indispensable to the Germans. The second largest ghetto in occupied Poland, after Warsaw, with a population of nearly two hundred thousand souls, it was the domain of Elder Chaim Rumkowski, who had adopted a policy of bending to German requirements as far as was possible so as to earn the favor of the occupier and thus, hopefully, preserve something of Jewish life. To this end, the ghetto had already been transformed into a hive of economic activity, exchanging finished goods for much-needed food, and Rumkowski had struck up a close relationship with the senior German administrator, Hans Biebow, in which it was said that his guiding principle was always to stay ten minutes ahead of German demands.

That principle would be tested to destruction in 1942. After the first round of deportations from the ghetto in the spring, a lull had followed, during which many had assumed, even hoped, that a new equilibrium might be established. Rumors had even circulated that the ghetto's workers would be granted a summer holiday. Such hopes would be dashed in the early autumn, when the patients in the hospitals were taken away by the Germans, and there were fresh rumors of a looming deportation of children, the elderly, and anyone else unable to work. "The panic in the city is incredible," one diarist wrote. "Nobody's working anywhere, everyone's running to secure work assignments for those in their family who are unemployed." The news was confirmed by Rumkowski himself in a public speech, delivered on the so-called Fireman's Square, on the afternoon of September 4. His face drawn and tearful, his snow-white hair hidden under a pale fedora, he looked like a broken man as he addressed the fearful, expectant crowd. "The ghetto has received a painful blow," he began. "They demand its most precious members—the children and the elderly." Explaining how he had sought, in vain, to temper German demands, he said he understood the tears of the mothers listening, the heartbreak of the fathers, but, he believed, "I must carry out this difficult and bloody operation," adding, "I come as a thief to take the greatest treasure you possess in the depths of your hearts." Finally, to the sound of "a tremendous, dreadful lament" from the crowd, Rumkowski spread his arms. "I beg you, brothers and sisters, give them to me! Fathers and Mothers, give me your children!"[25]

Though he spoke in euphemisms and allusions, Rumkowski made it abundantly clear that those deportees were being taken to

The delegates at the Évian Conference: hand-wringing and empty sympathy in equal measure

"Jews not wanted": the *St. Louis* in Havana harbor is harassed by small ships to prevent it dropping anchor.

Jews queue outside the Japanese consulate in Kaunas, Lithuania, desperate for a way out.

"Such a kind man"; the Japanese consul in Kaunas, Chiune Sugihara

Jan Zwartendijk, Dutch consul and coconspirator in the Sugihara operation

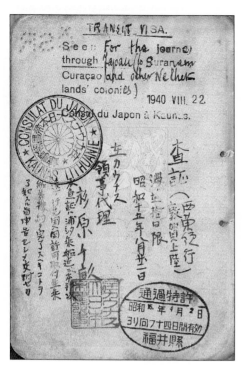

A Sugihara visa to Curaçao via Japan, the means to escape Europe for thousands of Jews

Tadeusz Romer, Polish ambassador to Tokyo, who did so much to help Sugihara's Jews

"A holy place": the Polish embassy building in Bern

Aleksander Ładoś (with cane, center left), with the Polish Second Rifle Division in Switzerland

A youthful Pierre Mendès-France, who escaped occupied Europe as the Pole "Jan Lemberg"

A business card for a fictional identity

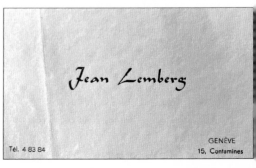

The Weingort family in happier times: Leo (left) would be one of the first to benefit from the Ładoś passport operation, but only Saul (right) would survive the Holocaust.

Dr. Heinrich Rothmund, the head of the Swiss Alien Police: xenophobia in a sharp suit

Polish ambassador to Switzerland
Aleksander Ładoś

Legation counselor
Stefan Ryniewicz

Consul Konstanty Rokicki

Attaché Juliusz Kühl

Abraham Silberschein, director of
RELICO, the Relief Committee
for Jewish War Victims

Chaim Eiss of Agudath Israel

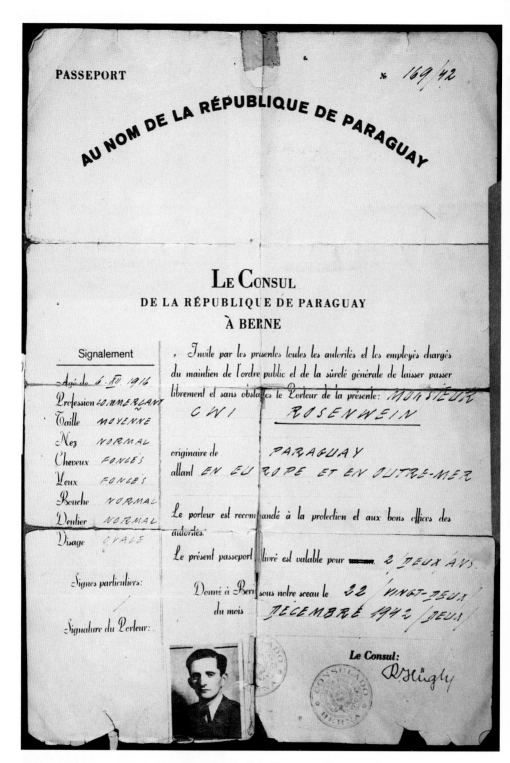

A Paraguayan passport issued by the Ładoś Group in Bern to Cwi Rosenwein, who would survive the Holocaust

Bern, den 30 Nowember 1942.

CONSULADO
DE LA
REPÚBLICA DEL PARAGUAY
EN BERNA

Sehr geehrter Herr Guzik,

Wir beehren uns Ihnen mitzuteilen, dass auf Grund der Bemühungen Ihrer Verwandten, sowohl Sie als auch Ihre Familie, die Staatszugehörigkeit von Paraguay erlangt haben.

Wir bitten Sie uns umgehend je zwei Lichtbilder sowie die genauen Personalien zusenden zu wollen, damit Ihnen der Pass ausgestellt und zugesandt werden kann.

Mit freundlichen Grüssen

Consul.

Herrn Dawid Guzik und Familie,
Warschau,
Niskastr.6.

A *promesa*, signed by honorary consul Rudolf Hügli, confirming Paraguayan citizenship in lieu of a passport

The quick and the dead: everyday tragedy on the streets of the Warsaw ghetto

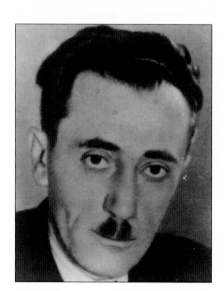

Szmul Zygielbojm, who would take his own life in protest at the unwillingness of the Allied powers to assist Europe's Jews

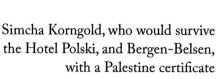

Simcha Korngold, who would survive the Hotel Polski, and Bergen-Belsen, with a Palestine certificate

Deportation of Jews from Warsaw, bound for the gas chambers of Treblinka

The Buchwajc and Laskier families from Będzin, holders of Honduran and Paraguayan papers. Only the latter would survive.

One of the hotels in the Vittel internment camp: a temporary "paradise" for Warsaw Jews

Yitzhak Katzenelson and his son Tzvi, who passed through the Hotel Polski and Vittel before being murdered in Auschwitz

The German internment and concentration camp of Bergen-Belsen, where "God himself was powerless"

The transit camp at Westerbork, the last stop before Auschwitz for thousands of Dutch Jews

The internment camp at Tittmoning, Bavaria, a curious haven

A group of "foreign Jews" in Tittmoning

Heinz Lichtenstern, whose Paraguayan passport would save him and his family from deportation to Auschwitz

The slip of paper that marked Heinz Lichtenstern as exempt from deportation

Ausgeschieden 3911 413-XXIV/7 Lichtenstern Heinz 1907

Frumka Płotnicka, a leading advocate of Jewish resistance against the Nazis and a holder of a Paraguayan passport. She would be killed during the liquidation of the ghetto in Będzin.

Nathan Eck in later life. He did much to convince his fellow Jews of the possibilities of rescue using false papers.

Bergen-Belsen after the liberation: more "days of dying"

Free at last: former Exchange Jews pose next to the train that took them from Belsen.

their deaths. He did not seek to sweeten the bitter pill of parting by feeding his audience the fiction of a new life for the deportees in a labor camp. Rather, he portrayed the action as a necessary sacrifice. He spoke of "cutting off limbs in order to save the body," giving the idea that though the young and the old would be sacrificed, the remainder—those who worked for the Germans— would thereby be spared. "What do you want," he asked, "to let eighty or ninety thousand Jews remain here, or, God forbid, see everyone destroyed?" It appears that Rumkowski, and a good proportion of his flock, were under few illusions about the fate that awaited the deported. It was finally and brutally clear that his policy of fulfillment of German demands was nothing more than a pact with the devil. In the days that followed, more than fifteen thousand ghetto inhabitants, the vast majority of them under the age of ten and over the age of sixty-five, would be "evacuated" from Łódź to the death camp at Chełmno; a further six hundred were shot by the Germans for trying to escape.[26]

IN THE MIDST OF THESE DEVELOPMENTS, A NEW CATEGORY of prisoners was entering the reckoning: western European Jews. Among the first to be affected were the Jews of Holland. Already in 1940, the 130,000-strong Dutch Jewish community—which included some 30,000 German Jews who had fled across the border in the years before the war—was facing considerable persecution, being banned from public service and increasingly marginalized. In January 1942, they began to be deported to the transit camp at Westerbork, near Assen in northern Holland. Conditions there were basic but not bad. "Nothing but desert," one inmate wrote, "despite a few lupins and campions." The camp had originally been constructed by the Dutch to house Jews fleeing Germany in the 1930s, and it was well equipped with wooden barrack blocks as well as brick cottages.[27]

Once the German authorities formally took over Westerbork in July 1942, those high standards were maintained, with a restaurant, hospital, school, and even a hairdresser on-site to lend a positive sheen to the prospects of deportation. The camp commandant, *SS-Obersturmführer* Albert Gemmeker, was a charmer who was scrupulously polite and always immaculately turned out. As one eyewitness recalled, he was "halfway between a dapper hairdresser's assistant and a stagedoor Johnny." Nonetheless, already that summer deportations out of Westerbork began, with the first train departing for the three-day journey to Auschwitz-Birkenau on July 15. Of the 1,132 people on that transport, over 800 were former refugees from Germany and Austria who had sought to escape the Nazi maelstrom. On arrival at Auschwitz, some four hundred of them—mainly the elderly and women with young children—were sent straight to the gas chambers, where their death throes were "unobtrusively observed" by Heinrich Himmler himself.[28]

In the months that followed, some ninety-seven trainloads of Jews left Westerbork. Most of them were bound for Auschwitz, with others heading to the gas chambers of Sobibór or to Theresienstadt in Bohemia. As Dutch Jew Etty Hillesum recalled, the deportees were crammed into empty goods wagons for the three-day journey: "Paper mattresses on the floor for the sick. For the rest bare boards with a bucket in the middle and roughly seventy people to a sealed wagon." She wondered how many of them would reach their destination alive. During the early deportations, at least, the German myths about Jews being deported to perform "labour service in the east" were maintained and even seem to have held some currency. Jewish social worker Gertrude van Tijn noted that, although deportees desperately sought a way to remove themselves from the deportation lists, they nonetheless departed "with utter docility," even with optimism, shouting, "We'll be back!" or "See you soon!" In due course, those Dutch Jews were joined by others. In a meeting in Berlin at the end of August, Adolf Eichmann demanded that all foreign Jews were to be "evacuated" by the end of June 1943. Already by the end of

1942, over forty thousand French Jews had been deported, as well as nearly twenty thousand from Belgium.[29]

As the deportations continued apace through 1942, some Dutch Jews went underground, seeking refuge in the attics and cellars of friends or among the wider networks of the Dutch resistance. The most famous example of the latter was Anne Frank, who went into hiding with her parents and sister that July, just as the systematic deportation of Dutch Jews began in earnest. Her story—and that of her ultimate betrayal, deportation, and death in Belsen—would be one of the seminal biographies of the Holocaust.

The story of the Salomonson family is more unusual, however. Hendrik—known as Hein—was an architect who was well-connected in the liberal and artistic milieu of prewar Amsterdam, with friends and acquaintances both within and beyond the Jewish community. Perhaps it was these contacts that gave Hein more options than most when the German occupation began to bite; he managed to procure false identity papers via a friend in the resistance and Paraguayan passports from the Ładoś Group in Switzerland. In that summer of 1942, Hein and his wife Hermine—known as Toussie—decided to split up and go into hiding separately, sending their two children, three-year-old Channa and infant Louise, into the care of two Dutch families. Hein went underground in Amsterdam, and Toussie joined the Dutch resistance. In that way, they thought, they would maximize the chances of at least one of them surviving. Through the months and years that followed, Toussie would throw herself into resistance work, while Hein would suffer terribly from the anxiety of separation and the fear of discovery. For both of them, their Paraguayan passports provided a last resort, a final throw of the dice to be held in reserve should they ever be required.[30]

NEWS OF THE NEXT PHASE OF THE HOLOCAUST PENE-trated the outside world only very slowly. There were piecemeal reports of the atrocities carried out against the Jews and others, which appeared in news roundups or in the intelligence briefings of the Allied powers, but there was, as yet, little appreciation of the vast scale of the crimes being committed. Moreover, for many, those fragmentary accounts emanating from occupied Poland were literally unbelievable. The idea that the German occupiers were systematically murdering European Jewry was quite simply unthinkable. This phenomenon was rather widespread. Holocaust survivor Primo Levi, for instance, recalled the profound and gnawing fear that many Jews had—even when inside Auschwitz—that should they survive to tell their stories, their sufferings would not be considered credible. The enormity of the Holocaust was such, he realized, that it simply defied belief.[31]

This was in evidence in the reaction to a report compiled by the Jewish socialist movement in Poland, the Bund, which reached the government-in-exile at the end of May 1942. The report gave extensive—and, as it turned out, correct—information about the Germans' ongoing extermination of the Jews on Polish soil, beginning with the *Einsatzgruppen* and progressing via the Chełmno gas vans to mass deportations "to an unknown destination." It concluded that seven hundred thousand Jews had already been killed and rightly predicted that the goal was to murder all of the Jews of Europe.[32]

Yet, even in the face of such apparently incontrovertible evidence, many in London found the report hard to believe. As Foreign Minister Edward Raczyński later recalled, "It seemed to me so devilish, it seemed to me so horrible, that at first I thought it was exaggerated." If Poland's senior ministers could not believe such reports, then it was all the more difficult to convince those—such as their British counterparts—who were further removed from events. It was a problem that was summed up by another member of the Polish government-in-exile in London, Adam Pragier, who wrote in his memoir, "How can one believe in the killing of 700,000 people? The Bund should have written that [the Germans] killed 7,000 people. Then we could provide the news to the British with a slight chance they would believe it." Such skepticism was not uncommon in Western capitals, but it would soon give way to a shocking realization.[33]

Things began to change in the summer of 1942, with a telegram from the secretary of the World Jewish Congress in Geneva, Gerhart Riegner. The information contained in it had come from a German industrialist named Eduard Schulte, who was well-connected with the Nazi elite in his home town of Breslau and had heard of Himmler's plan to step up the extermination of Polish Jewry. Schulte had communicated what he had picked up to contacts in Switzerland, where it was quickly passed to Gerhart Riegner, who went to the British and American consulates in Geneva to arrange for the information to be sent on to Rabbi Stephen Wise, the president of the American Jewish Congress, and the British MP Sydney Silverman, the organization's London representative. The telegram that Riegner sent on August 8 spoke of some "three and a half to four million" Jews being scheduled for deportation to the east, where "at one blow" they would be exterminated, possibly with "Prussic Acid." Riegner stated that the accuracy of the information "cannot be controlled" but added that the source nonetheless enjoyed "close connections with highest German authorities." According to one of the leading historians of the Holocaust, the Riegner telegram constituted "an astonishingly accurate piece of wartime intelligence."[34]

Yet the note fell on deaf ears. The Americans were dubious of the suggestion of an ongoing genocide, with State Department officials summarizing Riegner's telegram as "a wild rumor inspired by Jewish fears." They decided to sit on the revelations and withhold them from Rabbi Wise, instead asking Riegner for corroboration. On the British side, Silverman was a little more accepting and passed the contents of the telegram on to Wise, who in turn sent them to Sumner Welles at the State Department, where the telegram arrived three weeks after it had been wired.[35]

While Riegner's words were belatedly being assessed by their intended recipients, a second cable from Switzerland arrived, this time coming from the Polish legation in Bern. Just prior to the outbreak of war in 1939, the Polish legation building on Elfen-strasse had been equipped with a radio station in the attic, so as to facilitate communication with London in the event of conflict. After 1941 and the American entry into the war, postal correspondence between occupied Europe and the United States all but ceased, with what remained being routinely delayed for weeks or months by censorship. By 1942, therefore, the embassy's transmitting facilities had become vitally important and, as part of its ongoing collaboration with Jewish activist circles in the Swiss capital, were put at the latter's disposal.[36]

On September 3, 1942, Yitzchak and Recha Sternbuch sent a cable from the embassy's attic, via the Polish consulate in New York, to the president of Agudath Israel, Jacob Rosenheim. Unlike the Riegner telegram, it was unequivocal, declaring:

> According to recently received authentic information, the German authorities have evacuated the last ghetto in Warsaw, bestially murdering about one hundred thousand Jews. Mass murders continue. . . . The deportees from other occupied countries will meet the same fate. It must be supposed that only energetic reprisals on the part of America could halt these persecutions.

The Sternbuchs closed with a request to Rosenheim to "do whatever you can to cause an American reaction . . . stirring up statesmen, the press and the community." Rosenheim did not need telling twice. The following day, he contacted the Union of Orthodox Rabbis and the World Jewish Congress, belatedly spurring Rabbi Wise into calling a meeting of leading Jewish representatives to consider what action to take in response. The ball was finally rolling, it seemed, but it would take many more weeks before the State Department was willing to give the news its approval.[37]

In the meantime, Polish authorities in both London and occupied Poland were similarly groping toward an understanding not only of the Holocaust but also of how they might respond. A lead had been given in August 1942 by the publication of a leaflet called *Protest!* Its author was Zofia Kossak-Szczucka, a Catholic novelist known for her right-wing and—paradoxically, in the circumstances—anti-Semitic views. Like many in the interwar years, she had believed that the Jews of Poland represented a socioeconomic challenge to the Polish state, which was best eased through encouraging emigration. To her, the Nazi idea of a physical extermination of the Jews was totally abhorrent. *Protest!* therefore represented a call to arms, a demand that ordinary Poles, in spite of their own suffering, must acknowledge the genocide going on in their midst. "The world looks upon this murder, more horrible than anything else history has ever seen, and stays silent. The slaughter of millions of defenseless people is being carried out amid general sinister silence." That silence, she said, could no longer be tolerated. "Whoever is silent witnessing murder becomes a partner to the murder. Whoever does not condemn, consents."[38]

Kossak-Szczucka was clear that her views toward the Jews— that they were the "enemies of Poland"—had not changed, but her Catholic conscience demanded that she protest against their bestial killing. Hers was not an isolated case. Attitudes in Poland were beginning to shift with the horrors of the German occupation. While some Poles openly expressed anti-Semitic opinions, others who had previously shunned Jews were now willing to protest against their extermination on the grounds of their common humanity. Kossak-Szczucka had clearly hit a nerve, therefore. And, what is more, her opinion chimed with others in the Polish underground who were keen to do more than just protest.[39]

Consequently, at the end of September 1942, Kossak-Szczucka was appointed as joint head of a new underground aid organization, the Provisional Committee to Aid the Jewish People, which would later operate under the code name Żegota. Using funding supplied by the government-in-exile in London, Żegota expanded swiftly and by that autumn boasted representatives in fourteen Polish cities outside of Warsaw, including Lublin, Łódź, Sosnowiec, Radom, Przemyśl, and Zamość. Its activities spanned the spectrum, from establishing contacts with existing Jewish organizations to providing material assistance—money, clothing, and accommodation—to fugitive Jews. One of its specialties was the forging of official documents, from marriage and birth certificates to employment and identity papers, all of which were provided to Jews free of charge. It has been estimated that the organization produced some fifty thousand forged documents, on average around one hundred every day. By the middle of the war, indeed, fully 25 percent of work cards and 15 percent of identity cards used in occupied Warsaw were forgeries, the vast majority produced by the Polish underground. Poland's clandestine traditions of forging and falsification were being dusted off for a new generation.[40]

At the same time that Kossak-Szczucka was establishing what would become Żegota, underground courier Jan Karski was preparing for another mission to the free world. Karski had endured an eventful time since his last trip to the west in 1940. He had been captured by the Gestapo upon his return and had had his jaw broken during an interrogation, losing a number of teeth. After being freed by Polish commandos from a prison hospital in Nowy Sącz, he had lain low for a few months before taking command of an underground cell in Kraków in January 1941. He was being groomed for bigger things, however. Because of this background, and the huge amount of knowledge that he had gleaned about underground life and conditions in the country, he was considered the ideal candidate to carry documents and provide detailed briefings to the government-in-exile in London. However, as Karski himself recognized, he knew comparatively little about the fate of

Polish Jews, so to rectify this he would be smuggled into both the transit camp at Izbica and the Warsaw ghetto to see conditions there for himself. It was a harrowing experience:

> We just walked the streets. We did not talk to anybody. We walked probably for one hour. Sometimes he [his guide] would tell me: "Look at this Jew"—a Jew standing there, without moving. I said, "Is he dead?" "No, he is alive, but he is dying. Remember, he is dying. Look at him. Tell them over there you saw it. Don't forget." We walk again. It was macabre. Only from time to time he would whisper, "Remember this, remember this." Or he would tell me: "Look at her." Very many cases. I asked, "What are they doing here?" His answer: "They are dying, that's all. They are dying." We spent perhaps an hour, then we left. I could not take any more.[41]

Karski's journey westward that autumn—via Berlin, Brussels, Paris, Barcelona, and Gibraltar—was undertaken in the guise of a businessman, feigning a toothache throughout to avoid speaking. His forged papers, he recalled, were "in perfect order." In his luggage, he had a roll of film concealed in the handle of a razor and a second microfilm hidden in a key. He had memorized other shorter reports concerning conditions in occupied Poland and the fate of Poland's Jews, all of which he conveyed to Prime Minister Sikorski and the other leaders of the government-in-exile when he arrived in London.[42]

After meeting his Polish superiors, Karski met a slew of Allied politicians, including British foreign secretary Anthony Eden and the Leader of the Opposition, Arthur Greenwood. The information that he conveyed duly appeared in the British newspapers; *The Times*, for instance, reported on November 24 that a "systematic extermination of the Jewish inhabitants" at German hands was underway in Poland and that "all trace" of the deported had vanished. In addition, Karski's report coincided with State

Department recognition of the veracity of the Riegner telegram, giving an added impetus to developments. Slowly, then, the wheels of international diplomacy began to turn.[43]

On December 10, the Polish government-in-exile finally broke the official silence by issuing a note, in the name of the Polish foreign minister, Edward Raczyński, summarizing the existing available information about the Holocaust. Addressed to the governments of the United Nations and bluntly entitled "The Mass Extermination of Jews in German Occupied Europe," it was intended to elicit an international response to the crimes being committed by the Germans. It did not pull any punches, stating that the extermination of Poland's Jews constituted a horror that "surpasses anything known in the annals of history." Consequently, the Polish government saw it as its duty to "bring to the knowledge of the governments of all civilized countries . . . authentic information received from Poland." The hope was, the report concluded, that such crimes would not only be condemned but that some means might be found to restrain Germany from carrying out "her methods of mass extermination."[44]

Faced with such a significant, official intervention, Churchill's cabinet was unable to ignore the matter or allow it to be lost in the tangled bureaucracy of Whitehall. In response, Churchill himself requested more information on the genocide from the Foreign Office, while Foreign Secretary Eden presented a summary of the available intelligence to the war cabinet on December 14. After that, approval was given for the idea of a joint Allied declaration, the draft of which was quickly agreed with Washington and Moscow and was read by Eden to a packed House of Commons on December 17. "This bestial policy of cold-blooded extermination," Eden said, was to be condemned "in the strongest possible terms." "Such events," he declared, would "only strengthen the resolve of all freedom-loving peoples to overthrow the barbarous Hitlerite tyranny." In response, he said, the Allied governments had reaffirmed "their solemn resolution to ensure that those responsible for these crimes shall not escape retribution." In truth, no framework or agreement was yet in place to exact that retribution, but the dark reality of the Holocaust had now been made visible to the outside world.[45]

GIVEN THE GROWING EVIDENCE OF THE CRIMES THAT THE Germans were carrying out in occupied Poland, so the pressure grew on Jews to find a way to avoid their fate. Some attempted bribery, gathering together what remaining assets they had to try to escape via an amenable guard or policeman. Others prepared to resist, with the emerging Jewish resistance cells within the ghetto now determined that the next round of deportations would not go uncontested. In the autumn of 1942, arson attacks in the Warsaw ghetto grew in frequency, targeting German warehouses and businesses. More remarkable still, senior figures within the ghetto were targeted for assassination: German collaborators, for instance, or members of the Jewish police, fourteen of whom were murdered, including their commander Jakub Lejkin.[46]

Though such attacks might satisfy the urge for revenge, one of the best prospects for survival was still that offered by foreign passports. As the persecutions continued that autumn, those thought to be able to procure passports—like Saul Weingort and Abraham Silberschein in Switzerland—were soon inundated with desperate pleas for assistance. As the diarist Hillel Seidman noted, everyone in the Warsaw ghetto was searching desperately for "relatives, friends or acquaintances living abroad—particularly in Switzerland—to whom to write coded letters containing the urgent message: send passports!"[47]

Because of German censorship, code was often employed to avoid the attentions of the Gestapo. Writing in code was not easy, however. The trick was to be oblique enough to get past the censor and yet obvious enough to be understood by the recipient. Where there was a personal relationship or shared knowledge, of course, it was easier to conceal some sort of hidden message. Saul Weingort, for instance, received messages that referred obliquely to the passport that he had already procured for his brother: "Would like to receive what you sent Leo," one Berta Rosenblum wrote from Bochnia. Another pleaded, "My brother . . . is ill, needs medicine, like you sent your brother Leo. It is his only rescue." Others tried to use biblical references or subtly insert Hebrew words into their text, which is what Yitzchak Sternbuch and Isaac Domb did in their correspondence.[48]

It had been Domb's earlier procurement of a forged Swiss passport that had done so much to inspire others in Warsaw to follow the same course. Courtesy of that passport, Domb had been able to live outside the ghetto, but, as the German persecution of the Jews increased, he was now wary of being questioned too closely, fearing that his real identity might be discovered. Hence, Domb wrote to Sternbuch in the autumn of 1942 to request a Paraguayan passport, considering it preferable to a forged Swiss example. Yet, despite receiving an initial reply, no passport had yet been forthcoming from the embassy. So, on September 4, Domb wrote again, this time betraying the desperation that so many of his fellows in the ghetto must have felt. "I cry often," he wrote, "but tears can't help me." He complained bitterly at the lack of communication: "I'd rather know the truth than entertain foolish hopes." "Only when I receive word from Bern," he went on, "will I be able to keep myself afloat." In the final part of the letter, he slipped into a coded narrative of what was going on in the ghetto, explaining that he had spoken to "Mr. Jäger" (meaning "hunter" in German) who will invite "all members of the family" to his estate—called "Kever" (which means "grave" in Hebrew). If that wasn't clear enough, Domb added that "Uncle Gerusch is working in Warsaw. He is a very efficient worker. His friend Miso is now working with Uncle Gerusch together." As *gerusch* and *miso* are the Hebrew words for "deportation" and "death," the meaning of the message would have been immediately apparent to Sternbuch.[49]

In due course, Isaac Domb wrote to Sternbuch again. He had written previously, he said, in a state of extreme stress and "the utmost desperation," and he was embarrassed by the tone he had used. He now requested the address of "Herr Hügly," so that he could write to the Paraguayan honorary consul himself to inquire about the whereabouts of his passport. Domb's correspondence is unusual in the extent that he was evidently informed of the process by which his passport would be produced. Most recipients had very little idea of the wider system, knowing only the name of the primary contact—perhaps Abraham Silberschein or Yitzchak Sternbuch—to whom they had sent their photographs and details but with no knowledge of the other individuals involved.

Indeed, the passport production process included a number of individuals. The "application"—a letter containing photographs and life details—would usually arrive with representatives of one of the Jewish aid organizations, such as Agudath Israel or the World Jewish Congress. From there, the request would be forwarded to Juliusz Kühl at the Polish legation in Bern, where the details would be entered onto blank passport forms, normally by the Polish consul Konstanty Rokicki. The forms had been purchased by Kühl or Rokicki from the Paraguayan honorary consul Rudolf Hügli, using funds supplied by the Jewish aid agencies or by the Polish government-in-exile in London. Once the forms were filled out—in Rokicki's distinctive italic hand—they were returned to Hügli to be stamped and signed. Then they were generally notarized: a photostat copy would be made, certified by a local notary, who would keep the original document and return the notarized copy to Kühl, who would then send it on to the recipient. While Domb's letter shows that he knew the role that "Herr Hügly" was playing, the vast majority of recipients, and even some of those close to the operation, were wholly unaware of the process and of the central role played in it by the Polish legation.[50]

The code that was employed to evade the German censors did not always work. As Hillel Seidman recalled, often the recipient completely failed to comprehend what was required, with the result that urgent requests for "presents" would merely produce "packets of figs and tea." Saul Weingort recalled that visitors to him in Montreux, Switzerland, often had no idea that the errand they had been sent on concerned the procuring of forged documents.[51]

It was not just the vagaries of the censorship and the postal system that caused difficulty. Given the sheer volume of requests for passports that was being received in the autumn and winter of 1942, the Jewish activists and intermediaries in Switzerland were forced to make some difficult decisions about which applicants were considered the most deserving. A committee was therefore established by Abraham Silberschein and Chaim Eiss to ensure that there was no duplication or that "unauthorized persons" did not receive papers. In this, differing criteria could be applied. For the devoutly Orthodox Eiss and Agudath Israel, rabbis and religious scholars were often prioritized; Silberschein, meanwhile, tended to apply more secular criteria, as well as favoring those within his already extensive circle of acquaintances.[52]

To assist in those decisions, a committee was also established within the Warsaw ghetto, which drew up a list of those notables—rabbis, writers, artists, and other prominent individuals—who should be put at the head of the queue. This list was then sent to, among others, the Jewish aid agencies in Switzerland. In addition to such notables, Silberschein, who was keen to expand the operation to include members of Jewish youth organizations in occupied Poland, added some four hundred further names. In a struggle for their very existence, Warsaw's Jews sought to save the brightest and the best in the hope that something of Jewish life and culture could be preserved.[53]

One of those who applied for a passport was Nathan Eck, a prominent Zionist activist who had fled from Łódź to Warsaw in the autumn of 1939 to escape the attentions of the Gestapo. By the late summer of 1942, with the deportations already underway and Warsaw Jews in a state of panic, he escaped again, this time to Będzin in Upper Silesia. The Będzin ghetto was unusual in that it was not enclosed, but prior to Eck's arrival it had been subject to two deportations, with some eight thousand Jews having been sent to Auschwitz. In the aftermath, discussions raged among its residents about rival strategies for survival—whether to comply, resist, or attempt to escape. The community's elders broadly advocated compliance, while the young, especially the members of the Zionist organizations, tended toward resistance.

Those advocating escape were also growing in number that summer. Previously, the use of forged passports had not been taken seriously. As one survivor of the Będzin ghetto recalled, Jews wrote letters to the outside world begging for assistance and foreign papers, but they "did not believe that there was any possibility to leave occupied Poland." However, Eck's arrival galvanized the advocates of false passports as to the benefits that they promised and gave them a focus that they had previously lacked. Soon, thousands of letters were being sent to Abraham Silberschein and others in Switzerland containing photographs and coded requests for passports. Indeed, the demand was so great that Silberschein asked Eck to establish a committee in Będzin that, as in Warsaw, would draw up a list of those citizens who should be prioritized. The arguments for and against that escape route would rumble on for a few more months, but Będzin had woken up to the potential that false papers offered. Eck himself would be the first in the ghetto to receive a foreign passport.[54]

Other requests came from beyond Poland. When Clara Duschnitz was sent to Westerbork with her family that summer, she realized that the SS guards were not especially concerned with who was being deported, just that their lists, and their wagons, should be filled. She also noted that the possession of foreign passports seemed to preserve people from the threat of deportation. Through family contacts in Switzerland, therefore, she procured a Paraguayan passport for herself, her husband, Felix, and her daughter Marietta. Thereafter categorized by the Germans as "foreign Jews" eligible for *Rückstellungskategorie 1*—"reserve category 1"—all three were exempt from deportation.[55]

Despite such successes, for many of those desperately requesting help, the result was often the same: silence. As Hillel Seidman noted, it could be difficult to get a response, especially when one was writing on behalf of others: "Dr. Silverstein [*sic*] does not reply. . . . Rabbi Eiss also sends some passports to a select few religious Jews, but he seems to work extremely slowly and without warmth." "Meanwhile," he added bitterly, "the ground literally burns beneath one's feet."[56]

Rather than tardiness or an excessively selective attitude, the reality was that Silberschein and Eiss were simply overwhelmed with requests, which could not be processed quickly enough to meet the demand. To address the problem, Silberschein now approached other Latin American honorary consuls in Switzerland, seeking to speed up the procedure by requesting *promesas*—letters confirming citizenship, which did not require the time-consuming and costly production of photographs—rather than passports. He found a ready ally in Alfonso Bauer, the honorary consul of Honduras in Bern, who had been dismissed from his post in the spring of 1941 for illegally issuing Honduran passports but—having stolen the official consular seal—had continued to issue identity documents illicitly. In addition, Silberschein engaged other honorary consuls—including Max Brunner, consul for Haiti in Zürich, and José María Barreto, consul general for Peru in Geneva—to produce *promesas* in return for payment.[57]

Though the *promesas* were cheaper and quicker to produce, a Latin American passport remained the most sought-after document. It became something almost intangible, something to be longed for, more in hope than in expectation. That desire was expressed in a ditty composed by the poet Władysław Szlengel in the summer of 1942, which would have been recited in the Café Sztuka on Leszno Street, a renowned center of literary life in the

Warsaw ghetto. Szlengel was better known for his serious poetry, which captured the desperation of life in the ghetto and provided a chronicle of the hopes and fears of its inhabitants. "The Passports," however, was shorter and lighter in tone, almost doggerel in its frivolity, but it spoke of some of the profoundest hopes in the ghetto:

I would like to have a Uruguayan passport
Oh, what a beautiful land it is
How nice it must feel to be the subject
of the land called: Uruguay.

I would like to have a Paraguayan passport
Of gold and freedom is this land
Oh, how nice it must feel to be the subject
Of the land called: Paraguay.

I would like to have a Costa Rican passport
Celadon sky—eternal May
Oh, how nice it must feel to tell
That Costa Rica is my land.

I would like to have a Bolivian passport
Like a couple of friends of mine
Bolivian air—resin fragrant
Oh, what a beautiful land.

I would like to have a Honduran passport,
Honduras sounds like eastern paradise
It's nice to remark from time to time
Honduras, actually, is my land.

I would like to have a Uruguayan passport
Or Costa Rica, or Paraguay
Just so one can live peacefully in Warsaw
After all, it is the most beautiful of lands.[58]

IN DUE COURSE, THIS UPSURGE IN DEMAND FOR LATIN American passports would inevitably bring the forgery operation to the attention of the German authorities. Yet, their reaction was perhaps surprising. Nazi Germany was a racial state, whose guiding principles included the preservation of "good blood" and the elimination of "bad blood" within both the German population and those populations under German control. So, just as German racial policy was predicated upon the removal of the Jews and other supposedly "inferior" races, so it was also predicated upon the preservation and propagation of "good" German blood. This explains the Nazi regime's extraordinary efforts to encourage German women to have more children and to eliminate the mentally and physically handicapped through the T4 euthanasia campaign.

The principle of preserving "good blood" also extended beyond Germany's frontiers and illustrates why the Nazi regime went to such lengths to "rescue" the ethnic German populations of central and eastern Europe and bring them *Heim ins Reich*—home to the Reich. Moreover, where the lives and liberty of Germans beyond the direct reach of Hitler's forces were under threat, so they, too, had to be preserved as far as was possible. To this end, negotiations had already taken place between the Germans and the British—through Swiss intermediaries—resulting in two exchanges of German citizens living in the British protectorate of Palestine for citizens of the protectorate who had been trapped in Europe by the outbreak of hostilities.[59]

In addition, Nazi Germany had already made a temporary agreement with the United States whereby Axis nationals resident in America—predominantly diplomats but also ordinary German citizens—would be exchanged for American citizens who had fallen into German hands during the war. This action had borne fruit in a number of transatlantic sailings in 1942, most notably aboard the Swedish-registered SS *Drottningholm*, in which some two thousand German citizens were repatriated to Europe from the United States, while around 1,200 American nationals were sent in the other direction. Such exchanges were effectively suspended, however, in the summer of 1942, when American officials grew concerned that the new arrivals were "undesirable," complaining that many of them were Polish or German Jews, often with dubious paperwork, and only a minority even spoke English. As a German Foreign Office official sniffily put it: "The Americans have let it be known that that are not very satisfied with the quality of the human material they have received from Germany."[60]

There were other concerns. British objections about the wisdom of sending skilled men of fighting age back to aid the German war effort were taken seriously, resulting in an elaborate screening process, which effectively excluded all those who were willing to return to Germany at all. Moreover, US intelligence agencies were worried about the risk of espionage and raised objections to as many as 40 percent of applicants, despite the fact that only eight individuals were found to have actually been involved in spying. In such circumstances, the exchange scheme quickly foundered, with American officials finding a bureaucratic excuse to terminate the agreement.[61]

Though the arrangement with the United States broke down and that with the British appeared to have run its course, German officials were keen to continue to collect foreign Jews—especially those who were notable or politically valuable—in the hope of thereby persuading the Americans and their allies to resume the exchanges. In this they were driven not only by ideological concerns but also by simple mathematics; German citizens abroad comfortably outnumbered the foreign citizens resident in German-occupied Europe. Tellingly, at the Wannsee Conference in January 1942, the Foreign Office representative, Martin Luther, had insisted that foreign Jews were not to be deported to their deaths without express clearance from his department.[62]

Luther's Foreign Office, indeed, was the prime mover in the growing exchange plans, pursuing the rational goal of exchanging foreign Jews for Germans held abroad. That intention, however, meshed perfectly with the conspiracy theories of Heinrich Himmler and the SS, who wanted to hold foreign Jews effectively as hostages, so as to exert a degree of leverage against enemy nations that they believed were ruled by shadowy cabals of Jewish politicians. Given this coincidence of ideology and realpolitik, events moved swiftly, and in the summer of 1942, the Foreign Office and the SS agreed that some thirty thousand Jews might potentially be held back from the transports to the death camps so that they could be exchanged or otherwise leveraged. The criteria applied for the selection of those Jews included those who were prominent in their own right, those with significant foreign contacts, and, of course, those with foreign citizenship.[63]

So, at the very same time that Europe's Jews were waking up to the possibility that forged or otherwise illegitimate passports might offer them an escape from the Holocaust, so the Germans were keen to find as many foreign passport holders as possible to facilitate the exchange for German citizens abroad. What's more, the German authorities were not especially concerned whether the foreign passports they saw were genuine. So, while not actually colluding in a forgery operation, they were nonetheless willing to overlook its results and treat the passports thus produced as if they were genuine. With that, the concept of the "Exchange Jew" was born.[64]

6

ASKING AFTER AUNT DARKA

IN THE WINTER OF 1942–1943, GERMAN THINKING TOWARD the new category of Exchange Jews began to crystallize. In a series of memoranda, officials of the Reich Security Main Office (RSHA)—representing the SS and police—and the Foreign Ministry provided an outline of the new policy. "British and American Jews," one memo stated with a masterful display of euphemism, were to be "excepted from the measures taken against other Jews." Another stipulated that while stateless Jews and citizens of those countries under German occupation were to be included in the mass killing of the Holocaust, these measures should not be extended to include Jews "from enemy, neutral or even friendly states, belligerent or non-belligerent nations." Those individuals, the memo continued, were to be excluded from the "general measures" and were instead to be interned "for exchange against Germans living in enemy countries."[1]

In order to hold the resulting candidates for exchange, a new camp was required. The site chosen was a former POW camp north of Hanover, which could swiftly be converted to its new role as a "detention camp," or *Aufenthaltslager*, for foreign Jews. The designation would prove highly significant. Initially, the office of the SS responsible for the concentration camp system had announced the establishment of a "civilian internment camp" at the site. However, the name was subsequently changed to a "detention camp" for the simple reason that, according to the Geneva Convention, a civilian internment camp was required to be accessible to the Red Cross, while a detention camp was not. The SS was evidently keen that its new camp should evade any independent scrutiny. The order for the camp's establishment came, with Hitler's express agreement, in December 1942. It was called Bergen-Belsen.[2]

Despite the apparent urgency—given Nazi Germany's plans to exterminate European Jewry as soon as was possible—the transformation of Belsen proceeded rather slowly. In the spring, the camp was supplied with a new commandant to oversee the changes. SS captain Adolf Haas was a bullnecked former baker and First World War veteran who sported a fashionable toothbrush mustache and had been an early member of the SS. Having previously been commandant of the Niederhagen concentration camp near Paderborn, he was scarcely qualified for the slightly gentler task of running a "detention camp" for Exchange Jews. Nonetheless Haas presided over the transformation of the site, assembling a labor force of some five hundred concentration camp prisoners and French POWs to build new wooden barrack blocks and renovate those that remained from its previous iteration as a camp for prisoners of war. By midsummer 1943, Bergen-Belsen would be ready to receive its first transports of "detainees."[3]

While the new camp was being prepared, then, the German authorities began—in January 1943—to move those Jews holding foreign passports out of Warsaw and other cities. In truth, for those interned in the Pawiak prison in the heart of the Warsaw ghetto, it was not a moment too soon. They had been held there already for more than seven months, during which time the ghetto had been largely cleared around them, the sounds of gunshots and suffering echoing in the streets. On a number of occasions, executions were carried out by the Germans beneath the very walls of the Pawiak, while inside the prisoners cowered, crippled by hunger, infested with lice, praying that they would not be next.

Throughout that winter, the rumor mill in the prison had spun with stories of imminent departure, either to safety or to Treblinka. In mid-October, the prisoners had been informed that those with US papers would be sent away, leaving those who remained to worry about their own fate. A week later, the remaining internees were examined by a physician and the date of December 16 was set for their departure. But, when that day came around, they were told that the action had been postponed to the New Year. Many succumbed to despair. On New Year's Day 1943, Mary Berg noted in her diary that she had been plagued by nightmares of those she knew who had been deported and about the rumors of Treblinka: "I see before me the tiled bathhouses filled with naked people choking in the hot steam. How many of my relatives and friends have perished there? How many young, still unlived lives? I curse the coming of the New Year." She had good reason to think that she would never get out of the Pawiak.[4]

When the order finally came, some of the prisoners couldn't believe that it portended anything good. In the early hours of January 17, they were summoned down to the freezing courtyard with their belongings. After a roll call was taken, they were left to wait in the snow, sitting on their coats or their suitcases. From the treatment they received, many of them surmised that they were being sent to their deaths. Then, before dawn, they were finally loaded onto trucks, and as they were driven through the city they saw for the first time the scale of the devastation that had been wrought by the great deportation of the previous year. "Apartment windows hung open," Gutta Eisenzweig remembered. "There was no sign of life." Mary Berg saw the upturned furniture inside the buildings, the broken cupboards, the clothes strewn across the floors. "How much Jewish blood has been shed here?" she wondered. Her fears were not misplaced. Already the population of the Warsaw ghetto was only a tenth of what it had been a year before.[5]

Delivered to a suburban railway station, the prisoners were still unsure of their fate and so were alert for any hint that might betray their destination. They were relieved when they were loaded into passenger carriages, not the cattle cars that they knew were used for deportations to Treblinka. Still, they sat down cautiously on the hard, wooden seats, exhausted, not knowing where they were heading, carefully eyeing the German guards posted in each carriage. Only when the train pulled out westward did they realize that Treblinka was unlikely to be their destination.

Still, the prisoners had no idea where they were going, and—worse than that—most only had the paltry food supplies they had managed to bring with them from the Pawiak. For three days, their train trundled westward. When Mary Berg noticed that they were passing Zbąszyń on Poland's former western frontier, she realized that they were entering Germany. They then bypassed Berlin to the south, crossed the Rhine at Mainz, and passed through Saarbrücken, where she recalled seeing the first evidence of Allied bombing. Later that evening, the prisoners finally crossed into France, proceeding via Metz and Nancy to the town of Vittel, where they were unloaded and marched the short distance to their new home, an internment camp established in a spa resort. It was, as one of their number recalled, like "crossing the divide from hell to paradise."[6]

Established in 1941 in the heart of Vittel, the camp was centered on three hotels located in an elegant public park, now ringed with barbed wire and patrolled by soldiers. Two of the hotels—the Vittel Palace and the Ceres—were already occupied by British and American civilians who had been captured following the fall of France and the American entry into the war. The third hotel, the Grand, was earmarked for the new arrivals and would serve as a temporary internment site while Belsen was being renovated. As would befit its location, the camp was remarkably well equipped, with a library, casino, tennis courts, and a theater. Little wonder it was described by the Red Cross as "the best German camp in Europe." For Gutta Eisenzweig, the contrast between her new surroundings and where she had been only a few days earlier was overwhelming. She had come "from the starvation and cruelty of the Warsaw Ghetto," where the Germans "were shooting women and children . . . with mechanical efficiency." Now, in the elegant hotel lobby, she was greeted by courteous Wehrmacht soldiers who assigned the internees to their rooms and inquired politely if they would prefer a room with a balcony.[7]

It was all a world away from what they had known in Warsaw. There were no roll calls and few rules, except that they were to remain in the camp grounds. They were allowed to cook for themselves and eat in their rooms. They could send and receive post, and Red Cross parcels arrived regularly, containing corned beef, cheese, condensed milk, and cigarettes. Mary Berg relished the newfound freedom, walking the grounds, reading, and daydreaming. After the horrors of Warsaw, she wrote in her diary, "there is no more wonderful feeling." Others, it seems, remained profoundly scarred by their recent experiences. Sofka Skipwith was a former Russian princess who had fled the revolution, married a British baronet and moved to Paris, before being marooned there by the German invasion of 1940. Now interned in Vittel as a foreign national, she recalled that many of the new arrivals had the "air of sleep-walkers." "They appeared dazed. . . . They spoke little, never seemed to smile, walked slowly in the park, as though nervous of doing wrong . . . and seemed intent on avoiding all contact."[8]

WHILE THE DEPORTEES IN VITTEL WERE FREE TO ENJOY their comparative liberty, two developments elsewhere demonstrated that they were still far from safe. The first was an investigation by the Swiss authorities into the very source of their protection. Acting on intelligence gleaned at the end of the previous year, the

Swiss police invited the Paraguayan honorary consul in Bern, Rudolf Hügli, for an interview in the middle of January 1943. Hügli had been under investigation for some time. He had first come to the attention of the *Fremdenpolizei*—or Alien Police—in 1939, when it had emerged that he had been rather too generous in the distribution of Paraguayan visas to fugitive Austrian Jews the previous year. Though that investigation had been closed down, he was once again implicated in accusations of malfeasance in 1942 as evidence of the Ładoś passport operation began to leak out. His primary accuser was the Paraguayan honorary consul in Zürich, Walter Meyer, who wrote to the Alien Police in December 1942 to alert them to Hügli's illegal activities, giving details of the various cases that had come to his attention.[9]

These accusations chimed with a number of ongoing Swiss police investigations. The first was the strange case of Oskar Hörrle, a German national who had entered Switzerland illegally in September 1942, claiming to be a senior official in the Propaganda Ministry who had been forced to leave Germany because he had had a relationship with a Jewish woman. When Hügli gave him Paraguayan nationality and applied for him to be appointed as secretary to his honorary consulate, the Swiss authorities raised objections, suspecting (probably rightly) that Hörrle was a German agent.[10]

The second case involved another member of the Ładoś Group, Chaim Eiss, who purchased Paraguayan passports from Hügli in the autumn of 1942 for his daughter and son-in-law, who were then stranded in Antwerp in occupied Belgium. This purchase came to the attention of the authorities in Switzerland after the Swiss consulate in Antwerp attempted, unsuccessfully, to deliver the passports and duly reported the incident to the Foreign Ministry in Bern.[11]

By January 1943, therefore, the Swiss Alien Police were already quite well informed about Hügli's illicit activities, so brought him in for interrogation. Hügli held nothing back, stating that he had carried out his role as honorary consul "correctly" until the beginning of the German persecution of the Jews, at which point, he said, he had begun to be contacted by Jews seeking assistance, which he had been willing to give for a price. Thereafter, he admitted, he began the illegal production of Paraguayan passports and *promesas* for the benefit, primarily, of Polish Jews, but always with the proviso that such documents were only ever to be used to evade German persecution and were not intended to give their holders entry into Paraguay itself. He did not consider that he had done anything deserving of punishment.[12]

The interrogation swiftly revealed the central role played by the Polish legation in the affair, and, a few days later on January 18, 1943, Juliusz Kühl was called for an interview. As a mere employee of the legation, and so lacking diplomatic status and immunity, Kühl potentially faced dismissal and deportation from Switzerland, but he was nonetheless unequivocal. He confirmed the essentials of Hügli's testimony, explaining the origins of the passport scheme and outlining how the legation's cooperation with Hügli had evolved—how the blank forms were filled out by Konstanty Rokicki, then returned to Hügli for signature. The motivation, he said, had been saving Polish citizens from death in the German camps, and he stressed that neither the legation, nor the consulate, nor he himself had derived any material advantage from the action. Still, he was at pains to emphasize that he had not acted on his own initiative, rather "exclusively on the orders of chief consul Rokicki and legation counsellor Ryniewicz."[13]

In the weeks and months that followed, the Swiss authorities were left to ponder the significance of the passport scheme and consider what punishment would be appropriate for those involved. For the time being, however, the investigation was suspended. Despite the obvious breaches of diplomatic procedure, the admitted forgery, and the malpractice in public office, it was nonetheless clear that the case did not directly impact Swiss jurisdiction: none of the passports, it was noted, had so far been used to enter Switzerland. And, though the US embassy had raised the—admittedly rather distant—prospect that Hügli's forging activities might be exploited for the purposes of Axis espionage in North America, the Swiss authorities made clear that no complaint had yet been received from the Germans, although it could be "safely assumed" that Berlin was aware of the investigation.[14]

Berlin certainly was aware of the activities of the Ładoś Group. The mysterious case of Oskar Hörrle might have been an attempt at infiltration. The Swiss police certainly considered that a possibility, and Hörrle's disappearance soon after appeared to confirm such suspicions. If that had been the case, then the next attempt was not long in materializing.

In the spring of 1943, while the Swiss Alien Police were considering what should be done about Hügli and Kühl, a Viennese businessman named Heinrich Löri made contact with Jewish activist circles in Switzerland, seeking help for "friends of friends" in Kraków. Löri was a forty-one-year-old merchant who had arrived in Switzerland at the end of March. After fulfilling a couple of professional appointments in his official capacity as a representative of a silk company, he went to the home of Elia Boczko in Montreux, where he introduced himself as "Mr. Frank." According to Boczko, he presented himself as "not 100% German" and as an anti-Nazi who was "not in agreement" with the persecution of the Jews. He explained that he had brought a package from a "Mr. Fackler" from Karlsbad, which contained a roll of film, a list of names, and some passport photographs. In the accompanying letter, "Mr. Fackler" explained that he was hoping to get hold of passports for his associates.[15]

As a member of the council of Agudath Israel and the father-in-law of Saul Weingort, Boczko was well aware of the passport operation. Yet, he was cautious. He told Löri that there was nothing he could do personally and suggested that he contact Weingort directly. Weingort was similarly noncommittal, giving

Löri a message for "Mr. Fackler" that it would be very difficult to fulfill his request. For his part, Löri was cool, calm, and detached, giving the impression that he was only interested in passing on the package, nothing more. He even warned at one point that Switzerland was "crawling with German spies." With that, he left, leaving behind the package of photographs.[16]

Weingort did not suspect that he was speaking to a spy, but when Löri was picked up by Swiss police a few days later in Davos, his story began to fall apart. Under interrogation, he confessed to spying for Germany, having been recruited in Vienna in the spring of the previous year, with the intention of using his business interests as a cover for espionage. His task had been to leave the package of materials with Weingort, in the hope that a resulting positive contact to "Mr. Fackler" would demonstrate Weingort's proximity to the passport network. He presented himself in his testimony as a somewhat reluctant spy, acting under a sense of obligation to his country and keen to get the job over with as quickly as possible.[17]

Notwithstanding Löri's amateurish efforts at espionage, it was clear by the spring of 1943 that the situation had become perilous for the Ładoś Group. Not only were the Swiss authorities gathering evidence to close down the activities of Rudolf Hügli and Juliusz Kühl, but the Germans, too, were evidently aware of the passport operation. By way of a precaution, the Ładoś Group decided that all passports issued in 1943 were to be given an issue date of the end of 1942, so that they could plausibly claim to have halted their forgeries should the Swiss investigations continue. They knew that they were being watched.

THE SECOND DEVELOPMENT THAT CAST DOUBT ON THE long-term survival of the "foreign" Jews in Vittel was the start of active Jewish defiance in what remained of the Warsaw ghetto. Sporadic acts of resistance had already been in evidence the previous year, spurred by the emergence of the Jewish Combat

Organization, *Żydowska Organizacja Bojowa* (ŻOB), which had begun targeting collaborators and vowed to resist the next round of deportations. That moment came on January 18, 1943—the day after the internees had been taken from the Pawiak to Vittel—when a German roundup in the ghetto met with a violent response. For most of the day, the deportation had proceeded as usual, with random acts of brutality and with Jews totally helpless in the face of overwhelming German force. As one eyewitness recalled: "It did not help to show a work card. . . . There were no longer 'useful' and 'useless' Jews, all were condemned to death." Within hours, around five thousand Jews had been rounded up. Among them was diarist Abraham Lewin, who had dutifully recorded life in the ghetto since 1940. In his last diary entry, on January 16, he noted his fear of a new *Aktion* and wondered what would become of the deported. He would be murdered, along with his daughter Ora, in the gas chambers of Treblinka.[18]

The Germans were not expecting to meet resistance that day, but resistance was what they got. At first it was piecemeal. A soldier was ambushed and shot; another was disarmed and thrown from a third-floor window. "A different trick in every apartment," as one witness recalled, "blinding, boiling water, an axe . . . a hammer." Then, that afternoon, a group of ŻOB fighters infiltrated a column of prisoners being marched away and, on a given signal, stepped out of line to attack their German guards with handguns and grenades, calling on their fellow prisoners to run for their lives. In the skirmish that resulted, other Jewish fighters hurled petrol bombs, forcing the Germans to retreat and abandon their scheduled deportation, while the fighters disappeared back into their cellars and hideouts. Władysław Szpilman recalled the chaotic scene that followed the fighting:

> The streets of the ghetto were a shattering sight. Pavements were covered with glass from broken windows. The feathers of

slashed pillows clogged the gutter; there were feathers everywhere; every breath of wind raised great clouds of them, eddy-
ing in the air like a thick snowfall in reverse, going from earth
to sky. Every few paces we saw the bodies of murdered people.
There was such silence all around that our footsteps echoed back
from the walls of the buildings as if we were passing through a
rocky ravine in the mountains.[19]

According to German records, three soldiers were killed and
a further three wounded in the action; Jewish sources put the
total of German dead at twelve. The number of Jewish dead was
estimated at over six hundred. Despite the horrific death toll, the
revolt had a galvanizing effect on Jewish attitudes in the ghetto:
no longer did Warsaw Jews perceive themselves simply as defenseless victims. They were emboldened. As one eyewitness recalled,
"For the first time since the occupation we saw Germans clinging
to the walls, crawling along the ground, running for cover, hesitating before making a step in the fear of being hit by a Jewish
bullet." It remained to be seen how the Germans would respond
to such actions, and whether they would change their attitudes
toward those Jews whom they had resolved, however reluctantly,
to keep alive.[20]

In the weeks and months that followed, a tense standoff ensued, with the Germans increasingly unwilling to enter the ghetto,
and the Jews increasingly defiant. The atmosphere was fraught,
with the Jewish population terrorized by German death squads
that roamed the streets at night, looking for victims, whose corpses
would be found, dumped, the following morning. At one point,
the Germans even devised a ruse to undermine Jewish resolve,
when the largest remaining employer in the ghetto—Többens and
Schultz—told its workers to report for "relocation" to new factories near Lublin, assuring them that they had nothing to fear
if they complied. Few took the bait, however. Hope had at last

given way to a grim determination to make a stand. Weapons were sourced and bunkers and hideouts prepared.[21]

Some continued to look for a possible escape, using their foreign contacts in an effort to obtain Latin American passports. One Polish soldier wrote to Abraham Silberschein from the German POW camp at Murnau in Bavaria that April, to ask for help on behalf of his parents, Abraham and Stefania Gepner, who were still in the Warsaw ghetto. The soldier reminded Silberschein that Gepner had been prominent in Warsaw Jewish society and was a member of the ghetto's Jewish Council, and he asked if Silberschein could arrange a "gift of love," as he had done with a number of other prominent Jews. Silberschein took the hint. He replied that he had been a friend of Gepner, reassured the soldier that any resulting costs would be covered, and asked for an up-to-date address. Sadly, however, they were already too late. Two weeks after the soldier's letter was sent, Abraham and Stefania Gepner were murdered by German forces on the streets of Warsaw.[22]

Aside from such efforts, the Jewish resistance took steps of its own, nominating a few individuals as "condemned to life," whose task it was to escape the expected carnage so as to be able to tell the world of the genocide. One of those selected was Tosia Altman, a twenty-three-year-old courier and ŻOB activist who already acted as a messenger between the ghetto and "the Aryan side." She would be given a number of false identities. Not only did she receive a citizenship certificate for Honduras via the Ładoś Group in Bern, but her supporters among the Jewish aid organizations in Switzerland even petitioned Dr. Heinrich Rothmund, the head of the Alien Police and the Swiss representative at the Évian Conference in 1938, to grant her a Swiss passport. Surprisingly enough—given Rothmund's reputation as an anti-Semite and a stickler for rules and regulations—he obliged. In this way, the remaining Jews of Warsaw not only girded themselves for the confrontation to come, but they also prepared to tell the world of what had happened.[23]

The storm finally broke on the morning of April 19, 1943, when German forces—including Waffen-SS, Wehrmacht, and Ukrainian auxiliaries—surrounded the ghetto. Upon entering, they were met with a well-prepared armed response from Jewish fighters, but the disparity in firepower was plainly evident. The German forces, heavily armed and with air and artillery support, were ranged against ghetto fighters who possessed only a few pistols, rifles, and petrol bombs. The point, from a Jewish perspective, was not to win, however; it was to fight. After the myriad humiliations that the Germans had inflicted upon them, Jews wanted to be the masters of their fate, if only for a short time. There was also the simple matter of revenge. As one ghetto fighter recalled, "We saw German blood flowing in the streets of Warsaw. After so much Jewish blood and tears had previously flowed . . . we felt within us great rejoicing and it was of no importance what would happen the following day."[24]

Chastened by their first forays into the ghetto, German forces, led by *SS-Brigadeführer* Jürgen Stroop, altered their approach. When asked later in life if he had been surprised by the fighting prowess of the Jews, Stroop was unequivocal: "They astonished me on the morning of April nineteenth, and they kept astonishing me day after day. We obviously misjudged them." Clearly, a new method of fighting the insurgents had to be devised. Rather than be drawn into a dangerous, and potentially protracted, urban conflict, therefore, Stroop's forces resolved to simply destroy the ghetto—block by block, building by building—killing those who resisted and deporting the remainder to the death camps. Consequently, the Ghetto Uprising was characterized by some of the most egregious atrocities of an already bestial war. Fire became the Germans' weapon of choice, as buildings were routinely torched, their inhabitants gunned down as they sought to escape. Agonizing scenes ensued as the fires tore through the ghetto. In one instance, a woman in distress was observed on a second-floor balcony of a burning apartment block. "She disappeared inside the building, but returned a moment later, carrying a child and dragging a featherbed, which she flung to the pavement to break her fall. Clutching her child, she started to climb over the railing. A spray of bullets caught her midway—the child dropped to the street—the woman's body dangled lifeless from the railing."[25]

No prisoners were taken. Surrendering civilians were routinely shot out of hand, their bodies left where they fell. A German eye-witness recalled how a young woman emerged from a building with her five children in tow, seeking to escape the carnage. Spotted by an SS man, the group was ordered to stand still, before being mown down by a hail of machine-gun fire. "There they lay, in the middle of the market square, side by side, as they had stood. Some of the children were still alive; they waved their little arms and we heard their moans. The SS man approached the group, pulled out his pistol and shot the children in the head. Then he calmly returned whence he had come, as if nothing had happened." Massacres, too, were commonplace. When German forces entered the Jewish hospital in Czyste, they proceeded to work their way through the wards, systematically shooting the patients in their beds. When they were finished, they set fire to the building, leaving the remaining patients and staff, who had fled to the basement, to burn to death.[26]

By mid-May 1943, the resistance in the ghetto had essentially been quelled, and all that remained was for the Germans to deport the brutalized civilians who were left. For those who were willing to risk the attempt, however, escape was still possible. Though the ghetto fighters were determined to stay and did not expect to survive, they consistently sought to persuade civilians to attempt to get through to "the Aryan side." It was no easy task. The area outside the ghetto was heavily patrolled by German soldiers, with sentries routinely checking the papers of those who even strayed close to the walls, making it all but impossible for anyone outside to help. The only way out of the ghetto, therefore, was through makeshift tunnels or through the sewers. When German soldiers heard voices beneath their feet, they sought to prevent such escapes using smoke candles or tear gas.[27]

One of those who escaped in this way was Zivia Lubetkin, a twenty-nine-year-old from eastern Poland who had become active in the Jewish resistance against the Germans. In 1942, she had been one of the founding members of the ŻOB and, as a member of its central command, had participated in the first revolt in January 1943. When Jewish resistance faltered, she was ordered to leave the ghetto via the sewers, taking some of the wounded fighters with her. She escaped on May 10 and would go on to fight in the Warsaw Rising of the following year. It is testament to her central importance to the Jewish resistance in the ghetto that she had been issued a Paraguayan passport, supplied by the Ładoś Group.[28]

Tosia Altman was less fortunate. Though she initially escaped the ghetto a few days before Lubetkin, she was badly injured when a fire tore through her hideout—a celluloid factory—"on the Aryan side." Suffering from serious burns, she was handed over to the Germans but died from her injuries on May 26. On that very day, an underground courier arrived to deliver her Swiss passport. Finding her address deserted, he returned to Switzerland, where the passport was handed back to Dr. Rothmund.[29]

By the time of Altman's death, the Ghetto Uprising had already been crushed. Some days before, SS commander Stroop had brought the ghetto liquidation to a ceremonial close when he personally supervised the dynamiting of Warsaw's Great Synagogue. "What a marvellous sight it was," he gleefully recalled. "A fantastic piece of theatre." He went on:

I held the electrical device which would detonate all the charges simultaneously. . . . I glanced over at my brave officers and men, tired and dirty, silhouetted against the glow of the burning buildings. After prolonging the suspense for a moment, I shouted: "Heil Hitler" and pressed the button. With a thunderous, deafening bang and a rainbow burst of colors, the fiery explosion soared toward the clouds, an unforgettable tribute to our triumph over the Jews.

Soon after, Stroop triumphantly reported to his superiors in Berlin that "the Jewish Quarter in Warsaw is no more." He calculated that as many as fifty thousand Jews had been killed.[30]

ON APRIL 19, 1943, THE VERY SAME DAY THAT GERMAN forces had begun their destruction of the Warsaw ghetto, British and American representatives had gathered on the island of Bermuda to, once again, discuss the fate of Europe's Jews. Following on from the Polish government's note to the United Nations the previous winter, informing the world of the ongoing extermination of the Jews in occupied Poland, one might have imagined that the Bermuda gathering would have a seriousness of purpose that the earlier Évian Conference had so evidently lacked. But, despite the urgency of the hour, the meeting would be mired in the same exculpatory instincts that had beset its predecessor. Neither the British nor the Americans—the only two nations present— had sent high-level delegations. The former were represented by Richard Law, then the parliamentary undersecretary of state for foreign affairs, the latter by the president of Princeton University, Dr. Harold Dodds. Neither man had the authority to negotiate anything of substance.

The discussions that ensued took place behind closed doors, with only a limited press presence. Given that they lasted for twelve sun-kissed days, it is rather hard to imagine what the two delegations had to discuss. It seems that, as at Évian, both parties essentially sought to carry out a public-relations exercise: to quiet the growing chorus of voices that were demanding that some firm action should be taken to aid Europe's beleaguered Jews by deferring to some wider, ill-defined, international body to handle the problem. Meanwhile, both agreed to respect the other's areas of sensitivity. The British did not want any negotiation with the Germans or any discussion of opening Palestine to Jewish settlement, while the Americans were unwilling to discuss any loosening of their tight immigration policy.[31]

To give the delegates at Bermuda their due, then, one must recognize that they were operating within impossibly narrow parameters. Unable to contemplate the relaxation of American immigration quotas or the opening up of Palestine, there was little that they could practically suggest to aid the Jews of German-occupied Europe. In addition, the belief of both parties—that rescue should be achieved solely through military victory—effectively precluded any alternatives, which could easily be portrayed as unnecessary distractions from that primary imperative. Even to question that policy, according to American representative Dodds, "would not only be foolish, it would be criminal." Consequently, in the discussions that followed, any suggestion of rescue operations to aid European Jews would be rejected out of hand. Even the sending of aid packages to the camps and ghettos was rejected on the grounds that it represented a diversion of vital resources that would achieve only limited results. There was also no appetite to reactivate the moribund Intergovernmental Committee on Refugees that had been established at Évian.[32]

One rabbi's verdict on the discussions at Bermuda was scathing: "If 6,000,000 cattle had been slaughtered," he said, "there would have been more interest." The result was a rather shameful collusion in inaction, accurately summed up by British representative Richard Law as a "formal agreement about what is impossible," which left the possible to be handled by "some kind of intergovernmental machinery." If the Jews of Warsaw and elsewhere were hoping for the help of some outside power, it seemed they were to be bitterly disappointed.[33]

That disappointment was not confined to the ghettos and the camps. In London, Szmul Zygielbojm, a Jewish member of the National Council of the Polish government-in-exile, felt it very keenly. A veteran of the Bund—the Jewish labor movement—Zygielbojm had initially remained in Poland after the German occupation and had served as a member of the Jewish Council in occupied Warsaw, before escaping to Belgium, then France, then the UK. As a prominent speaker on the dark fate of Poland's Jews, he realized that it was an uphill task to convince the world of the seriousness of the Jewish predicament, and he showed his desperation when he wrote, in December 1942, "It will actually be a shame to go on living, to belong to the human race, if steps are not taken to halt the greatest crime in human history."[34]

On the morning of May 12, after the Warsaw ghetto had been liquidated, and the Bermuda conference had reiterated the fundamental unwillingness of the Allied powers to assist Europe's Jews, Zygielbojm took his own life. He left a long letter, addressed to the president and prime minister of the Polish government-in-exile, in which he had written: "I cannot continue to live and to be silent, while the remnants of Polish Jewry, whose representative I am, are being murdered. My comrades in the Warsaw ghetto fell with weapons in their hands in the last heroic battle. I was not permitted to fall like them, together with them, but I belong with them, [in] their mass grave." By his death, he said, he wished to express his "most profound protest against the inaction in which the world watches and permits the destruction of the Jewish people. He hoped that he could "arouse from lethargy" those who were still able to save the remaining Polish Jews "from certain destruction." With that, he took leave "from everything and from everybody" that he had loved. According to Jan Karski, Zygielbojm's suicide—as an expression of the helplessness of the Jews and the indifference of the Allies—summed up the Jewish tragedy.[35]

By a curious irony, on the same day that Zygielbojm took his life to protest Allied inaction, the wheels of diplomatic intervention were beginning to turn. On that day, May 12, Abraham Silberschein penned a dispatch to the Polish embassy in Washington, DC, in which he explained the background to the passport operation, noting that those who had been helped were kept "in decent conditions" by the Germans and were thereby saved from almost certain death. In this way, he added, a number of prominent Jewish personalities had already been rescued. He now warned that unfounded American fears about espionage could undermine the operation and asked that Polish diplomatic officials in the US capital engage with the State Department, as well as with the diplomatic representatives of the Latin American countries, to ensure that the passport scheme could continue unhindered. He closed by adding that he had been "fully supported" by the Polish legation in Bern, and, by way of proof, Aleksander Ładoś appended his own message of support in a coda.[36]

As strange as it seems, this appears to be the first that Polish diplomatic circles and, most significantly, the Polish Ministry of Foreign Affairs in London, had heard about the passport scheme devised in Bern. Ładoś would have refrained from telling his superiors for a combination of reasons. For one thing, basic operational security demanded that as few people as possible—only those who needed to know—were informed. What's more, communication with London, whether by cipher or via courier, always carried the risk of interception by German intelligence, so there was little reason to inform the government-in-exile of the action if doing so served no vital purpose. In addition, Ładoś would no doubt have been wary of informing his superiors for fear that they might feel duty bound to rein him in.

On this last point, the Polish envoy need not have worried. A week after Silberschein's message had been sent, a reply was dispatched to the Polish legation in Bern by the Ministry of Foreign Affairs, which outlined the workings of the passport operation seemingly in ignorance of the legation's central role in it. It explained that the ministry had recently been informed by Jewish organizations of an "alleged possibility of rescuing individual Jews" via passports from Latin American countries, which, "it is said," were issued by the representatives of those countries in Switzerland. Passport holders, the message informed them, were mainly placed in Vittel—"a spa town in France." Having had the basic workings of their own operation thus patiently explained to them, Ładoś and his fellows would have been relieved to read that the ministry wholeheartedly supported the scheme. The situation demanded a "strictly humanitarian" response, the message said, an action of "the broadest possible extent." It closed by requesting a breakdown of the legation's efforts in this regard and their results.[37]

In the following months, Polish diplomatic traffic on the matter pursued two primary avenues. Firstly, the Foreign Ministry inquired whether the officials in Bern could produce passports upon request, providing a list of names of possible candidates and asking for clarification of procedures and costs. Bern replied that each passport cost between five hundred and one thousand Swiss francs, though they added that the Jewish organizations might subsidize the cost if they considered the individuals concerned especially worthy of help. Moreover, it was stipulated that, rather than using the passports as a general method of rescue, the recipients should only be Jews, to avoid arousing suspicion should they be subjected to closer scrutiny by the Germans. Procedures thus confirmed, the Foreign Ministry requested passports for a number of individuals, clarifying that the Polish Treasury and Social Welfare Ministries would cover the resulting costs.[38]

At the same time, the ministry was making inquiries about the possibility of an exchange of Polish Jews for German citizens in Latin America, essentially echoing the Exchange Jew ideas of the Germans. In late June, for instance, the minister of foreign affairs, Edward Raczyński, cabled the Polish legation in Rio de Janeiro, asking them to discuss with the Brazilian government the possibility of effecting an exchange. Another cable, some days later, asked the legation in Buenos Aires to extend that inquiry to all Latin American governments. Responses were far from encouraging, however. The Argentinian Foreign Ministry replied that such an exchange was "virtually unfeasible."[39]

If Latin American governments feared that they would find themselves inundated with Jewish refugees, those fears were misplaced. As Abraham Silberschein and others had explained to the Swiss police earlier that year, the intention of the passport program was not actually to send Jews to Latin America; it was merely to preserve imperiled Jews from certain death at German hands by granting them the temporary protection that citizenship would confer. Raczyński's request, therefore, was rather missing the point of the scheme and was perhaps an expression of his own misconceptions. Yet it was symptomatic of a wider problem, which too many of those now involved failed to see: the imagined complications of any exchange were obscuring the benefits that a much simpler course of action—that of a public recognition of the passports—would bring. Merely by declaring that they would recognize the illegally produced passports, the Latin American governments could give thousands of desperate Jews a real chance of survival, without any of them ever leaving European shores. If these countries refused, however, then the passports were worthless, and those who held them would be robbed of what little legal protection they had.

To make matters worse, there were powerful voices arguing against that recognition. Most important among them were the Americans, who were still far from convinced of the utility—or advisability—of pursuing rescue through the forging of passports. In the spring of 1943, the US consul in Bern, John Madonne, asked Rothmund's deputy to clamp down on the Ładoś Group and put an end to the passport operation because of the espionage risks that he thought it represented. Elsewhere, the State Department was airing the same fears to its Latin American counterparts. While the Warsaw ghetto was still burning, Washington had advised its diplomatic missions in Latin America to point out "the necessity" of examining each individual case "before approving such repatriations." Latin American governments were thereby being urged to reject the planned exchange of those whose need was greatest: those Jews with false papers. It was surely only a matter of time before they took heed.[40]

WHILE THE DIPLOMATS CAJOLED AND AGONIZED, THE Netherlands was being systematically cleared of Jews. For much of the previous year, the German authorities had been deporting Jews piecemeal, on the pretense that the deportees would be taken to labor camps, but in the early summer of 1943, the pace was stepped up. The Jewish Council, which had acted as the interface with the occupation regime, was told that seven thousand of its own staff were to make up the next group of deportees. When less than half responded, a punitive raid was launched by the police and SS in Amsterdam to make up the numbers.[41]

Where the roundups were carried out on a voluntary basis, the procedure was rather different. Deportees would be informed, via the Jewish Council, of their impending departure and told what items they were permitted to take with them. Then, at the appropriate time, they would be escorted to the waiting trains. As one deportee recalled, it all transpired with minimal drama:

> We knew we were going to be collected, we could hear the boots early in the morning already on the pavements, and we knew what was coming. We had packed a few things, what we thought we might be allowed to take with us. We were wearing several layers of clothing, though it was a very hot June day, in case we might be separated from what little we could carry. And we ate for breakfast anything that we couldn't take. . . . And, early in the morning, they came up to our flat, they counted us—one, two, three, four, five—and said "Come down."[42]

The Kanarek family, then living in Amsterdam, were among those deported that summer. Parents Salke and Rosy and their seven-year-old daughter, Zahava, were visited by the SS on May 26, 1943, and forced out into the city's main square, with only three precious suitcases for their journey into the unknown. The family had prepared for this moment, however. For one thing, they had arranged for their infant son, eighteen-month-old Yehudi, to be taken to safety with contacts in the Dutch resistance, in the hope that he would be unable to betray either his family or himself. Moreover, the family had applied for immigration certificates for Palestine and had secured a Honduran passport, which had arrived the previous month, via Abraham Silberschein and the former Honduran honorary consul in Bern, Alfonso Bauer. It remained to be seen what good it would all do, so they departed from Amsterdam in trepidation.[43]

After the roundups, deportees—like the Kanareks—were usually taken by train to the transit camp of Westerbork. They could spend days, weeks, or months there, depending on luck, their status, and whether they were able to bribe or cajole the authorities so as to temporarily avoid onward transport "to the east." The deportation trains generally left Westerbork on a Tuesday, bound—in the main—for Auschwitz; a list of those to be deported was usually read out the day before in alphabetical order. The authorities maintained the fiction that the deportees were being sent for "labor service," though the dark reality was becoming increasingly apparent, not least in the fact that none of those thus deported were ever heard from again. Rumors abounded, and the name of Auschwitz was occasionally invoked like a mysterious curse, but reliable information was absent.

In such circumstances, many in Westerbork were desperate to have their names put on one of the lists of exemptions drawn up by the Jewish Council and tolerated—at least temporarily—by the German authorities. In his diary, prisoner Philip Mechanicus mentioned the numerous categories of exemption, such as the Puttkamer list, which required the simple payment of a substantial bribe; or the Calmeyer list, which depended on the acceptance of dubious genealogical paperwork by the eponymous Calmeyer, a sympathetic official in the German administration. The papers of the lucky ones were marked with various deferment stamps, usually a colored Z, for *Zurückstellung*. Such exemptions were rarely permanent, however, as Mechanicus noted: "Many who thought they were safe because of their stamps see the danger of deportation suddenly looming up out of the deep abyss." It was, he said, "a tragi-comic stamp game . . . deportation by stages. Again and again the Jews let themselves be taken in and they hold tightly to their stamps which, when the time comes, do not turn out to be gilt-edged securities after all."[44]

As it transpired, one of the more reliable methods to avoid the deportation trains was to procure foreign passports. Already that summer, the German occupation authorities in Holland had announced that Exchange Jews—those with foreign nationality, or even merely foreign contacts—should come forward. And, when word reached Westerbork that the Germans were drawing up lists of Jews eligible for exchange, it was a prospect that electrified the camp. To some, the word "exchange" seemed to hold the promise of liberation; one deportee was confident enough to tell his family that their Paraguayan passports would protect them from deportation. Others believed it to be just another cruel German ruse. After all, Philip Mechanicus quipped, "exchange joke"—*Austauschwitz* in German—"sounds so very like Auschwitz."[45]

Nonetheless, some prisoners began to seek out the contacts by which they might get Latin American passports. A key player in the shadowy network by which Ładoś passports made their way to the Netherlands was one W. E. A. de Graaff. As an employee of the company Philips in the Netherlands and a longtime confidant of German intelligence services, de Graaff had cultivated extensive contacts within the offices of the *Sicherheitsdienst* (SD), the SS security service. According to the files of his employers, he gave "the SD in The Hague the impression that he was working for their Brussels bureau, while in Brussels he alluded to his relations with the Düsseldorf Gestapo, and in Düsseldorf he led the Gestapo to believe that he was in the service of the SD in The Hague." In addition, he suggested throughout that he "enjoyed high-level support from Berlin." It was "a house of cards," he later confessed, but one that enabled him to travel to Switzerland a total of twenty-two times during the war.[46]

It was during those journeys that he acted as a courier, not only for the Dutch resistance—carrying microfilms and verbal messages that he would deliver to the Dutch mission in Bern— but also for those producing and supplying Ładoś passports. It seems that, in November 1943, he was approached by Dutch contacts close to Abraham Silberschein who were aware of his travels, and they asked him to smuggle illegal passports into the occupied Netherlands. De Graaff agreed and subsequently carried the names, addresses, and passport photographs in one direction and later returned in the other with the finished passports, some of which were sewn into the lining of his jacket.[47]

In all, it is thought that de Graaff delivered ninety-nine Ładoś passports to the Dutch underground. One of the recipients was Eva van Amerongen from Haarlem. After her family's arrest in 1943, her husband, Louis, had volunteered for a work camp, in the hope that by laboring for the occupier, his family would be spared further persecution. However, when he was deported to his death, she and her teenage son David went underground, finding refuge in Amsterdam, before their capture in the spring of 1944. Confined to the punishment barracks in Westerbork, from where the pair could ordinarily expect a swift deportation to Auschwitz, Eva and her son were saved by their Paraguayan passport, which she had sourced while in Amsterdam. It had been delivered by W. E. A. de Graaff.[48]

Eva van Amerongen was not the only beneficiary. Indeed, such was the prevalence of Latin American passports in Westerbork that one wit referred to the camp as "the capital of Honduras." For Irene Hasenberg's family, Ecuadorean passports arrived, sent by a contact of her father. Irene had hardly heard of Ecuador at the time, she recalled, but "it was ripe with promise, because it was anywhere but here." Others were scarcely more knowledgeable about their new savior states. One inmate procured seven foreign passports for himself, all from Latin American countries, but he was perennially confused as to which capital was which. Some newly minted citizens of Paraguay or Haiti struggled even to spell the names of their new motherlands correctly.[49]

Understandably, therefore, the German administration took a rather cynical view of the new South Americans in the camp. One official even complained to his superiors about a "highly undesirable" Jew, whom he had known from Düsseldorf, who was now in possession of a Latin American passport. "We shall be very glad to get rid of him," he said. There were some tentative countermeasures. The assistant to the local Gestapo head, one Gertrude Slottke, was a regular visitor to Westerbork, where she quizzed applicants as to their suitability for exchange, asking about the geography of the country of which they claimed to be citizens or demanding that they name its capital. Such was her power to add or remove people from the deportation lists that Slottke—a "small, bitter and stubborn" woman—was viewed in the camp with a curious mixture of reverence and terror. Critically, she would ask all those detainees who were on multiple lists or had multiple deferments which one they wanted to be recognized. "It was extremely difficult to make the right decision," one prisoner recalled. They were told that a Palestine certificate or Paraguayan passport would result in a transfer to an "Exchange Camp," while proof of service in the Great War would permit a transfer to Theresienstadt. It was an agonizing choice, as "one did not know which option would seal [one's] fate."[50]

Nonetheless, large numbers of Dutch Jews in Westerbork would procure Latin American passports and successfully pass themselves off as citizens of Paraguay, Honduras, or Costa Rica. Alfred Wiener's family was among them. He had escaped Germany with his wife, Margarethe, and their three daughters—Ruth, Eva, and Mirjam—after the Nazis came to power in 1933. Settled in Amsterdam, Alfred had gathered material on the Nazi movement—which would, in time, form the basis of the renowned Wiener Library in London—while his daughters went to the same school as the young Anne Frank. The German invasion of May 1940 caught them unprepared: Alfred was in London and was forced to leave his family to fend for themselves in the German occupation. Deported to Westerbork in June 1943, Margarethe and the three girls were saved from an onward transport to Auschwitz by the arrival of Paraguayan passports, prepared by the Ładoś Group in Bern and sourced by Alfred via a family contact in Switzerland, one Camilla Aronson, who—as fate would have it—was a sister-in-law of Juliusz Kühl. While other members of the wider family were taken away to their deaths, Margarethe Wiener and her daughters were spared deportation. As Exchange Jews, they discovered that they would be sent to the new internment camp at Bergen-Belsen.[51]

For the Wieners and for many others like them, the future was still desperately uncertain, but the rumor that their deportation train was bound not for Auschwitz but for Celle, the nearest town to Bergen-Belsen, at least held the promise of salvation. Such was the excitement, indeed, that the name became almost a mantra in itself: "Celle, Celle, Celle," Philip Mechanicus wrote. "Wherever you go in the camp the residents are speaking of Celle."[52]

BY THE TIME THAT DUTCH JEWS WERE ENTERING THE grim reckoning of the Holocaust, most Polish Jews had already been driven toward oblivion. The liquidation of the Warsaw ghetto, in the spring of 1943, had coincided with a number of other forced clearances. The Kraków ghetto, for example, had been liquidated in March of that year, and a number of other smaller ghettos had been amalgamated, their populations decimated or exterminated entirely.

One of those that remained was the ghetto at Będzin. Like Łódź, it was one of the few ghettos to be located in territory annexed directly to the Reich in 1939, and so it existed under rather different conditions than those in occupied Poland. Będzin was spared some of the everyday horrors witnessed in Warsaw, for instance, and the postal system was more reliable and less prone to interception and interference from the Gestapo. Moreover, as in Łódź, the head of the Będzin Jewish Council, Moshe Merin, believed that by cooperating with the Germans as far as was possible, some element of Jewish life—not least his own—could be preserved. To this end, Merin even assisted the Germans with the deportations: drawing up the lists of deportees, overseeing the roundups, and then personally handing over the unfortunates to the German authorities. A speech he made in early 1943 demonstrated both the predicament that he faced and his twisted thinking:

> I am in a cage confronted by a raging hungry lion. I stuff flesh down his throat, human flesh, my brothers' and sisters' flesh. . . . Why? Because I am trying to keep the lion in his cage, so that he doesn't get out and trample and devour every one of us at once. . . . No one will dissuade me from this course. . . . I shall continue to gorge the lion with my brothers' and sisters' flesh! I shall fight all those men who would disrupt my work.[53]

Many in Będzin disagreed with Merin's policy of compliance, however, and a growing resistance movement emerged. After a number of deportations in the previous year, the population of the ghetto had been reduced to around eighteen thousand by the early summer of 1943, while the proximity of the town to Ausch-witz, which was only forty kilometers (twenty-five miles) away, meant that few of those who remained harbored any illusions about what deportation meant. Consequently, many in the ghetto were keen to avenge themselves on the Germans. As the Zionist activist Chajka Klinger explained, "We cultivated the hate in our hearts. . . . We were burning, seething. . . . Desire for vengeance [was] blazing inside us like a red-hot iron." For Klinger, and many like her, resistance was more of an emotional than a logical deci-sion. As in Warsaw, the Jews of Będzin knew very well that they couldn't defeat the Germans, but they could, as she put it, at least "die a human death."[54]

Yet, for all that desire for revenge and resistance, some in Będzin were also considering ways of escape. Since the start of 1943, Jewish organizations abroad had been advocating the use of Latin American passports—of the sort that the Ładoś Group was producing—to exploit the German Exchange Jews program and so enable as many as possible to evade the looming slaughter. In this, the Jews of Będzin had distinct advantages, not least be-cause two of Abraham Silberschein's closest aides, Nathan Schwalb and Alfred Szwarcbaum, had links to the town. An example of the vital role played by these personal and familial relations is that of the Laskier family—Michał, Chana, and their son Yehuda—all of whom received Paraguayan passports via Alfred Szwarcbaum in 1943. The links did not stop there, however. Their friends and acquaintances, the Buchwajc and Szenberg families, all received Honduran passports, in total numbering some twenty individuals. As a result of such connections, the ghetto saw a rapid uptake in the number of passports being requested in the first half of 1943. Indeed, over 1,200 Ładoś passports were sent to Będzin and neighboring Sosnowiec and Dąbrowa Górnicza, more than three times the number that were sent to Warsaw and fully one-third of the total for which details have survived.[55]

As elsewhere, the correspondence had to be conducted in code to evade the attentions of the German censors. Often an apparently familiar tone would be employed, asking after loved ones and giving information about family members. However, the names used held a meaning that would immediately be apparent to those with a knowledge of Hebrew. A request to send news about Mr. Tmunawasky, for instance, was a coded demand to send a photograph—*tmunah* is "picture" in Hebrew. "Sister Esrah" meant "help," "Aunt Darka"—from *darkon*—referred to the passports.[56]

Frumka Płotnicka's experience was typical. Sent to Będzin by the Warsaw resistance in the autumn of 1942, with the intention of encouraging further resistance operations, she employed numerous ruses and codes in her correspondence with the Jewish agencies in Switzerland to request a passport. In one letter, she wrote of a planned marriage, asking for advice and stating that she wanted her brother-in-law to be included in the "exchange." In another she stated that she had celebrated her twenty-eighth birthday the day before, thereby providing her date of birth. She enclosed her photograph "as a souvenir." In a later letter, she said that she hoped to meet "with Darka" soon. She would, in due course, receive a Paraguayan passport from Bern.[57]

Such was the volume of applications that some grew suspicious about the silence of the German authorities, fearing that the operation must have been compromised. "All letters that I received from Upper Silesia . . . had been opened by the German censors," Heini Bornstein, a Jewish activist in Switzerland, recalled. "The fact that all of them contained photographs with personal dedications, must have aroused the attention of the censor. How many cousins or family members could I, or Nathan Schwalb, have in Będzin?" Unsurprisingly, therefore, many applicants began to doubt that the scheme was genuine. In the meantime, lacking any independent confirmation, all they could do was hope.[58]

Yet, as the applications for Latin American passports from Będzin increased through 1943, another problem emerged: some Jews in the ghetto became opposed to the very idea of escape. The prospect of rescue was perceived by some activists as detrimental to solidarity within the ghetto and to the efforts of those who were advocating resistance. As Chajka Klinger complained, if everyone of fighting age received passports, then the planned defense of the ghetto would be doomed before it began.[59]

This fundamental question was complicated by two additional factors. Firstly, petty rivalries among the various youth organizations in the ghetto were piqued when one group, Gordonia, started to receive passports, while others were still hesitating or deciding whether to apply. A solution was eventually found when the advocates of resistance, such as Frumka Płotnicka, proposed asking for passports for everyone who wanted one, on the proviso that they might only be used at the moment of deportation. Unsurprisingly, it was a proposal that satisfied no one. Chajka Klinger was blunt in her assessment: "We cursed the entire passport operation," she later wrote. "It caused a great deal of damage."[60]

Secondly, and more seriously perhaps, the head of the Jewish Council, Moshe Merin, was very keen for any such operation to be under his exclusive control. He was worried that the hasty actions of the ghetto's youth movements would disturb his fragile peace, and, crucially, he wanted to be able to decide who received a passport and who didn't. In early June, he sent Alfred Szwarcbaum a letter "politely requesting" that he and his "other friends" stop communicating directly with people in Będzin. If they had any further business with the ghetto, Merin added, he was at their disposal. In due course, he would order outgoing letters bound for Switzerland to be confiscated, and he threatened to betray the operation to the Germans if he did not get his way.[61]

For the remainder of that summer, then, the wrangling continued. Those advocating resistance criticized those wanting to leave, and the "king of Będzin" maneuvered between them to try to gain control of something of which he disapproved. All the while, those who had already received the precious passports waited— both for the expected German "liquidation" of the ghetto and for their own possible salvation.

7

NO TIME TO LOSE

THE AGONIES THEN BEING ENDURED IN BĘDZIN WERE shared in Warsaw. Though the ghetto had already been destroyed, the former Polish capital was far from *judenrein*, or "cleansed of Jews," with as many as thirty thousand Jews still living in the city, according to one estimate. The majority survived "on the Aryan side," often using false papers, having escaped the ghetto either before or during its destruction. The remainder inhabited the smoking ruins of the ghetto, hiding out in a troglodyte existence in bunkers and cellars, hoping to be able to wait out the German occupation.[1]

That plan was borne more of desperation than expectation, of course, but holding out for Germany's defeat was not an entirely unrealistic prospect in the summer of 1943. Though it would be another year at least before German forces would start to be pushed out of central Poland, the war on the eastern front had already demonstrably turned. Stalingrad had been held by the Soviets over the previous winter, while in July the great confrontation at Kursk had destroyed much of Hitler's strategic reserve, and Allied troops had landed in Sicily, foreshadowing the end of Mussolini's Fascist regime. Sadly, however, such reversals in military fortune had only spurred a renewed determination in Berlin to deal decisively with the Jewish question. As Himmler would explain to senior SS personnel at Posen (now Poznań in Poland) that autumn, exterminating the Jews had become a strategic necessity. "We know how difficult we would have made it for ourselves," he said, "if, on top of the bombing raids, the burdens and the deprivations of the war, we still had Jews in every town as secret saboteurs, agitators and trouble makers." He closed by telling them that "we had the moral right, the duty to our people to destroy this people which wanted to destroy us."[2]

To a Nazi mind, then, those surviving "Jewish elements" in Warsaw urgently needed to be rooted out and destroyed, not only for matters of "racial hygiene" but because of the security threat that it was believed they posed. For the SS and the Gestapo, the prospect that those with foreign papers might be exchanged, therefore, was another step toward the overriding goal of making Europe *judenrein*. This was the brutal logic of *SS-Obergruppenführer* Hans Rauter, the senior SS officer in the Netherlands, who stated in June 1943 that the program of Exchange Jews might lure as many as twenty thousand Dutch Jews out of hiding. At the same time, representatives of the German Foreign Ministry and others were investigating the possibility that foreign and prominent Jews could be leveraged as a way of "redeeming" German blood abroad. It was in the narrow intersection of those two positions that one of the most remarkable episodes of the passport saga would play out.[3]

With the destruction of the Warsaw ghetto, the Germans needed a facility from where they could still process those foreign Jews—and those merely holding foreign passports—who were still present in the former Polish capital. Initially, a reception center was established at the Hotel Royal, close to the Central Station, where, remarkably, Jews, Poles, and Germans still mingled, "sharing the same lobby, eating in the same restaurant," while the German authorities assured them that those with valid papers would be taken to a transfer camp. The skeptical had their suspicions doused when, on May 18, 1943, only two days after the demolition of the Great Synagogue, some sixty-four Jews departed from Warsaw in a sealed train carriage, bound for the transit camp at Vittel.[4]

One of those who left Warsaw that day was the renowned writer Yitzhak Katzenelson, who had chronicled the suffering of Warsaw's Jews in his poems and plays. Forced to watch his wife, Chana, and two younger sons be deported to Treblinka in July 1942, he was crushed by his loss and was spirited out of the ghetto at the outbreak of the rising to a hiding place "on the Aryan side." Now, in the summer of 1943, and in possession of a Honduran passport for himself and his eldest son, Tzvi, he was included in the transport to Vittel. Once there, Katzenelson was plagued by depression and the fear that the reprieve that he and his son were enjoying would prove to be only temporary and that their status as foreign citizens would not be honored. He consoled himself by writing his masterpiece, *The Song of the Massacred Jewish People*, an epic poem that he dedicated to his dead wife. Viscerally moving, it stands as both a personal and a collective lament:

> *Sing! Take your curved and light harp in hand*
> *and throw your fingers at its subtle strings.*
> *Heartsick, sorrowful, sing the last song,*
> *of the last Jews on European earth.*
>
> *But how can I sing, even open my mouth, as I'm*
> *so very much alone? My wife and two children. . . . What a*
> *horror! I'm shuddering. . . and I'm hearing weeping,*
> *weeping everywhere.*[5]

After the departure of that first train to Vittel, more and more Jews still hiding in Warsaw came forward, brandishing their identity documents, while others desperately sought to buy passports for themselves and their families. Given everything that had gone before, they were not unaware of the very real possibility that the action could be some sort of devious scheme to flush out Warsaw's remaining Jews, but, after the years of privation and hardship, and the horrors of the ghetto's liquidation, they were exhausted. It was not that they believed German promises, but rather that some of them no longer had the energy to fight on. Yitzhak Zukerman, for instance, who had been one of the leaders of the ŻOB during the Ghetto Uprising, recalled that some of his fighters who had escaped in the aftermath were "crushed" and "desperate." They had simply lost the will to carry on "on the Aryan side."[6]

For those who lived illegally outside the ghetto, the strain of survival was considerable. It was not only the sense of overwhelming mourning for all that had been lost; it was also the fear of capture by the Germans and the everyday worry about giving oneself away, being spotted by an old school friend or former neighbor. Yiddish accents and verbal mannerisms could be hard to hide, and even those who were careful and well practiced could find themselves inexplicably compromised. One fugitive Jew, who considered herself very well assimilated and lived openly beyond the ghetto, had a sobering experience at a Warsaw market stall. After asking the price of some lemons, she exclaimed, "Jesus, Maria!" as a good Catholic would. The stallholder was unconvinced, however, and replied sarcastically, "You've known them such a short time, missy, and already you're on first-name terms." She had no idea how the man could tell that she was Jewish.[7]

Then there was the terror of being exposed by *szmalcownicy*, blackmailers who targeted the desperate, "roaming the city's streets, smelling a Jew in every passer-by," as one ghetto veteran recalled. Blackmailers were an inevitable product of a society that had been driven to madness by the brute realities of the German occupation. Mostly established petty criminals, they operated as individuals or in small gangs, and would seek out fugitive Jews to then demand payment not to reveal their secret to the Germans.

Vladka Meed recalled being accosted on a Warsaw street by three *szmalcownicy*—"ruffians" as she called them—who claimed that they knew she was Jewish and demanded three thousand zloty to leave her alone. Though she managed to bluff her way out of the situation, she noted that many other Jews were not as fortunate and were thus deprived of their last possessions while being forced to live in constant fear of denunciation.[8]

Given these dangers, it is perhaps not surprising that so many embraced the exit route that the Hotel Royal appeared to offer. It helped that the operation seemed to be legitimate, or at least legitimate enough to be worth the risk. It was reported that the local director of the American Jewish Joint Distribution Committee, David Guzik, was present in the foyer of the hotel, legalizing documents and even adding the names of those without papers to lists so that they might in due course receive them. What's more, letters arriving from Vittel provided convincing proof that those already taken away had not ended their days in the horror of Auschwitz or Treblinka. And the more people who came out of hiding, the more convincing the operation appeared to be to others. Calel Perechodnik, the ghetto policeman who had joined the force in a futile attempt to spare his wife and daughter, was himself skeptical. But he explained the logic: "These were wealthy people, possessing both money and Polish friends. . . . If these people went there, it could not be a suspicious affair."[9]

As the numbers of Jews coming forward increased, the Germans decided that they needed a larger facility to deal with the influx. Rather than the Hotel Royal, therefore, they opted for the Hotel Polski—the former Witosławski Palace—an elegant eighteenth-century building on Długa Street, just to the east of what remained of the Warsaw ghetto. They also brought in two Jewish Gestapo collaborators, Lolek Skosowski and Adam Żurawin, to act as the public face of the operation.

Skosowski, a Jew from Łódź, was a former member of the Thirteen, the group set up by Abraham Gancwajch to supposedly

combat corruption and smuggling in the ghetto. After the disso-
lution of that group, Skosowski continued as a Gestapo informant
while also providing information on the Gestapo to the Polish
underground. This role as a double agent did not prevent him
from being targeted in an assassination attempt by members of a
ŻOB hit squad in the spring of 1943, not long before the Hotel
Polski operation got underway. Adam Żurawin, meanwhile, was
a former smuggler and informant who seemed to have claimed
that his contacts with the Germans were purely incidental, despite
the fact that he regularly received Gestapo officers at his home in
Warsaw. A Polish underground report on him concluded that "the
Germans treat him with much gentleness and it is obvious that
[he] is very important to them."[10]

Skosowski and Żurawin endeavored to lure more Jews to
the Hotel Polski. Word was spread that those possessing foreign
passports would be transferred out of Warsaw to safety by the
Germans, as had previously happened to those who had stayed at
the Hotel Royal. In addition, it was said that surplus foreign passports would be available to those without papers. The explanation
ran that Skosowski and Żurawin were in possession of numerous passports that had been procured by people who had since
been deported from the ghetto or were otherwise deceased, and
they now offered them for sale. The new owner would merely have
to adopt the name on the document and in due course would be
transported to the safety of the detention camp at Vittel. These
passports were not cheap, however. Reportedly, the two collaborators earned enormous sums of money for their German masters,
with the cost of each passport running to "100,000, 200,000,
500,000 zlotys, or diamonds, dollars, gold." Desperation made for
big business.[11]

Once word of the possibility of escape circulated, large numbers of Jews came forward. In this, they were driven not only by
the prospect of survival but also by the pressure that the Germans
were now exerting on those who were hiding them. German

regulations threatening the death penalty for those harboring fugitives from the ghetto appeared all over the city that summer, and this resulted in Jews being driven out of their hiding places and finding it impossible to secure a new refuge. The response was immediate, as one eyewitness recalled:

> Wealthy Jews began to abandon their best hideouts and children were being retrieved from shelters at churches and orphanages so as to be ready to leave for France at a moment's notice. Anyone who could get his name on the emigration register considered himself as good as saved. Jews sold their last trinkets—rings, gold chains, diamonds—to raise the money needed for the coveted passports.[12]

They would then present themselves at the Hotel Polski, where the words "*Jestem Żydem, chcę wejść*" (I am a Jew and want to come in) were enough to secure entry. As one resident remembered, the hotel now became "an island," the only place in occupied Poland where Jews lived legally "under the eyes of the Gestapo." Once inside, the hopeful were sorted into categories. Those who already had papers and had been added to an emigration list were assigned hotel rooms, where they could rest and receive visitors and mail prior to their expected transport out of Warsaw. The remainder fell into two groups: those who were trying to purchase documents and so-called squatters—Jews who had no papers and no money to buy them and were simply hoping that by being in the hotel they might strike lucky.[13]

Given the sheer numbers of people gathered there—estimated by some sources at over two thousand—the hotel's public areas were rather chaotic. "People were sitting on their stuff in hallways, on the stairs or in the hotel courtyard," one resident remembered, "all fidgeting nervously, talking and telling one another stories of the fate of their loved ones who had fallen into the hands of Germans." Another account described an atmosphere that felt almost like peacetime: Jewish ladies in elegant dresses, gentlemen drinking beer in the hotel restaurant, and no one threatening them or demanding money with menaces. Vladka Meed, who had gone to the Hotel Polski to see what the fuss was about, noted that men and women kept "dashing inside to see whether the office was already open for business." They would return and converse in hushed whispers: "Did you talk to them?" "How much do they want?" "What kind of passport will you get?"[14]

While Skosowski and Żurawin clearly acted as the public face of the operation for the Gestapo, it seems they also had a personal stake in it. The first names that the two men put on the emigration lists were those of their immediate families: five members of the Skosowski family, three Żurawins, and five of Żurawin's in-laws, the Krystenfraynd family, all received Honduran passports or citizenship certificates in 1943. Although they may well have harbored doubts about the operation they were fronting, putting their own families on the list suggests that they must have considered that the possibility that the enterprise was genuine made it worth the risk.[15]

In the meantime, Skosowski and Żurawin made good money. The prices they asked for their passports seem to have fluctuated according to demand and consequently varied enormously, ranging from 30,000 zloty ($300) to as much as 750,000 zloty ($7,500). According to a report prepared by the Polish underground, prices for Latin American passports were generally in the range of 200,000 to 250,000 zloty ($2,500). *Promesas* were considerably cheaper than that, while immigration certificates for Palestine were cheaper still and were sometimes even given away for free, reflecting the belief that such certificates were worthless, as they would not be recognized. Haggling could bring results. One recipient, Warsaw merchant Simcha Korngold, bartered hard and paid only thirty thousand zloty for identity papers for eight people. Appeals to emotion could also succeed. Felicja Blum had no money but recalled that Skosowski took one look at her three-year-old daughter and declared, "I cannot let this child perish!"[16]

For those lacking resources, the presence in the hotel of the Warsaw director of the Joint, David Guzik, provided a lifeline. He routinely handed out certificates for Palestine and gave money to those who could not cover their expenses. He even appears to have held back a few Latin American passports for prominent applicants, such as former ghetto fighters Israel Kanal and Eliezer Geller and the writer Jehoszua Perle.[17]

Once in possession of the necessary papers, many would-be emigrants thought it prudent to learn their new identities, so as not to be caught out at the last minute. Anna Szpiro discovered the pitfalls of having a new name when, at a later roll call, she forgot she had been given the name Brande. After hearing the name called a few times, she finally realized that they meant her, and she went to explain to the German guards. The guard replied icily, "It isn't enough that you were robbed and that you're sick. You're also unconscious." For another memoirist, the change of name was highly symbolic, proof almost of his impending salvation. He recalled that he had entered the Hotel Polski as a Polish Jew, "defenseless to the caprices of the German executioners," but in exchange for $1,000, he now had identity papers in the name of Bretsztein. "I became, at least in principle, a free man," he said. "I was no longer just a Jew, but a citizen of Paraguay."[18]

Given that many of the passports had originally been made out to a family rather than to an individual, some of the new recipients found that they had to adopt new relatives as well as a new identity. Though it was unclear whether the German authorities were especially concerned about such matters, "completing" a family group might help to avoid scrutiny and at least provided the possibility that further fugitives might be rescued. For this reason, additional individuals of the approximate age of those listed on the documents were often sought to complete the family group. Lone children would be "adopted" and would thereafter share the fate of their new family. One eyewitness remembered shell-shocked families that were often complemented by friends or strangers who had lost their own. "There were 'sisters' who were no relation to anybody," she wrote, "husbands and wives who barely knew one another, a 'mother' or a 'father' from the house next door," children who were so traumatized that they "never seemed to speak."[19]

Of course, such considerations did not cloud out the predicament that those in the Hotel Polski faced: they were willingly entrusting their fate to those who, only weeks before, would have killed them without a second thought. The change in attitude on the part of German soldiers was remarkable. Vladka Meed remembered being told the story of a man, registered at the hotel, who went out into "the Aryan side" to retrieve some belongings that he had left with a Gentile friend. When the friend refused to hand the items over, the man complained to the officials at the Hotel Polski, and two German soldiers were duly dispatched to help him reclaim his property. More remarkably still, it is said that one of the German officers present at the hotel was *SS-Untersturmführer* Karl Georg Brandt, a man who had been well-known in the ghetto for his sadistic treatment of Jews during the deportations, yet in the hotel was remarkably restrained and polite.[20]

It must all have appeared too good to believe. Unsurprisingly, therefore, the nagging fear that the operation was an elaborate trap to ensnare fugitive Jews never really abated. "Isn't it all one big swindle?" one man wrote to his wife from inside the hotel. "I am inclined to believe that this is a bald lie." For those on the outside, the doubts loomed even larger. Tadeusz Obremski was living in hiding in Warsaw, while his brother Leon was in the Hotel Polski, having purchased a Bolivian passport, and was now awaiting transport. Tadeusz was tempted to join the scheme but had second thoughts. "My wife and I began to think about it," he recalled. "Foreign citizenship? Fictional names? All those things were believable enough, but not when the whole affair was run by the Gestapo." He arrived at the conclusion that the operation was deeply suspect. "I wrote to Leon straight away, explaining our position and asking him, regardless of the expenses already made, to flee from the hotel immediately, since it was the mouth of a lion which might devour him at any time." Leon replied that, in pure rational terms, he agreed with his brother's assessment. He knew that the Germans could not be trusted, but he felt he had to take the chance, if only because he didn't want to meekly submit to his fate. Tadeusz would continue to write to his brother, trying to convince him that the Hotel Polski was a trap, but to no avail. "It was herd instinct," he recalled. "No-one was thinking. It was all in vain. They were spell-bound."[21]

When a large transport of some 1,300 Jews left the Hotel Polski in an orderly manner on July 5, 1943, bound for a transit camp in Germany, it seemed to prove wrong all those who had said that the operation was an elaborate trap. Indeed, those who left Warsaw that day were seemingly so convinced that they were heading for freedom that they penned a letter of thanks to Skosowski and Żurawin, praising their "effort, toil and sacrifice," their "moral and material help," and promising that their "selfless and madly courageous action" would never be forgotten.[22]

Consequently, though the pressure at the hotel was eased momentarily, the successful departure merely convinced many hundreds more hopeful candidates to come out of the shadows. As one eyewitness recalled, "The hotel wasn't any less crowded, due to the constant influx of unfortunates who came to save themselves, or simply to hide." That cautious confidence was shared by the Polish underground, whose report on the Hotel Polski affair, dated the same week as that departure, expressed belief in the legitimacy of the operation, stating that it "looks like something set up by the proper agencies," even though it was evidently being run for profit by the Warsaw Gestapo.[23]

ON JULY 12, BARBARA RUCINSKA VISITED HER SISTER, WHO was already at the Hotel Polski seeking a way out of Warsaw. She had been dubious of the operation, not least as her husband had expressed his doubts, but she had gone there to see her sister and in the process had decided to try, in vain, to charm Skosowski into adding their names to the departure list. When that failed, she resolved to stay in the hotel overnight, as her sister was expected to depart the next day. That night, however, Barbara's husband arrived at the hotel, demanding that she return home with him. "I wanted to stay with my sister for at least that night," she recalled. "But my husband was unbending. After getting home, he told me that he had heard one of the Poles in the hotel tell another that the Jews were stupid to let themselves be trapped like this."[24]

At dawn the following morning, July 13, German gendarmes surrounded the hotel and told all residents to prepare for departure within the hour. Trucks were brought into the courtyard, and, as the guests gathered with their belongings, names were called out from a list of those holding Latin American passports, *promesas*, and Palestine certificates. Some six hundred Jews, including Barbara Rucinska's sister, were loaded onto the trucks and taken away to the train station. They were treated courteously by the Germans, reminded not to push and helped with their luggage. One of those present recalled that "the mood of the people was good, even cheerful. We were treated like real foreigners."[25]

That care and courtesy continued when the group reached the Danzig Station, in the north of the city center, where a special passenger train was waiting for them. "Everyone had a seat," one of the departing Jews remembered. "We seemed to be treated like normal people." As they were preparing to depart, carts arrived on the platform piled high with food parcels, which were then distributed through the train windows. One account even claimed that *SS-Brigadeführer* Stroop himself, who had masterminded the destruction of the ghetto, was present at the station, ensuring his men were treating the departing Jews with due decorum. With that, the eyewitness noted, "the last lingering sense of fear left us, to be replaced by joy." When the train finally left Warsaw, he was flushed with relief. "After all that I've lived through recently, it feels like I am on leave, granted me indefinitely by the prison authorities."[26]

Initially, the journey progressed smoothly. Simcha Korngold remembered that the passengers looked at each other, unsure what to make of their situation: "We were free! We were afraid to say a bad word, but everyone sat with a pounding heart. In spite of everything that had happened to us, we weren't sure whether it was all real." The relief of departure led to an outpouring of emotion, and the passengers were soon speaking eagerly with one another, sharing their experiences, counting their blessings, and mourning the lost. At the stations where they stopped, they bartered for water or food, marveling at the German towns, which were as yet largely unscarred by the war.[27]

In time, however, darker thoughts came to the fore. "In the next compartment," Mina Tomkiewicz recalled, "an elderly woman was complaining in a tearful voice that she had let herself be drawn into this trap—why had no one dissuaded her from taking this mad step?" For Tomkiewicz, it was a scene that illustrated the profound insecurity of the majority of the travelers. Most of them, she recalled, had no valid documents at all and were in possession only of dubious foreign passports in false names. Most of them had been dragged from their hiding places "on the Aryan side," pushed onto a train, and were now hurrying to an unknown destination: "Everyone felt uncertain."[28]

Their arrival, at Celle, later that same day only appeared to confirm such apprehensions. The veneer of civility that had been shown to the prisoners by the SS in Warsaw was finally wrenched away and, once again, they were treated harshly. As one man recalled, "We got off at a siding guarded by the SS. We were brutally separated from the women and children, amid screams and blows and pushing with rifle butts. The women and children were herded into lorries, and the men were lined up to march. We immediately lost all our illusions."[29]

For the women, loaded into covered trucks for the short journey to Belsen, the tension could be unbearable. Expecting to be killed, many comforted their children or took the opportunity to impart some last instructions or wisdom. Some gave whispered voice to recriminations, blaming their husbands for not listening to them or themselves for believing foolish promises. Others aired their darkest fears: "This is what they did in Treblinka," one woman said. "We are lost," exclaimed another, prompting yet more tears and anguish. For a nurse from Lublin, it was all too much. With a fearful voice, she cried out: "Say goodbye to Zygmunt for me—I've had enough," then took cyanide.[30]

For the men, meanwhile, there was a twenty-kilometer (twelve-mile) night march to reach the camp, closely flanked by SS guards. One prisoner remembered walking alongside a doctor, who worried that they would be "shot like dogs" and that nobody would ever know where their bodies were left. Finally, the exhausted men discerned the vague outlines of the camp's wooden barracks and guard towers emerging out of the darkness. Driven into the barrack huts, which were furnished with only straw mattresses and "filthy blankets strewn on the bare floor," they found sleep impossible and were "overwhelmed with a sense of hopelessness and despair."[31]

One of the new arrivals was Józef Gitler-Barski, a forty-five-year-old Jewish activist from Warsaw, whose earlier escape from the ghetto had been organized by the underground aid organization Żegota. He spent his first morning in Belsen trying to settle into life in the barrack, as he and the other prisoners arranged the bunks and drew their allocated supplies—a cup, bowls, and spoons—from the camp stores. They were also informed of the camp routine: reveille at 5:30, roll call at 6:00, followed by breakfast and cleaning until midday, when soup was served. In the afternoon, various duties were prescribed, followed by another roll call and soup for supper. In all, and despite the shock of their arrival, Gitler-Barski was cautiously optimistic. The food was scarce and the living conditions were primitive, he recalled, but after the horrors of Warsaw, it gave "some measure of relaxation."[32]

That same month, similar transports arrived in Bergen-Belsen from other locations across German-occupied Poland. On July 7, deportation trains brought some 224 "foreign Jews" from Kraków and Lwów, followed by more trains from Radom, Bochnia, and Warsaw later that week, which delivered a further seven hundred people. One inmate remembered the arrival of the Jews from Bochnia and Kraków and the rivalries that it exposed. The new inmates were "tremendously sure of themselves," she wrote. "They pretended, even to each other, that everything with them was 100 percent kosher and they looked at us with disdain, pointing out the phoniness of our papers."[33]

One of those who arrived from Bochnia was twelve-year-old Henryk Schönker, whose artist father, Leon, had forged a connection with an SS officer, who had urged the family to get hold of false papers. Arriving at Belsen that summer, Schönker remembered a comparatively civil reception: "No one was shouting, no one was driving us on." Instead, he was greeted by people seated behind a long row of tables, each one bearing a typewriter and a board with the name of a country:

> There were the names of different South American countries, Palestine, USA and others. We were overjoyed and excited. We were sure that they were the envoys who were to take us abroad. Long queues formed in front of some of the tables. I noticed they were all South American countries. We headed for the table that said "Palestine." The people behind the desks turned out to be Jews from the camp, who had been ordered to register us. I noticed that each had a lapel pin with the flag of the country of his citizenship.

The Schönker family was told that they had arrived at the *Aufenthaltslager* Bergen-Belsen, where they would be interned until they could be exchanged.[34]

More transports from Warsaw and Kraków followed, with smaller numbers, into the autumn. In total, it is thought that 2,533 Polish Jews were deported to Bergen-Belsen that summer, the vast majority of whom were holding passports or *promesas* from Honduras, Paraguay, and other Latin American countries. All of them were flushed with relief at their escape from occupied Poland, certainly, but they were also desperately hoping that their papers would continue to preserve them from harm.[35]

FOR THOSE WHO HAD REMAINED IN THE HOTEL POLSKI—mainly those without any papers—the outlook was rather more worrying. For one thing, on July 13, 1943, they suddenly found themselves locked in. Whereas the hotel had previously been open to visitors, the entrances and doorways usually unguarded, it was now locked down, with German vehicles blocking the street outside and soldiers and Gestapo officials shouting instructions that all remaining residents were to gather in the courtyard, giving them no time to collect their possessions. When the order was given, Vladka Meed remembered, "there was an eruption of clamor and tumult," with many hurrying to Skosowski's office seeking an explanation but being met only by more guards and police. "Some refused to get into the vehicles," she wrote, "but protests proved futile."[36]

Maria Rajcher watched events unfold from across the street. She had traveled to the Hotel Polski that day to bring a Jewish child, Stasia Goldszlak, whom she had been hiding, to her parents, who were in the hotel hoping to leave Warsaw. Having delivered the girl earlier that day, she returned to the hotel to find that the building was already surrounded. "I hid in a gateway across the street," she recalled. "The siege lasted until 2:00 o'clock. Then the lorries began to pull out, filled with people. In the tenth lorry, I saw Stasia, in her father's arms. He was white as a sheet. His wife was standing next to him." She noted that all the prisoners' possessions were strewn across the courtyard.[37]

Loaded into trucks with the customary brutality of the Germans, the four hundred or so residents who were still at the hotel that morning, including the Goldszlaks, were driven the short distance to the Pawiak prison, amid what remained of the former ghetto. There, those with foreign papers—around ninety-four in all—were told that they would be deported to Bergen-Belsen. The remainder, those with no such documents, were treated simply as Jewish fugitives. Two days after their arrival, that second group would be led, in batches of ten, the short distance to the ruins of a nearby building. As an eyewitness remembered, "Ukrainians, armed with enormous clubs, drove them across Dzielna Street, into the gate of no. 27. Across the front of the courtyard, there was a wide trench dug with a small wooden bridge over it. The victims were driven onto that bridge, and then a series of shots was fired. . . . All that was left was corpses in a ditch." Stanisław Wróblewski watched in impotent horror as his wife and child were taken across Dzielna Street to be killed. According to his testimony, a work party of ten Jews then piled the corpses up, threw some wooden planks on top, and doused the pyre in gasoline before setting light to it. The workmen were later shot.[38]

The bloody end to the Hotel Polski operation left those remaining in the Jewish ghettos in occupied Poland in limbo. While the wholesale murder of those without papers outside the Pawiak presaged nothing good, those looking for positive auguries could point to the fact that many hundreds more with passports and identity papers had been evacuated to Bergen-Belsen and other camps, where they appeared to be safe and have some chance of survival.

Jews in Będzin who had already procured their passports, for instance, would have been heartened by a message to the leaders of the resistance in the ghetto from a Jewish activist already in

Palestine, advising them to "pursue all paths to rescue," to do all they could to save themselves so that at least a remnant of Będzin's Jewish community would survive. A similar message arrived from the surviving leaders of the Warsaw resistance. In a letter, two former ŻOB commanders in the capital, Yitzhak Zukerman and Zivia Lubetkin, declared that—after the bitter experience of Warsaw—they had changed their minds about the utility of armed resistance. "Spiritually exhausted," they had come to the conclusion that the sacrifice had not been worth it.[39]

Some had already heeded the message. Since his arrival in Będzin the previous year, Nathan Eck had done much to galvanize those who advocated escape from the ghetto and—as the first there to receive a Paraguayan passport—had been something of a trailblazer. When he was arrested by the Germans in March 1943, it proved to be an acid test of the passport scheme: Would he be sent to Auschwitz or to a camp for Exchange Jews? That question was answered some days later when a letter arrived from Eck to his friend Arie Liwer in Będzin, confirming that he had been sent to an internment camp for foreigners at Tittmoning in Bavaria.[40]

That letter, and those that followed, caused a ferment in Będzin and spurred many who had previously thought the passport scheme implausible to apply for passports themselves. One of them was Arie Liwer, who received his Paraguayan passport just prior to his arrest in April 1943. The following month, he would join Nathan Eck in the comparative comfort of "Internment Camp VII/Z" at Tittmoning, located in a thirteenth-century castle, which had once been the summer residence of the prince-archbishops of Salzburg.

They escaped Będzin just in time. In June, thirty-four Jewish activists there were arrested and deported to Auschwitz, despite having Paraguayan passports. It is not clear whether they were already known to the Gestapo or if they had been betrayed, possibly by Moshe Merin, the head of the Jewish Council, as part of his ongoing struggle to control the passport operation in the city. A couple of weeks later, Merin himself would share their fate. On June 19, 1943, he was called to a meeting with the SS. With the Będzin ghetto slated for liquidation, he had finally outlived his usefulness to the Germans, and he and his entourage were arrested, dispatched to Auschwitz, and murdered on arrival.[41]

In such circumstances, those advocating resistance in the ghetto redoubled their efforts and tried to forget the bloody example of Warsaw. Chajka Klinger noted in her diary that the ghetto fighters of the capital had been overwhelmed by events: "Afraid of what they had started with their own hands, and that the responsibility that had fallen on their shoulders was too great." But, Będzin was different, she wrote. Będzin wanted to fight. Anything else would have been "more than dishonourable."[42]

A few days later, the liquidation of the Będzin ghetto began, with the Germans pulling people from their homes and rounding them up for deportation, including all of those—militiamen, informants, and members of the Jewish Council—who had thought that they would be preserved from harm by their collaboration. As one eyewitness noted, "They didn't spare anybody, women or children, old or young. People unable to walk out were shot immediately." Of the 4,100 Jews deported to Auschwitz at that time, only twenty-five—six women and nineteen men—were selected for labor. The remainder were gassed.[43]

Those who had decided to resist hurried to their bunkers and cellars to prepare for the inevitable onslaught. They had a long wait, however. By accident or design, the final clearing of the Będzin ghetto took place more than a month later, in the first week of August. By that time, many of the would-be resisters were already exhausted, running short of food and water and suffering horribly in the unsanitary conditions. Some attempted to survive by drinking their own urine; others risked capture by venturing out to seek supplies. All of them had to listen to the screams and gunfire as the ghetto was systematically cleared around them.[44]

Nonetheless, there was resistance. In the desultory fighting that accompanied the deportation operations, around three thousand people were killed, including Frumka Płotnicka who, according to an eyewitness, "did not let go of her pistol for one moment" and was finally kicked to death by an SS man. Chajka Klinger was captured and handed over to the Gestapo for interrogation, from which she would escape. Like her, some did not give up until the very end, continuing the fight even on that final journey to Auschwitz. One trainload of deportees from Będzin was so mutinous, it was rumored that they were not unloaded on arrival at Auschwitz; rather, they were simply machine-gunned by the SS. In all that autumn, some thirty thousand Jews were deported from Będzin and Sosnowiec to meet their fate in the gas chambers of Auschwitz-Birkenau.[45]

At the end of that summer, then, Jewish life in Warsaw and Będzin had been brutally extinguished, while other ghettos, too—Białystok, Tarnów, Częstochowa, Vilnius—had seen partial or complete liquidation. The German authorities had thereby made it clear that the policy of ghettoization—of permitting Jewish communities to temporarily survive for the purposes of labor—had been superseded by wholesale extermination, with no quarter given, even to those who were able to work or who had collaborated with them. Where Jews remained, in hiding or under assumed identities, they feared for their lives each and every day. Only those who were slated for "exchange" in camps like Vittel, Tittmoning, and Bergen-Belsen—many of them holding Paraguayan passports or Honduran *promesas*—could view the future with any degree of optimism. It remained to be seen whether that optimism would prove justified.

ON THE MORNING OF OCTOBER 13, 1943, ALEKSANDER Ładoś arrived at the Swiss Federal Palace in the heart of Bern for an interview with the foreign minister, Marcel Pilet-Golaz. More than anyone else, perhaps, Pilet-Golaz had been responsible for charting Switzerland's neutral course during the war, steering the country between the demands of its totalitarian neighbors and the promises of the Western Allies. Lauded by some as a shrewd pragmatist, he was viewed by others as an appeaser, even as a Nazi sympathizer. Indeed, with his lank combover and incongruous toothbrush mustache, Pilet-Golaz could almost have been mistaken for a cut-price impersonator of the dictator across Switzerland's northern frontier.[46]

Ładoś had been summoned as part of the ongoing Swiss investigation into the illegal activities of his staff in procuring Latin American passports. The interrogations of Rudolf Hügli, Chaim Eiss, and Juliusz Kühl, among others, earlier that year had revealed the scale of the passport operation, but when the case had come to court in May, the charges against Hügli had been dismissed because, in the judge's assessment, no Swiss laws had been broken. If Hügli had been issuing Paraguayan passports contrary to regulations, it was a matter for the Paraguayan government, not the Swiss. Moreover, given that only photocopies of the passports were being sent out of the country, there were no grounds for further action by the Swiss police.[47]

Nonetheless, the police investigation into the case was not formally closed, and in due course the Swiss authorities began, instead, to target the sympathetic diplomats. Pending conferral with the Paraguayan authorities, it was suggested that Rudolf Hügli should have his recognition as honorary consul withdrawn. Moreover, José María Barreto, the Peruvian consul in Geneva, was dismissed by his superiors in August 1943, when his forging activities—he had issued some twenty-seven passports—were discovered. The former consul of Honduras, Alfonso Bauer, was also singled out. He had been dismissed already in April 1941 for issuing passports illegally but had continued to do so, using the official seal and flag of Honduras to adorn his residence. In July 1943, he was ordered by the Swiss authorities, on pain of prosecution, to cease all such activities.[48]

By the late summer, then, the investigations were closing in on Abraham Silberschein and his activities as a middleman in the operation. On September 1, he was arrested, and a search of his home revealed a cache of new Latin American passports "from diverse states." Under interrogation, Silberschein explained how the passport operation had come into being and how it had worked, naming Konstanty Rokicki and Stefan Ryniewicz from the Polish legation for their role in bringing him into the fold. In an effort to assist his confederate, Ładoś sent Ryniewicz to meet with the chief of the Swiss Alien Police, Heinrich Rothmund, to explain the circumstances surrounding Silberschein's involvement. Rothmund was less than sympathetic, however, informing Ryniewicz that the legal process against Silberschein had to run its course and pointing out to him "very firmly" that the forgery of passports was indefensible. Though he was aware that the operation had been intended to save Jewish victims from the hands of the Gestapo, Rothmund was adamant that it "should not have been done from Swiss soil."[49]

At the end of that summer, the Swiss Political Department summed up the results of their "thorough investigation." Hügli had been removed from his post, his position revoked by the authorities in Asunción, and his recognition withdrawn by the Swiss. In addition, "several Polish diplomatic officials" were identified as being "personally involved in the matter," naming Juliusz Kühl, Stefan Ryniewicz, and Konstanty Rokicki as the culprits, all three of whom had taken part in the "falsification of passports" and had therefore committed actions prohibited by Swiss law. Due to the severity of the case, the note went on, it was necessary to impose sanctions. It was recommended that Rokicki and Ryniewicz were to be formally reprimanded and warned to cease such activities and that Kühl should be dismissed as an employee of the Polish legation, which meant his ration cards would be withdrawn and his right to remain in Switzerland revoked. With that, it appeared that the passport operation had finally run its course.[50]

It was in this context, then, that Ładoś had arrived at the Foreign Ministry that October morning. He was coming to fight his corner, to support his staff, and to plead for the passport operation to continue. Given that Pilet-Golaz valued his close contacts with foreign diplomats, Ładoś was doubtless received cordially; however, as the record of the meeting shows, he was agitated. Referring to an earlier report of the Swiss investigation into his activities, Ładoś gave his frustration free rein, asking why he was not consulted, stressing that his government would not accept its findings, and arguing that the passport operation had nothing to do with Switzerland; it was solely the concern of the Poles and the government of Paraguay. To Pilet-Golaz's contention that a serious offense like the forging of passports necessitated Swiss intervention, Ładoś argued that the operation was not about falsifying passports, because they were issued in the conventional manner. Pilet-Golaz calmly replied that the passports were nonetheless invalid.[51]

Sensing the conversation turning against him, perhaps, Ładoś grew more agitated still—as Pilet-Golaz laconically noted, "*Il s'excite un peu.*" He told Pilet-Golaz that the Polish government-in-exile would not accept the Swiss decision to shut down the passport operation, especially as it had been inspired by a "very noble intention": to save the lives of good people. Pilet-Golaz, however, was unmoved, even when Ładoś provocatively suggested that the Swiss intervention had been motivated by anti-Semitism. Finally, when asked to reconsider his decision, the foreign minister said he would continue to gather information, but he concluded, "*Les choses en sont là*"—there the matter rests. It was checkmate.[52]

WHILE ŁADOŚ AND PILET-GOLAZ WERE DISCUSSING THE precise definition of a forged passport, the beneficiaries of those documents were still clinging to the hope that their luck, and the credibility of their papers, would hold. That autumn, those who had been sent to Belsen from the Hotel Polski in Warsaw were finally "processed" by the German authorities. They had already discovered that conditions there were much more challenging than the comparative luxury reported from Vittel.

Because of the peculiarities of its development, Belsen was a hybrid camp, with various sub-camps established within it that were sealed off from the rest and run under different regimes. The result, according to one historian, was a "proliferation of com-pounds," which turned the camp into "a shantytown of barracks and tents." At its heart was the so-called *Sternlager* or "star camp," where mainly Dutch and Greek Jews were accommodated. In addition, a *Neutralenlager* or "neutrals' camp" was home to those Jews who were citizens of neutral states.[53]

The Hotel Polski prisoners—now designated as Exchange Jews—were housed in the so-called *Sonderlager*, or "special camp," where they lived in wooden barrack blocks. There, they were not only kept isolated, so far as was possible, from the rest of the camp, but they were also banned from any correspondence with the out-side world, presumably because their SS captors had no wish for word of the murderous realities of the Jewish fate in occupied Poland to spread. Nonetheless, preserved as they were for future exchange—at least nominally—they had some privileges: they did not have to work and were permitted to keep their luggage and dress in civilian clothes.[54]

Despite the privations, life was not unbearable, at least to begin with. Simcha Korngold recalled that food was initially plentiful: there was bread, soup, margarine, and marmalade, and "everyone could help himself to as much as he wanted." The richer prisoners among them, he noted, even turned down the offered soup, preferring to eat the supplies that they had brought with them—canned meat, sausages, and other items—no doubt in the expectation that they would not be detained in the camp for long. Others tried to prepare for their hoped-for exchange, learning

English or rehearsing their new identities. Henryk Schönker recalled one example:

> There was a large group of some thirty people, who were all one family. Their name was Róża and they were from Warsaw. They had false papers of some South-American country. Every day before noon, they sat in some secluded place by the barrack wall and one of them taught the rest one after another, what his name was, when he was born, and how he or she was related to the others.[55]

Mina Tomkiewicz remembered some of the women wearing their most stylish clothes—"silk and velvet"—as if to defy their surroundings. Another prisoner wrote of social life blossoming between the barrack blocks, with regular meetings between friends, where experiences would be compared or the events of the day discussed. In addition, the prisoners' enforced inactivity made them hungry for more intellectual pursuits. Newspapers, smuggled into the barracks from the camp officers' mess, provided ample information for discussion and spurred the establishment of an "oral newspaper"—named *Tramwaj*—which would be "proclaimed in the barracks" and provided editorials as well as commentary on current events and the progress of the war. Lectures were soon organized on art history, literature, architecture, and theology, and courses were set up for language learning. A school was even organized for the smaller children—many of whom had hardly known formal schooling—where the wooden slats from the beds were used as writing tablets, before being cleaned and replaced to be removed again the following day. The teachers were paid in bread.[56]

The sense of community that existed within the *Sonderlager* came to the aid of a prisoner with a peculiar story. In the autumn of 1943, a mysterious "Professor Chaim Ajzenman" arrived in the barrack who avoided all conversation and merely lay on his bunk all day "with fear in his eyes," thereby spurring all manner of tall stories and conspiracy theories. It transpired that the "professor" was a gravedigger by the name of Mendelsohn, who had discovered the corpse of the real Professor Ajzenman on a Warsaw street and, noting a vague physical resemblance, had searched through his pockets and stolen his foreign papers. However, when he registered with the Germans, he discovered that he was much sought-after as an Exchange Jew and was swiftly sent to Belsen. This simple man, who spoke only Yiddish and had very poor Polish, was now terrified that the Germans would discover the ruse and that he would be murdered out of hand as an imposter. He had therefore decided to play mute and feign memory loss. When "the professor" finally confessed all to the barrack elders, it was decided to keep the whole affair secret, to protect his identity. With that, an eyewitness recalled, "everyone walked up to him and shook his hand. A few people kissed him. Ajzenman was moved to tears. For the first time in a long time, he could be himself." As it turned out, the lucky professor would later be the subject of an elaborate exchange, arriving to a bemused reception committee in Montreux.[57]

The most serious threat the Exchange Jews faced was not the veracity of their identity, however, but that their status would be brought into question. Though the Jewish agencies outside occupied Europe were keen to push forward with an exchange program of the scale that had been foreseen by Himmler the previous year, the wider circumstances had now altered somewhat. For one thing, the British, who were key to any proposed exodus into Palestine, were now rather more hostile to the idea, not only because of the detrimental effect that it would have on their relations with Palestinian Arabs but also because they had committed themselves in Bermuda to a policy of not negotiating with the Germans.

The Germans, too, were having second thoughts about the utility of the exchange program. There were a number of reasons. One, certainly, was the desire to keep their own murderous activities under wraps. Given the horrific progress of the Holocaust in occupied Poland, German officials were understandably less than keen to allow witnesses to escape to the outside world. Already in 1941, the experiences of a group of Exchange Jews who had arrived in Palestine had been widely publicized, leaving no doubt as to the scale of Nazi genocide and the identity of the perpetrators. Thus, an SS instruction from March 1943 suggested that, in the event of a collapse of the exchange program, the extermination of Polish and other eastern European Jews was to be prioritized over that of their fellows from Holland, France, and Norway—the logic being that such "Western Jews" were not only more valuable as hostages but also unburdened by knowledge of the grim realities of the Holocaust.[58]

More importantly, perhaps, concerns were growing that the Latin American countries involved would not honor the dubious documentation being held by large numbers of Exchange Jews. As the specter of nonrecognition was raised, the administrative squabbles in Berlin between the SS and the German Foreign Ministry took on a new immediacy. Earlier in the summer, the ministry had prevailed in its opinion that the successful furthering of the exchange scheme might require overlooking the dubious nature of some of the passports. On June 18, for instance, an instruction from its legal department to its rather more zealous partners in the SS had stated that, in the interests of those Germans in enemy territory abroad, particularly the Central and Latin American states, "the inclusion of Jews considered for exchange in the general Jewish measures [i.e., the Holocaust] was to be avoided at all costs." This ruling was to apply, the instruction went on, "even if the application, or the passports themselves, give cause for suspicion." In other words, the success of the exchange scheme was of paramount importance, and therefore trumped the validity or otherwise of the passports involved.[59]

Once the Latin American nations began to question the validity of the passports, however, that policy faltered. Paraguay, it seems, was the first to discern a problem, alerted to the dubious activities of its honorary consul in Bern, Rudolf Hügli, by his—rather more fastidious—counterpart in Zürich, Walter Meyer. In addition, it may be that Paraguay's reaction was prompted by the story of a Jewish passport holder who actually tried to enter the country, spurring fears in Asunción that they would soon be inundated with Jewish refugees. Whatever the reason, the Paraguayans now refused to recognize the illegal documents, sending a list of the valid Paraguayan passport holders in Axis-occupied Europe and instructing the Spanish ambassador in Berlin, Paraguay's official proxy, that all others were to be disregarded.[60]

Other countries soon followed suit. In early August, the Peruvian authorities instructed their consul in Geneva that he was no longer permitted to issue passports. In response, Ładoś sent a note to the Polish ambassador in Peru, Jerzy Potocki, requesting that he put pressure on the Peruvian authorities to recognize passports issued "without authorization" in Geneva. He reminded his colleague that such documents had been produced "in order to save Polish citizens from the concentration camps" and were not intended for use to travel to Peru. Potocki received no response.[61]

At the same time, wheels were beginning to turn within the SS. That month, *SS-Hauptsturmführer* Alois Brunner, then commandant of the transit camp at Drancy, outside Paris, sent a letter to his superior, Adolf Eichmann, which raised the question of what was to be done with the Latin American Jews that were already in Vittel. Brunner's derisive tone betrayed how he thought the issue should be settled. The Jews in Vittel, he said, had purchased their nationality and had never seen their "so-called homeland." Their passports had been inappropriately issued, he went on, and they represented the "worst Jewish criminals" from Warsaw. Brunner demanded a screening process of those already in Vittel to assess the validity of the evacuees' claims to citizenship. Fraudulently issued papers, he said, should not be permitted to enable "Jewish criminals" to escape the Reich. In its battle with the Foreign Ministry, the SS was starting to flex its muscles.[62]

The consequences of this shift were most grievously felt by those prospective Exchange Jews already in Bergen-Belsen. Soon after their arrival from Warsaw, in August 1943, the former residents of the Hotel Polski began to be interviewed by a representative of the Gestapo, *SS-Hauptsturmführer* Dr. Siegfried Seidl—a thin-lipped Austrian "with razor sharp eyes," who already had a long history of participation in Jewish "resettlements." Seidl summoned each of the prisoners in turn, asked their name, place of birth, and who had supplied them with their papers, noting everything down with scarcely another word. Without the protection of the exchange scheme, some 1,800 individuals, mostly holders of Latin American passports, were duly deemed "worthless."[63]

Those affected were not informed of this decision, of course. Instead, they were told that they would be sent to another transit camp, a place called "Bergau" near Dresden. The news was greeted with enthusiasm. The assumption that those heading for Bergau were being allowed to leave Germany was so widespread in the camp that many of those who remained bewailed the fact that they were not going, too. As Henryk Schönker remembered, "They began calling out names [of those to be deported], first a few I did not know, and then the whole Róża family. In my heart, I pleaded with God for our names to be called as well, but it didn't happen, though we waited several hours." Another eyewitness recalled the camp commandant, Captain Haas, telling a prisoner how beautiful the Bergau camp was, with living conditions and food so much better there than at Bergen-Belsen.[64]

In truth, however, "Bergau" did not exist. It was another German ruse, a promise of salvation to ensure passivity and compliance. On October 21, 1943, barely a week after Pilet-Golaz and Ładoś had met in Bern, those 1,800 "worthless" Exchange Jews were loaded back onto the train carriages. Mina Tomkiewicz remembered them dressed in all their finery: "Everyone wore the best that he or she had, thinking that the 'foreigners' should look very chic. Some women wore overcoats with foxes or minks, and large velvet hats in the fashionable manner of the Aryan side, with gauze stockings and special travelling shoes. They carried pigskin handbags and English plaid blankets thrown across the shoulder." They didn't know that they were on their way to Auschwitz-Birkenau.[65]

When they arrived at the camp, the pretense that they were en route to freedom was maintained. Whereas most Jews were brutally segregated on the ramp at Birkenau on arrival, with those deemed unable to work almost immediately herded away to their deaths, the Belsen Jews were treated rather more gently. The *Sonderkommando* prisoners were kept out of sight, for fear that the true purpose of Birkenau might leak out, and the gas chambers and changing areas had been meticulously cleaned and even fragranced. Arriving in trucks, the prisoners were helped down, with none of the usual shouting, beating, and harassment. "They were treated very politely," one Birkenau prisoner remembered, adding that they looked most unlike the Jews who arrived from the ghettos. "They were elegantly dressed. . . . A few of the women had fur coats and gold jewellery. They looked as if they had come from another world."[66]

An SS officer in plain clothes, posing as an official from the German Foreign Ministry, welcomed the new arrivals, telling them most politely that they were to be disinfected before continuing their onward journey the following morning. He told them to have their documents ready for inspection and wished them a pleasant trip. Many of those present instinctively reached into their breast pockets to check that their precious passports were still there, one eyewitness recalled: "At that moment, they meant more to them than anything else in the world."[67]

Soon after, the prisoners all moved off in the direction of the gas chambers—long, single-story, brick buildings at the western end of the main camp road. There, they began to undress under constant instruction from the SS. The "Foreign Office official" reappeared to apologize for this "unavoidable procedure," claiming that it was all at the insistence of the Swiss authorities. It was at this point, however, that events took an unexpected turn. Some of the prisoners had grown suspicious and hesitated, instinctively sensing that something wasn't right. After all, rumors about the Germans' methods of mass killing had been widespread, especially among Polish Jews, so it was unsurprising, perhaps, that some of them were cautious. In response, the SS guards grew nervous, and, after ushering those already undressed into the gas chamber, they dropped the pretense of civility and began ordering the remaining prisoners to undress, threatening them and beating them with truncheons if they did not comply.[68]

Having seemingly mastered the situation, the SS guards surveyed the mass of terrified, humiliated prisoners. There are conflicting accounts of what happened next. According to one, a young woman caught the eye of Josef Schillinger, a guard renowned in the camp for his sadism. He and his fellow officer Wilhelm Emmerich began taunting the woman, leering at her. In another account, the woman threw her bra in Schillinger's face, causing him to drop his pistol. In the most lurid version of events, the woman drew the guards in by performing a seductive striptease, lifting her skirt to show a glimpse of thigh. When the two drew closer, she slammed the heel of her shoe into Emmerich's forehead before grabbing his pistol and shooting Schillinger twice in the stomach. The identity of the woman is disputed but is thought to have been Franceska Mann, a young Polish ballerina who had enjoyed some success in prewar Warsaw. Whoever she was, following her example, the Belsen Jews now attacked the SS men with their bare hands. One was even said to have bitten off a guard's nose.[69]

In the chaos that followed, the SS quickly exited the changing room, dragging the fatally wounded Schillinger with them, and bolted the door. Filip Müller, a Slovak Jew and a member of the *Sonderkommando*, found himself locked inside with the prisoners. There was now a great commotion, he recalled, with some preparing to resist, while others were "weeping and bemoaning their fate, some were praying, others bidding each other farewell." Noticing Müller's striped prison uniform, one man demanded to know what was going on. "I don't understand what this is all about," he said. "After all, we have valid entry visas for Paraguay: and what's more, we paid the Gestapo a great deal of money to get our exit permits!" Müller was spared the necessity of explaining the grim truth of the man's predicament by the arrival of the SS, who opened the doors again and demanded that all members of the *Sonderkommando* leave the building. Soon after, Müller recalled, there was a rattle of machine-gun fire as the changing room was brutally cleared. It was all a reminder, he would later write, that there was no chance of escape: "The promises of the SS . . . were nothing but barefaced deception, as they had proved to be for these wretched people who had wanted to emigrate to Paraguay."[70]

A few months later, in a glaring example of the administrative chaos that lurked at the heart of the Nazi regime, an inquiry from the German Foreign Office arrived at the Reich Security Main Office regarding the whereabouts of the Herzog family. Osias and Mina Herzog and their children—twenty-one-year-old Sylvia and thirteen-year-old Norbert—were Honduran citizens, formerly resident in Lwów in eastern Poland, whose last known address was the internment camp at Bergen-Belsen. The Foreign Office was evidently unaware of what had happened to many former Exchange Jews. The response they received from the RSHA was brutally brief. The Herzog family, it said, had left Bergen-Belsen on October 22, 1943, therefore they were "no longer available for exchange." In the months that followed, two further transports would carry a thousand more Exchange Jews to their deaths in Auschwitz.[71]

THAT AUTUMN, FOLLOWING THE EXTERMINATION OF THE failed Exchange Jews from Bergen-Belsen, the noose also began to tighten around others holding Latin American passports. While life for the Jews in the camp at Vittel went on more or less as normal that autumn and winter, word of the growing crisis surrounding recognition was not slow to arrive. Gutta Eisenzweig recalled that the internees in Vittel were permitted to write letters—subject to German censorship—and one frequent recipient was the Spanish ambassador in Berlin, whom they asked to extend protection to those Jews with Latin American papers who were still in the ghettos and camps of German-occupied Poland. When a reply arrived from the Spanish embassy informing them that—according to the instructions received from Asunción—Paraguayan passports would no longer be recognized, a veritable panic broke out.[72]

In response, there was a frenzy of further letter writing. "We wrote to Jewish organizations and acquaintances in Switzerland and England," Eisenzweig remembered. "Some of these letters were mailed via the International Red Cross, and others were sown into the clothing of American, British and Palestinian citizens who were exchanged by the Nazis for German nationals. . . . Hillel Seidman wrote desperate messages in Hebrew and German to the Jewish community, begging for their help." Among the recipients were Agudath Israel in London and New York and Abraham Silberschein in Geneva, as well as ambassadors, politicians, and anyone who was thought able to exert some influence.[73]

Former Russian princess Sofka Skipwith remembered the predicament of the Polish Jews in Vittel all too clearly. For one thing, she recalled, they were not free from the prejudice of their fellows, noting that the exclusive practices of the Orthodox aroused "acute irritation" among some of the other detainees. Another Vittel inmate reported that some of the other prisoners tried to investigate the Polish Jews "in the most unsympathetic matter" as to the origin of their identity papers, and even wrote anonymous letters of denunciation to the German authorities.[74]

Skipwith recalled that it was "only too obvious" that the Latin American papers that the new arrivals brandished "were worth nothing." Yet, she wrote, "their possessors still clung to their faith in the efficacy of the documents as their last hope." She did what she could to help them, offering English lessons, writing letters on request, even engaging in clandestine activity. "I was given the full list of names," Skipwith wrote in her memoir, "and with the aid of a fine mapping pen and a magnifying glass, learned to write out the two hundred and fifty names as well as a few words of message on a couple of cigarette papers, which were concealed in a capsule which a messenger could easily swallow or destroy." In this way, word of the plight of some of the Jews in Vittel was sent "in all directions." In addition, Skipwith wrote to the Board of Deputies of British Jews, the British embassy in Moscow, and the Home Office in London, giving the names of those affected, explaining their situation, and begging that they be granted Palestinian citizenship by the British government.[75]

In the midst of this frenzy of clandestine communication, on November 13, 1943, Chaim Eiss died. As one of the inner circle of the Ładoś Group, who knew all aspects of the operation, his was a grievous loss. In the weeks and months that followed, his son Joseph initially took up the reins of his rescue work, relying on Saul Weingort for advice, but soon after, another figure on the periphery of the group, Yitzchak Sternbuch, took over Eiss's position as the representative of Agudath Israel in Switzerland.

Occurring the same month that the fruits of the passport operation were being called into question for the first time, Eiss's death must have seemed a dark portent of troubles to come.[76]

A few days before Eiss passed away, another death, this time in Warsaw, provided a peculiar coda to the Hotel Polski story. Lolek Skosowski, who, along with Adam Żurawin, had been the public face of the Hotel Polski operation, met his end in early November 1943. While Żurawin had taken advantage of the exchange scheme to make his escape to Vittel along with his family, Skosowski had opted to remain in Warsaw, presumably to continue his lucrative role as go-between, fixer, and double agent. It was this uneasy balancing act, rather than his involvement with the Hotel Polski deportations, that had spelled his end. Though the political arm of the Polish underground, the so-called *Delegatura*, had been willing to use Skosowski as an informer and agent of influence, some within the military arm—the *Armia Krajowa*—were wary of the potential effect on morale if Gestapo collaborators were allowed to continue their actions undeterred. In Skosowski's case, it seems, the latter opinion won the day. Lured to a meeting in a Warsaw bar, he was shot three times in the head by an underground hit squad. That same evening, his mistress Ewa Sobolewska and two other associates were also assassinated. Skosowski's chauffeur and his mistress's sister were killed in another hit a couple of weeks later. With that, Skosowski's "cell" was considered to have been liquidated, and a powerful message was sent to those Varsovians who might still have considered collaborating with the Germans.[77]

Those who had escaped Warsaw thanks to Skosowski's scheming likely never heard about his violent demise, yet within weeks they, too, were faced once again with the threat of deportation. On the morning of December 10, 1943, a commission of German Foreign Office officials arrived in Vittel, demanding—as Brunner had suggested to Eichmann—to examine the documents of the Jewish internees. The result, according to Mary Berg, was "a terrible panic," as rumors spread that the Jews might be sent back to Poland, or to Palestine, or deported elsewhere. More worryingly still, the Germans confiscated the identity documents of the camp's Latin American "citizens," with the justification that the papers were to be sent to Berlin for review. They would never be returned.[78]

Just as the Germans were deciding what to do with the Latin American passport holders, the Ładoś Group and their Jewish allies were desperately trying to alert the international community to the threat that the surviving Jews faced. Juliusz Kühl tried to enlist the help of the Vatican to use its influence in Latin America, asking his friend Philippe Bernardini, the papal nuncio in Bern—with whom he played table tennis in their free time—to intervene directly with the pope. That December, Ładoś forwarded a message from Yitzchak Sternbuch to the Polish Foreign Ministry, which gave a stark assessment of the situation. "Deportation and death loom over the holders of Paraguayan passports," Sternbuch warned, because of the refusal by Latin American governments to recognize the documents. He went on to request that Jewish organizations "cause every possible intervention" to overturn that decision. "Those people's lives now depend only on South American governments," he urged. "We've got no time to lose."[79]

Ładoś, too, wrote to his superiors in the Polish Foreign Ministry in London in mid-December, informing them about the German investigative commission, newly arrived in Vittel, and requesting that a "vigorous intervention" be undertaken with "all relevant governments," including those of Britain, the United States, Paraguay, Honduras, Peru, Ecuador, Costa Rica, Nicaragua, Haiti, Chile, and Venezuela, as well as the Pan-American Union. The goal was to secure the recognition of the passports, which, he said, had been issued "solely for humanitarian purposes, to save people from certain death," and imposed no obligations on the respective governments. The matter, he said, was "very urgent." A few days later, the new Polish foreign minister, Tadeusz Romer, obliged, sending a circular to the Polish missions throughout Latin America echoing Ładoś, asking for swift interventions with all the governments concerned. He asked that the results of those interventions be reported back to London forthwith.[80]

At the same time, Saul Weingort was writing to correspondents in Istanbul, Tel Aviv, and New York, pleading for assistance for "our families in Vittel." He also met with representatives of the Red Cross and the YMCA in an effort to persuade them to intercede with the Spanish and Paraguayan governments. "Every minute could be fatal for my parents and friends," he pleaded. Abraham Silberschein, meanwhile, provided a thoroughgoing summary of events to his contacts in New York in the first days of January 1944. Through the passport operation, he wrote, they had "saved around 10,000 persons from hell," who were now threatened by the prospect of nonrecognition and the brutal actions of the Germans. "It is certain," he warned, "that if the question of the passports is answered in an unfavourable direction," all those Jews would face death.[81]

In the months that followed, the diplomatic wires fairly hummed with correspondence on the question of the Latin American passports. The auguries were initially positive. Already on January 4, the Polish consul general in New York could report to the Polish Foreign Ministry in London that the interventions had borne fruit: the Paraguayan government had belatedly informed their colleagues in the US State Department that they would recognize the passports issued in Bern. Indeed, the consul added, the Paraguayans did not understand why the Spanish ambassador in Berlin had responded in the way he did. The note closed by stating that the papal nuncio in Washington had requested that the pope himself intervene to stop the deportations. The following day, a letter from the Polish envoy in Havana to the embassy in Washington brought more good news, explaining that the intervention with the government of Haiti had brought a positive response, and that, thanks to the good relations between Haiti and Poland, the desired outcome was to be expected.[82]

In addition to the diplomatic traffic, there was also a lively correspondence between Yitzchak Sternbuch and Agudath Israel in New York, which was transmitted via the Polish legation in Bern and the Polish embassy in Washington, DC. Agudath Israel representatives reported to Sternbuch on January 26 that the Paraguayans were now accepting the questionable passports, and added a week later that Peru had followed suit. Although the following month brought the bad news that the Venezuelan and Ecuadorean governments would refuse to recognize irregularly issued passports—due in part, according to the Polish envoy in Bogotá, to anti-Semitic sentiment—the responses on the question of recognition were still reasonably positive. Those most closely involved must have hoped that their worst fears would not be realized.[83]

8

DEATH CASTS ITS SHADOW

HOPE ALSO BEGAN TO FLOURISH AGAIN IN BERGEN-BELSEN. After the departure of the "Bergau" group, barely four hundred Polish Jews remained in the camp, almost exclusively those holding Palestine certificates. They had once been the least envied of the Exchange Jews. Described by other prisoners as "desperate beggars" and "fourth class passengers," they had often received their certificates at no cost, as it had been widely assumed that they would prove worthless. Now, thanks to the hesitant international recognition of the papers held by the Exchange Jews, the humble Palestine certificate—never formally disavowed by the British and so still nominally valid—had emerged as something of a lifeline.[1]

The remaining Polish prisoners did not want for space, certainly, but they had to endure the gradual decline in living conditions—in particular, bad food and the perennial rumors of further deportations—in isolation from their fellows elsewhere in the camp. Typical of the period, perhaps, was the diary entry of Józef Gitler-Barski, who wrote on November 18, 1943: "A very hungry day. Awful soup made of stinging nettles. They are waiting for a list of names for the next departure."[2]

The somber mood was lifted somewhat by the arrival, on January 11, 1944, of a transport of over a thousand Jews from Westerbork, the majority of whom were candidates for the exchange program, holding certificates for Palestine or Latin American passports. It was the first of a number of transports arriving that spring, as the camp in Holland was gradually cleared of the remaining "privileged" and "deferred" prisoners. In all, over 3,500 Jews would be transported from there to Bergen-Belsen in the early months of 1944, meaning that Dutch Exchange Jews supplanted Poles as the biggest group in the camp.[3]

This marked a deliberate shift. The German authorities had long been concerned that surviving Polish Jews had effectively seen too much to be lightly permitted to survive. The brutal experience of German occupation in Poland—ghettoization, deportations, and the various ghetto risings—had unequivocally revealed to Polish Jews that German policy toward them was genocidal, and that was a message that few senior Nazi officials wanted to allow to be broadcast to the outside world. Consequently, one strand of Nazi thinking through the previous year had been to use western European Jews for exchange where possible, precisely because they had not seen the horrors that were commonplace further east. Dutch Jews in particular were considered to be the perfect candidates for exchange.[4]

For the prisoners in Westerbork, therefore, that first transport to Bergen-Belsen was markedly different from those that routinely carried deportees to Auschwitz. For one thing, it had departed the camp in the middle of the day, rather than in the early morning. What's more, passengers had been allowed to take their belongings with them, rather than being limited to a single bag. Even the mistress of the Gestapo lists, Frau Slottke, had said to a waverer, "This is a unique transport. But it's up to you."[5]

Despite a lack of firm knowledge about the deportees' destination, the resulting air of positivity had been infectious. Philip

Mechanicus noted that those leaving Westerbork "departed in a procession with a final farewell, with a wave or a clap of the hand at the open windows. . . . There was a flicker of hope about this transport." Mirjam Wiener, who was ten years old at the time, remembered that they journeyed "in an ordinary train, not a cattle truck," which, she thought, "boded well." It seems that the air of hope was sustained through the journey to Bergen-Belsen, as the official record noted that the group arrived in a "rather positive mood."[6]

Others leaving that spring shared that sense of optimism. Irene Hasenberg, who was deported from Westerbork in early February, recalled feeling "almost giddy" with excitement as the train departed. The fact that there was a toilet aboard, she remembered, was a sure sign "that things were improving." Renata Laqueur was similarly hopeful. She had been arrested in Amsterdam in November 1943 and sent to Westerbork, where her Paraguayan passport—issued by the Ładoś Group—had prevented her immediate onward deportation to Auschwitz. Scheduled for transport to Celle in the spring of 1944, she remembered how the mood had lifted: "We hoped to find, in Bergen-Belsen, a camp perhaps under the control of the International Red Cross; hoped to be treated as foreigners, with the possibility of exchange; and perhaps with central heating and warm running water?"[7]

Yet amid the enthusiasm, there was also concern. Philip Mechanicus remembered that those who left the camp bound for Celle on January 31, 1944, departed "with sorrow in their hearts"—anxious to be leaving Dutch soil, certainly, but also fearful of what the future held. "Whatever Celle is like, they feel suspicious," he wrote. "They know that the Germans are taking the Jews to Celle for a sordid barter deal and, if it miscarries, they will be flung on the dunghill like the hundred thousand other Jews, most of whom were carried off to Poland in cattle trucks." It would prove to be a prescient observation.[8]

This awareness of the caprice of fate, of how life could turn in a moment, was widespread and is a common feature of the reminiscences of those who survived the Holocaust. A poignant example is the story of Charles Siegman, a Dutch Jew who was seven years old when he was deported to Westerbork early in 1944. In an effort to escape deportation, Siegman's mother had placed him and his elder brother Leo in an orphanage in Amsterdam, but she had succeeded only in delaying the inevitable. By the time they arrived at Westerbork, their mother and other siblings had already been deported onward to Auschwitz, leaving only a postcard in which she reminded the boys to take good care of each other. She had signed off with "See you again!" It was the last they would hear from her.

Charles and Leo would have followed their mother and siblings to Auschwitz but for the intervention of fate. After their arrival in Westerbork, there was an outbreak of scarlet fever, resulting in a weeklong quarantine, during which all transports in and out of the camp were suspended. By the time the deportations were resumed—with Charles and his brother on the list—a telegram had arrived from Amsterdam informing the camp authorities that the Siegman family had received Honduran passports, which had been sourced from the Ładoś Group in Switzerland. Those passports, coupled with the disease-induced delay, would save the boys' lives.[9]

For all of them—the optimistic and the suspicious—arrival at Belsen was chastening. The treatment that the prisoners received there and at the railhead at Celle was certainly harsher than what they had experienced at Westerbork. Irene Hasenberg was torn from her reveries by snarling dogs and barked instructions, with a guard shouting: "*Raus! Raus!* This train is too good for your kind!" When a man remonstrated with an SS officer, telling him that there had been some mistake, that they were due to be exchanged and should surely be sent to a different camp, he received a violent slap across the face and was ordered to get back in line. Thus cowed, the prisoners proceeded—at the double and under guard—to Bergen-Belsen.[10]

For Renata Laqueur, the camp was a far cry from the Red Cross facility she had hoped for, and she was dismayed to see a large white sign at the entrance, which read "SS Camp of the SS Death's Head Regiment." Her spirits sank: "I am without hope. This is the end." When Gertrude van Tijn arrived at Belsen in March 1944, she described the camp as "the most dismal place" she had ever seen: a vista of barbed wire, SS guards, and watchtowers. What shocked her most, however, was the state of those prisoners from Westerbork—many of whom she knew personally—who had arrived there in the previous transports. They had left Holland "in good mental and physical condition," she noted, but "already the men looked emaciated, ill-kept, cowed—a shadow of their former selves." Almost all of them were suffering from dysentery.[11]

While conditions in Belsen had originally been perhaps better than in most other concentration camps, not least as many of the inmates were being preserved there for some purpose or other, they were now quickly deteriorating. The scarcity and poor quality of the food available that winter was the most immediate signal of hard times to come. Meals generally consisted of a small portion of dry bread and some turnip broth. If the prisoners were lucky, the soup would be augmented by the presence of some scraps of meat of indeterminate origin; if they were not, there would be no soup at all and they would receive a spoonful of jam or cheese curds instead. The most fortunate among them were able to supplement their meager diet through food parcels from home, but most just went hungry. Józef Gitler-Barski—whose diary is one of the best records of life in the *Sonderlager*—was dependent only on the food provided by the Germans and the occasional generosity of others. Hunger was his constant companion. It was most severe, he wrote in his diary, "in the evenings, while I lie in my cot. . . . It is difficult to fall asleep. I chase away thoughts of hunger, but later—a dream about food."[12]

Other prisoners would have sympathized. Mirjam Wiener recalled desperately scraping the containers out after the food had been served. Irene Hasenberg remembered how "food was power" in Bergen-Belsen. When the daily soup was being distributed, she wrote, the barrack leader knew even without looking who was next in line, and used the ladle accordingly: digging deep for those he favored, barely scooping the surface for those he didn't. Irene, to her chagrin, always received a weak portion, which reminded her of laundry water.[13]

Other perils began to make themselves felt. Given that the *Sonderlager* now housed a fraction of the numbers it once had, its inmates were obliged to move to another part of the camp to make way for newcomers. In February 1944, the arrival of the Dutch Jews forced the smaller contingent of Polish Jews to vacate their barrack blocks. They were obliged to leave their blankets, mattresses, and bowls for their Dutch fellows, taking only their few remaining possessions with them. Inevitably, they found that their new barracks were dirtier, colder, more cramped, and more lice infested than those they had left. "Every such move worsens our conditions," one inmate wrote.[14]

The innate brutality of camp life also came to the fore. One eyewitness described Belsen as a curious microcosm of the outside world: "A deformed small cosmos where the extremes were magnified to absurdity." All human life was there, she remembered, the ordinary and the extraordinary. There were ghetto fighters and intellectuals, the silent and depressed, but also "collaborators, scoundrels and hooligans with lots of money and few scruples." Given that the majority of the Exchange Jews present in the camp were in possession of forged or illegally issued papers, it was perhaps inevitable that some of them were ruthless, criminal even, and willing to sacrifice anything and anyone to survive.[15]

Theft became commonplace, driven by hunger, scarcity, and opportunity. The lack of food made some of the prisoners feral. "Food and clothing, even the smallest scrap and swatch, disappeared," one prisoner recalled. "Starvation made us sick and slow, but for some stoked a desire to survive so strong that they stole others' means for surviving. It was every soul for its own." Simcha Korngold was unsparing in his descriptions of some of his fellows: they were "scoundrels," "tough guys," "murderers," "a motley group of criminals and German agents."[16]

Unsurprisingly, such conditions did little to assuage the emotional damage already affecting many of the prisoners. A sense of loss was a universal condition. Everybody had lost someone or was mourning someone—siblings, children, spouses, or parents—whose absence was felt most keenly on anniversaries and birthdays, or simply spurred by a glance, a random comment, or the presence of children of a similar age to those being mourned. One inmate wrote of a Mrs. Rubin, who eased her own pain by helping others in the camp, yet would occasionally reveal the empty world behind the mask of her smile. "Sometimes, in the middle of the night, she would talk to her husband whom she had adored, and to her two small children, all of whom she had lost during the deportations." An example remembered by Henryk Schönker showed the visceral pain that some prisoners endured. He recalled meeting a woman who had been so convinced, while she was on the deportation train, that they were being taken to their deaths that she had thrown her small child through the carriage window. Now in the relative safety of Belsen, she was inconsolable. "She screamed in her sleep every night, 'Give me back my child! Give me back my child!' People would wake her up and try to calm her down, but she began shouting again as soon as she fell asleep."[17]

WHILE BERGEN-BELSEN WAS BEGINNING ITS GRADUAL deterioration into a "regular" concentration camp, with all the attendant horrors, the camp at Vittel was still a comparative haven of civility and hope. That February, some of its internees were being registered for departure. They included Mary Berg, who held an American passport and suffered the agony of being first included on exchange lists, then removed at the last moment as the Germans changed their criteria for inclusion. It reminded her of what had happened in the Pawiak: "There, too, they changed their minds every minute, apparently for the sole purpose of torturing us." But for all the inexplicable changes and apparent backsliding, two days after she wrote those words, on March 1, 1944, Berg was on a train headed for Biarritz, Lisbon, and freedom. To those she left behind in Vittel, her departure must have seemed a good omen.[18]

Any resulting optimism among the Latin American passport holders in Vittel was to be short-lived, however. On March 18, they were informed by the camp's commandant that, because their passports had not been recognized, they were no longer considered eligible for exchange and so would not be permitted to remain in Vittel. They were to be moved to another hotel, the "Beau-Site," some distance away from the camp and separated from it by a barbed-wire fence. There the internees were held initially in isolation; it was only after protests that they were allowed to access the main compound of the camp, as long as they wore a tag to identify themselves and were back in the Beau-Site by six o'clock in the evening. To calm their fears, they were informed that the transfer was only a technicality and they would be sent to another camp, similar to Vittel, some fifty kilometers (thirty-one miles) away. Nonetheless, the move sparked alarm, and for many it brought back their darkest fears that it was all only a prelude to another deportation. One internee was so desperate that she committed suicide by throwing herself down the hotel stairwell.[19]

Unknown to the internees in Vittel, the reason for their distress was partly down to diplomatic infighting and inertia. By this time, the Germans were well aware that many Latin American countries—and, crucially, the United States—were raising objections to the passport scheme. The US State Department had long been opposed to the principle of rescue through false papers, motivated by the disappointing results of previous, small-scale exchanges and by intelligence concerns about the possibilities for espionage that such schemes appeared to present. Consequently, through 1943, US diplomats in Latin America had been nudging their host governments toward a careful scrutiny of all such exchanges and a rejection of false or illegally produced papers. In September, the State Department had gone a step further and sent word to German officials, via the Swiss, to inform them that Jews holding false papers would not be considered eligible for exchange. Then, as if to deepen the confusion, they relented, following pressure from the World Jewish Congress, and in December 1943 informed the Latin American governments that, though the United States did not approve of the unauthorized production and sale of identity documents, the perilous situation for Jews was such that cancellation of false passports should at least be delayed, so that the holders "might remain alive." Nonetheless, for US officials, at least, considerable squeamishness on the matter remained.[20]

Unsurprisingly, the result was confusion and logjam in Washington. So, in January 1944, when President Franklin D. Roosevelt found himself under increasing pressure from both Jewish organizations and members of his own administration, he decided to establish the War Refugee Board (WRB) to carry out an official US program of rescue and relief for civilian victims—especially Jews—of the Axis powers. The WRB began to set up relief networks, but it also started an information campaign both to tell the world of the crimes being committed by the Germans and to deter any would-be perpetrators by reminding them that they would, ultimately, be brought to justice. The WRB also took up the issue of the Latin American passports, perhaps sensing an opportunity to prove its worth by bypassing sclerotic and recalcitrant government departments. In mid-February, in response to the ongoing crisis, the WRB drafted a telegram demanding that the Swiss—as the de facto representatives of many Latin American countries in Europe—pressure Germany to accept the Latin American documents as valid. That telegram was duly passed on to the State Department for transmission to the American legation in Bern.[21]

However, the State Department—still smarting from its enforced volte-face of the previous year—had some ideas of its own. Not only did it object to the WRB's rather more dynamic methods of diplomacy, but—like the Swiss police—it still harbored profound reservations about the propriety of recognizing fraudulent passports. Consequently, State Department officials "protested vehemently" against the scheme and refused to transmit the WRB telegram to Bern. So, while Agudath Israel, Polish diplomats, and others believed that action was being taken by the US government to force the recognition of the Latin American passports, in truth little had been done. In March 1944, an internal report from the State Department stated defiantly that

> this government's view regarding the issuance of fraudulent documents has not changed. . . . It is an oversimplification to say that several hundreds or thousands of Jewish refugees will be killed if South American passports are not supplied to them. . . . We should not be forced, and we should not willingly accept, a proposal which is essentially fraudulent and improper.

State Department intervention, it seemed, would not be as straightforward as many of those in the world beyond had hoped.[22]

While State Department officials dragged their feet on points of principle, others continued to do their best. In early March, Yitzchak Sternbuch cabled Agudath Israel in New York from the Polish legation in Bern, informing them of the "good news" that the instruction that the Latin American passports were to be recognized had apparently reached the camp at Vittel. On a more sobering note, he stated that the destination for many Exchange Jews, the camp at Bergen-Belsen, was still effectively out of bounds—as the SS had intended. "We have no names," he wrote. "Nobody can send us any letters from there, even the Red Cross has no way to contact the camp." He asked that Agudath Israel use whatever influence it had to investigate. Despite their valiant efforts, it was becoming increasingly clear to all those seeking to assist the Exchange Jews that they were effectively working in the dark.[23]

It was testament to the illusion that the passports issue had been rectified, and perhaps to a fundamental misunderstanding of the plight of Exchange Jews, that the response from Agudath Israel later that month was upbeat, appending the names of various prominent missing Jews—from Hungarian rabbis to the mother of the violinist Bronisław Huberman—and requesting that Sternbuch try to find them and supply them with papers. Sternbuch did his best, but all too often his answer amounted to little more than "whereabouts unknown."[24]

At the same time, however, a note from Isaac Lewin of Agudath Israel in New York to the Polish ambassador in Buenos Aires, Mirosław Arciszewski, betrayed the seriousness of the situation. Lewin outlined the origins of the passport operation and the predicament that Exchange Jews in Vittel and Bergen-Belsen now faced if their papers were not recognized. He explained that the Polish government-in-exile in London had intervened to assist those affected by attempting to ensure the recognition of the South American passports, adding that the papal nuncio in Asunción and—as he thought—the State Department were also pressuring the Paraguayan government to that end. However, Lewin wrote, those holding Latin American passports were still in great danger, as the Germans knew that something was "not right" and so were keeping them alive only as long as they considered them to be useful as "material for exchange." Consequently, he asked the ambassador to intervene directly with the Paraguayan government to ensure not only recognition of the passports but to begin the process of exchange.[25]

But the Paraguayans and other Latin American governments were unmoved by Polish requests. Those that were directly affected by the Ładoś operation—Paraguay, Honduras, Haiti, and Chile—displayed a spectrum of reactions. Paraguay, whose passports made up the overwhelming majority of those illegally issued in Bern, continued to waver, while Honduras failed to respond to the Polish approaches at all. Chile and Haiti, meanwhile, refused to make any commitments and promised to judge any upcoming cases solely on their merits.[26]

Those countries that adopted a more resolute stance on the rejection of the passports were supported by the State Department, which still sought to undermine the War Refugee Board. The resulting deadlock in American policy was only broken in early April, when three New York rabbis headed to Washington to make an emotional plea directly to Henry Morgenthau—secretary of the Treasury and one of those behind the WRB—to agree to immediate intervention. Morgenthau called Cordell Hull at the State Department, and the WRB telegram intended to pressure the Swiss into forcing the Germans' hands on recognition was finally sent to Bern, after fully seven weeks of delay.

Still, one of the recipients of that telegram, the first legation secretary in the Swiss capital, George Tait, shared the objections of many in Washington. In a note to his superiors, he complained, "I do not like this matter at all, in any of its aspects." Of Jews with Latin American passports languishing in the German camps, he was brutally unequivocal: "This group of persons has obtained false papers to which they have no claim and has endeavored to obtain special treatment which they would not otherwise have received. We are being placed in the position of acting as nursemaid to persons who have no claim to our protection." Even at this late stage of the Holocaust, human sympathy could still be trumped by bureaucratic propriety.[27]

Thankfully for those still awaiting their fate in Vittel and Bergen-Belsen, Tait was overruled. However, the delayed telegram and the resumption of American diplomatic pressure arrived too late for many of those most grievously affected. This time, it was not only the Americans who were to blame; the Swiss were now unwilling to confront the German authorities on the matter. After the WRB telegram arrived on April 7, the Swiss hesitated, seeking to downplay the urgency of the situation, and only passed a verbal summary of the communication on to the Germans—eleven days later. By that time, the situation in Vittel had developed into a full-blown crisis.[28]

AFTER THE LATIN AMERICAN PASSPORT HOLDERS IN VITTEL had been sent to the Beau-Site hotel that March, Yitzchak Sternbuch informed his correspondents in New York of the new development. "All the people in Vittel have been arrested and are at risk of being sent to certain death," he wrote. "Immediate intervention is necessary. Please reply at once." A few days later, the Polish foreign minister, Tadeusz Romer—who had been ambassador in Tokyo during the Sugihara operation in 1940— also lent a shoulder to the wheel, sending a circular to all Polish diplomatic representatives in Latin America. Referring to the removal of the prisoners from Vittel, he explained that the lives of the passport holders were still at risk and urged his diplomats in the region to once again intervene on their behalf with the Latin American governments. A simple official statement that exchange was possible, he believed, could be enough to save countless lives.[29]

In Vittel, meanwhile, life had settled down somewhat after the upheaval of the previous month. But then the arrival of a train with boarded-up windows in a siding close to the camp caused new panic. "To us," Sofka Skipwith recalled, "deportation was just a word," but the Poles in the camp knew "only too well" what that train indicated. On the morning of April 19, the internees of Beau-Site were awakened by SS men pounding on the doors of their rooms, ordering them to pack their things and go down to the hotel lobby. "We sat there as though paralyzed," Gutta Eisenzweig wrote. "The word 'Treblinka' was on all our minds, although no one dared speak it."[30]

Eisenzweig's mother, Sarah, however, was determined to resist their deportation. "She knew that we had to do everything we could to keep from leaving," Gutta wrote. "She ran through the hallways, shouting, 'Don't let them take you! Don't go! Resist, do whatever you can!'" Some of the internees did not want to hear her prognostications of doom and tried to shout her down. Her response was phlegmatic. She told her daughter, "They don't know that they are already dead."[31]

Such protests would not stop the inevitable, and some 163 people were duly deported from Vittel. Sofka Skipwith remembered them walking off in a long column, with their rabbis at the head, flanked by German guards. Among them were some forty-one members of the Rapaport family and eleven members of the Frankiel family from Bielsko, all of whom were holding Paraguayan papers. Also deported was Leo Weingort, who had received one of the very first Paraguayan passports back in the spring of 1941. The Yiddish poet Yitzhak Katzenelson and his seventeen-year-old son, Tzvi, the last survivors of a family already destroyed by the Holocaust, also left that day. All of them were taken initially to Drancy, the makeshift camp outside Paris where they were kept in isolation for around ten days. They were not informed of their ultimate destination.[32]

Some of the Vittel internees preferred not to wait for a transport into the unknown. Of those slated for deportation that day, as many as seventeen are thought to have attempted suicide. Three of them succeeded: Tamara Schorr, a "dignified upright figure, with piled snowy hair," and Joel and Bluma Bauminger, holders of

Paraguayan passports. As Skipwith recalled, the favored methods employed were poisoning, slashing one's wrists, or jumping from the hotel's upper floors, but success was rarely guaranteed. Some of those who had obtained poison discovered that it was ineffective, producing "only sickness, blindness or paralysis." Those who leaped from windows would be similarly frustrated. Felicia Kohn jumped from a fifth-floor window but landed on soft ground and sustained only minor injuries. She was taken to the hospital, where she spent the next seven months feigning paralysis, successfully fooling her German doctors until the day of liberation arrived.[33]

Gutta Eisenzweig also tried to end her life. When the deportation had begun, she and her mother had decided to hide in the hotel basement, where there were large ovens for baking bread. Along with two others, they crawled into one of the ovens, head first, pulling the door shut behind them. "I felt suffocated," she recalled, "crippled by panic." Their hiding place was not discovered, but when they reemerged two days later, they were confronted by one of the camp elders appointed by the Germans, who loudly and angrily proclaimed: "*Ir zent noch do!*" (You are still here!) Fearing that she would be betrayed to the Germans, Eisenzweig picked up a bottle of cleaning fluid and drank it. She collapsed unconscious, and when she awoke, she found herself in the camp hospital.[34]

One of the peculiarities of the deportations from western Europe and from the Reich itself was that they tended to be carried out "correctly." While deportations from the ghettos of occupied Poland were routinely accompanied by bestial brutality, those from Berlin, Paris, or indeed Vittel had the veneer of civility: baggage was still permitted, and the deportees generally had to be considered medically fit enough to travel. This meant that, as Gutta Eisenzweig and Felicia Kohn discovered, those who had harmed themselves in the process of avoiding their deportation needed to be nursed back to health before they could be sent to their deaths.[35]

At the end of April, Yitzchak Sternbuch informed Agudath Israel in New York, via Polish diplomatic channels, that the internees in Vittel had been deported and were now in Drancy. He added that, according to two deportees who had absconded from the train en route, German officials had not yet been informed that the passports would be recognized. Sternbuch warned that responsibility for this failing lay at the door of Agudath Israel, and he urged them to intervene with the Spanish and Swiss authorities forthwith: "Otherwise," he stated, "all these people are lost." Unknown to him, two days after he wrote those words, on April 29, the Vittel prisoners at Drancy were deported once again, this time to Auschwitz, as part of a transport of over one thousand mainly French Jews, which arrived in the camp on May 1. Almost all of them were gassed immediately upon arrival.[36]

Belatedly, responses to the note that Polish foreign minister Tadeusz Romer had sent the previous month now began to arrive. The auguries were not good. The chargé d'affaires in Lima, Peru, informed Romer that, despite his entreaties, the Peruvian government stood by its original assessment that the passports had been issued "against the law" and there was "not much hope" that they would change their decision. In early May, the Polish envoy in Havana, Cuba, informed his superiors that the Haitian government considered the irregular issuing of identity papers as an "abuse." He added that further negotiation on the issue with the Dominican and Haitian republics was hampered by the fact that officials there followed the "prevailing custom" of ignoring the substance of his letters. In the circumstances, he concluded regretfully, the matter was better left in the hands of the American ambassador.[37]

The Paraguayans, meanwhile, had gone ominously quiet. In his report to the Ministry of Foreign Affairs in London, the Polish envoy to Buenos Aires, Mirosław Arciszewski, explained that, while the previous Paraguayan foreign minister had been positively predisposed to the matter of passport recognition, his successor had failed to respond to Arciszewski's inquiries for the full five months that he had been in post. The resulting uncertainty did nothing to help those Jews in German-occupied Europe whose survival was entirely dependent on the official recognition of their Paraguayan passports. In a letter to Abraham Silberschein in May 1944, Klara Eck, wife of Zionist activist Nathan, summed up the predicament of those who were left in Vittel: "You have assured us that our nationality is guaranteed, but unfortunately the German authorities are not in agreement. Don't waste any time! Make every effort to inform the Germans that we are recognised and ready for exchange!"[38]

So it was that Gutta Eisenzweig, lying in the hospital in Vittel, waited in fear for the day that she was deemed well enough to travel. That moment came in the middle of May, when another train pulled into the siding close to the Vittel camp. Soon after, the remaining internees—those in the hospital as well as those who had otherwise avoided the first deportation—were ushered onto the train. Eisenzweig remembered the hospital patients weeping as they were carried out on stretchers. Sofka Skipwith recalled others walking between armed guards, "stumbling along with blood dripping from slashed wrists roughly bound."[39]

Eisenzweig was not among the last wave of deportees, however. When on the day of the deportation a German officer had entered her hospital room, filled with terror she had jumped out of bed, run to the window, and begun to open it. Yet the man tried to calm her, telling her not to be scared and promising that she wouldn't be deported. To her protestations of disbelief, he replied, "I give you my word as an officer," before calling the nurses and leaving the room. Eisenzweig never knew why the officer decided to spare her life.[40]

Like the first, that second deportation from Vittel proceeded via Drancy, with the forty-eight prisoners carried in two passenger carriages, the doors and windows crudely boarded up. As one of them recalled, it was a mystery why so few of the deportees tried to escape, given that the train stopped at a number of stations and French railway personnel called out to them offering their help. The only prisoner to brave an escape attempt, one source alleged, was Nathan Eck, who, along with his mistress Lola Radzejewska, is said to have squeezed his way out of a lavatory window as the train pulled into the Gare de l'Est in Paris. He left his wife, Klara, behind in the carriage loudly demanding to know where he had gone. As another prisoner quipped, "The way to life and happiness sometimes leads through a tiny window in the loo."[41]

A few days later, on May 30, the group was sent on to Auschwitz—this time in a cattle car—as part of a larger transport of some one thousand Jewish men, women, and children. "We have passed three dreadful nights," one of them remembered. "People do not realize that they are going to their death; they don't want to, cannot, believe it. They are deluding and comforting themselves that they are going to a labor camp." Some now began to talk of escape. Adam Żurawin, who had helped to organize the Hotel Polski operation but who was now also on the train, promised as soon as he was free to call reliable German contacts in Berlin to stop the deportation, before jumping from the train and disappearing into the darkness. Others followed his example.[42]

Those of the former Vittel internees who remained aboard—among them Żurawin's in-laws, the Krystenfraynd family; Lolek Skosowski's brother Izidor, along with his silent adopted "sister" Szaja; Nathan Eck's abandoned wife, Klara; and Abraham Weingort and his wife, Mathilde, whose son Saul had been one of the instigators of the passport scheme—rode the train all the way to Auschwitz, where they were among the 627 prisoners who were murdered upon arrival.[43]

WITH THE EFFECTIVE LIQUIDATION OF VITTEL THAT SUMmer, Bergen-Belsen was left as the primary internment camp for the remaining Exchange Jews. Conditions there had been deteriorating for much of the previous year, with the food supply increasingly intermittent and disease beginning to take its toll on the prisoners. For the Polish Jews in the *Sonderlager*, now numbering around six hundred, boredom vied with hunger as the main existential threat. In his diary, Józef Gitler-Barski recalled the occasional intrusion of the outside world—such as new arrivals in the camp or the news of the Normandy landings in June—but otherwise the prisoners were isolated from events, confined to a peculiar world of indolence, self-improvement, and gnawing hunger. He described a typical morning in his barrack:

> In a corner between the cots and the loo, I study *The Renaissance in Rome* (I've borrowed a book from Szenker). On a cot in front of me, Szajn plays cards with someone. Next to them, young Berger teaches someone arithmetic on a plank removed from the cot. A bit farther from us, a group of men in tallis shawls pray aloud. Next to them, Tomkiewicz is studying English, and next to him Bojman and Lindberg are studying French. In another corner, a doctor-prisoner examines a sick companion in adversity. Next to them, Ajerman haggles with Prajs trying to buy clothes from him in exchange for bread. On the cot above me, Dąb bandages his boils, and almost right next to him, Degenszajn picks lice out of his shirt. . . . This is, more-or-less, a normal picture of life.[44]

For the Exchange Jews in the nearby *Sternlager*, meanwhile, life was similar. While the *Sonderlager* dwindled, the *Sternlager* became the main holding site for Exchange Jews, primarily those from Holland. It had some advantages over its neighboring subcamps, not least a degree of self-administration through a Jewish Council, which—though largely cosmetic—did protect it from some of the more egregious excesses of the SS. Labor duties, for instance, could be rotated to ameliorate the worst effects of exhaustion. *Sternlager* prisoners were engaged in road building or tree felling, and many were put to work in Belsen's primary economic enterprise, the "shoe factory." Here they were salvaging usable scraps of leather from the thousands of pairs of old shoes that were brought to the camp from all around German-occupied Europe and—as one inmate soon realized—also from Auschwitz. It was hard, dirty work, which left the laborers filthy and choking with dust.[45]

Another horror was the roll calls that the SS guards regularly held, often numerous times per day, rain or shine. The prisoners were lined up five abreast, in barrack-block order, then counted and recounted to ensure that they were all present, including the sick. "Malnourishment was common," one inmate remembered. "There were fleas, lice and rats. Epidemics broke out constantly. . . . It is astonishing how many people died right there at the roll call." Irene Hasenberg recalled how an elderly lady sat down during a two-hour roll call in the camp, due to exhaustion. Those around her whispered to her to get up, reminding her that it was not allowed to sit down and that she risked invoking a collective punishment, but she was adamant. "Tired," came the defiant reply. Very quickly she attracted the attention of the SS guard, who called her "filth" and ordered her to get up. Before she could obey, he beat her with his whip, causing a trickle of blood to run down the back of her neck. With the second whipping, Hasenberg wrote, the guard flushed, his arm "pumping in blunt strokes, up and down, up and down. The whip ends wrapped over the old woman's shoulders and curled around her neck. . . . She hissed and screamed like a cornered cat, spitting and weeping. Then silence." The woman was taken away in a wheelbarrow. She was never seen again.[46]

Aside from the hard labor and the casual brutality, the main daily challenge for the prisoners was the food. Dutch Jew Louis Tas was an especially thoughtful chronicler of life in the camp, and he devoted much of his postwar memoir to the difficulties that the prisoners faced in feeding themselves. The twenty-three-year-old had arrived in Belsen from Westerbork in April 1944 with his parents, all of them in possession not only of Paraguayan passports supplied by the Ładoś Group but also of papers for El Salvador and Palestinian certificates. All three of them were put to work, the two men on daily labor details and the mother in the shoe factory. Tas quickly began to complain about the food in his diary. "One can live on 300g of bread, a litre of soup and 10g of margarine per day," he wrote. "The question is, for how long?" In another entry he stressed that food "is the most important thing there is": while in the outside world "politics, morals, law, litera-ture and commerce" all have importance, inside the camp, only food had any real significance.[47]

Incarceration in Bergen-Belsen, even for those not forced to work, took a significant toll on the prisoners' mental health. Abel Herzberg, a Dutch Jew in possession of a certificate for Palestine, kept an extensive diary, in which he recorded his thoughts as con-ditions in the camp deteriorated that autumn. "Time no longer exists here," he wrote in November 1944.

> The days pass by but sometimes it seems as if they do not fol-low one another but coincide, and that what happens today occurs simultaneously with that of yesterday and tomorrow. This imprisonment is like a book that is handed to us, of which all the days are pages. One need only turn the pages, the time is up to us, things happen and all simultaneously, except that we cannot read and absorb everything at once.[48]

Part of the collapse in morale was caused by the fading belief in the prospect of ever being exchanged. That, of course, was the reason they were there and why they had avoided deportation to Auschwitz. To start with, they had witnessed, or at least heard about, transports out of the camp—even if it was only the ficti-tious deportation of the failed "Latin Americans" to "Bergau"—so there was hope that they, too, might see freedom. As the year wore on, however, that faith gradually waned. After his arrival in the camp in the autumn of 1943, Józef Gitler-Barski had noted in his diary the frequent rumors of an imminent departure and recorded small-scale transports to Theresienstadt and elsewhere. Yet by the autumn of 1944, he was doubtful that he would ever get out. "It's been 15 months since our deportation from Warsaw," he wrote in mid-September. "Will we live to see the end?"[49]

As conditions in Belsen deteriorated further, the death toll rose inexorably. Death, Irene Hasenberg remembered, became a constant companion:

> Before Bergen-Belsen death was only an idea, like Switzerland or Africa, something you would think or talk about, but was unknown. Then death started soaring closer, like a rare bird you might glimpse from time to time, and finally it just came and went as it pleased, like dozens of pigeons you paid no heed. Death was daily, and like all daily things, it was tied to little things. It could be as simple as just not being able to get up.

Louis Tas was more prosaic in his assessment: "The mortality rate is climbing," he wrote. "Death casts its shadow over all of us."[50]

The preferential treatment that the Exchange Jews had once enjoyed in Bergen-Belsen was now increasingly being more honored in the breach than in observance. Conditions for most of them were no better than they were for prisoners in the other German concentration camps. If the diplomats and activists in the outside world were to save any of them, they would need to act fast. The problem was, however, that the outside world had little idea of where the remaining Exchange Jews were.

WHEN THE CAMP AT VITTEL WAS LIQUIDATED IN THE summer of 1944, the outside world lost contact with the surviving Exchange Jews. For all the hardships they had endured in Vittel, the internees had never been entirely cut off: clandestine and semiofficial channels for the transmission of information had remained; letters could be written and smuggled out without difficulty. With Vittel closed, however, those channels effectively dried up. Now, with the remaining Exchange Jews in Bergen-Belsen prevented from communicating with the outside world and the Red Cross forbidden from visiting the camp, those who were agitating for international recognition of the Ładoś passports lacked any up-to-date information on those they were endeavoring to save.

The problem was first raised by Yitzchak Sternbuch in June 1944, when he wrote to inform his colleagues at Agudath Israel in New York that the whereabouts of the Exchange Jews from Vittel were now unknown. He advised that there was a rumor that they had been sent to Drancy, but, he added, it was "probably not true." He went on to explain that neither the American legation in Bern nor the Swiss embassy in Berlin was able to investigate the matter further, and that the German Foreign Office had merely confirmed that the Vittel prisoners had been deported "in an unknown direction." As it was already two months since the Vittel Jews had been taken away, and no new information about their whereabouts had been forthcoming, it would have been hard to escape the thought that they had been deported to the death camps.[51]

The following month, a report from a survivor of the Vittel camp—Sofka Skipwith, who was interviewed in Lisbon, en route to freedom—muddied the waters still further. She recalled that while the earlier transports were thought to have gone to Drancy, the camp's commandant himself had stated that the final clearance of the camp had seen the remaining prisoners sent to Bergen-Belsen. But this, Skipwith explained in her testimony, "proved to be untrue." She thought that the last deportees were "probably in some Jewish Camp in Upper Silesia."[52]

When the Swiss legation in Berlin reported back to the Poles on what it had learned from its inquiries, it shed little light on events. The German Foreign Ministry had told the Swiss that the internees from Vittel had been handed over to the Gestapo, and so their fate depended ultimately on Himmler. On the question of the whereabouts of the internees, there were "different versions," but the Foreign Ministry source suggested that they were in "one of the camps near Hanover," which was almost certainly a reference to Bergen-Belsen. The German Foreign Ministry had promised the Swiss that it would look into the case further but had given no guarantees as to tangible results. It was little wonder that Saul Weingort was thrown into despair, writing in July 1944, "When one thinks that, with God's help, we had saved these people this far, and now, after two years, we have lost sight of them, one can go insane."[53]

In such circumstances, it was imperative to have someone to make inquiries on the spot. In this, Juliusz Kühl, from the Polish embassy staff in Bern, was considered to be a good candidate, given that his Swiss passport would make travel across recently liberated France comparatively easy. As Yitzchak Sternbuch explained, Kühl's primary task was to establish the whereabouts of the Vittel Jews, especially as a new lead had suggested that they might have been sent to Louvain in Belgium. When he set off that October, accompanied by Yitzchak Sternbuch's brother Eli, it was, to a large extent, a journey into the unknown. The newly liberated territories were still reeling from four years of war and occupation: the trains were not running, no hotels were open, and the roads were clogged with refugees and military traffic. Nonetheless, Kühl and Sternbuch would loop through southern France—via Grenoble, Nice, Montpellier, and Toulouse—before heading north to Limoges and on to Paris, Brussels, and Antwerp. For all their efforts, however, the pair achieved comparatively little. At Aix-les-Bains, in French Savoy, they were informed that the Vittel Jews had been deported to Auschwitz. Meanwhile, a chance discovery at the former internment camp at Gurs, in southwest France, brought home the urgency of their task. Gurs had been used by the Vichy regime to hold foreign Jews and had been closed in the autumn of 1943, so Kühl found little there to assist in his search. He did, however, find a tattered, handwritten list that he picked up from the floor of an abandoned barrack block—it contained the names of some of the Jews deported from there to Auschwitz.[54]

At the same time that Juliusz Kühl was searching in France, Yitzchak Sternbuch approached the former Swiss president, Jean-Marie Musy, to undertake a mission to Berlin. As an acquaintance of Heinrich Himmler and an ideological fellow traveler of the Nazis—some thought of him as a potential Swiss quisling—Musy was considered the ideal emissary to ask the Germans directly about the whereabouts of the former Exchange Jews from Vittel. A car, fuel, and travel expenses were provided for the journey, and Musy set off for Berlin, together with his son Benoît, in October 1944, by which time his remit had grown to that of negotiating for the lives of *all* the remaining Jews in German concentration camps.[55]

In this wider goal, Musy was, to some extent, pushing at an open door. According to Walter Schellenberg, head of the German Secret Service, Himmler was willing to consider the idea of releasing some of the imprisoned Jews, as "he genuinely wanted to free himself from his past record on the Jewish question." It would be this exculpatory impulse on Himmler's part that would facilitate some of the other rescue attempts being mounted in the closing months of the war, but Musy's efforts achieved only modest success. Falling foul of that section of Jewish opinion that objected to doing deals with the Nazis, he was able to secure the release of only a single transport, numbering some 1,200 Jews, from Theresienstadt, in return for the promise of one million US dollars and some favorable headlines for Nazi Germany in the world's press. When it came to the fate of the Exchange Jews from Vittel, meanwhile, Musy was able to confirm what many had already suspected: that they had been deported to Auschwitz in the summer of 1944 and murdered.[56]

THOSE EXCHANGE JEWS WHO HAD BEEN PERMITTED TO remain in Belsen might have considered themselves fortunate, therefore, but by the autumn and winter of 1944, they most certainly did not feel that way. The camp now saw a large influx of new prisoners. Already in June, the SS administration had decided to establish a new transit camp within Belsen to cope with the large numbers of prisoners evacuated from the eastern fringes of German-occupied territory who were still considered able to work. Among the first to arrive were some four thousand Polish women and children, many of whom had been deported from Warsaw and who brought with them word of the brave rising of the Polish Home Army against the Germans—news that briefly electrified the camp, as it seemed to foreshadow the collapse of German rule. Smuggled newspapers confirmed the rumors, but the German authorities were nonetheless keen to isolate the new arrivals, so that word of their experiences did not "contaminate" the other prisoners. Consequently, the small number of arriving Poles who possessed Latin American passports were forced to stay with their fellows rather than being placed with the remaining Exchange Jews in the *Sternlager*.[57]

As a Communist, Józef Gitler-Barski was less than sympathetic to the Polish Home Army, and his comment on the arrival of the prisoners from Warsaw was brutally lapidary: "Soup rations have been decreased." But then, for those still languishing in the camps in the autumn of 1944, almost everything was now measured in food. Shortages and dwindling supplies so dominated the prisoners' thoughts, consumed their waking hours, and tormented their sleep that hardly anything else appeared to matter.[58]

There were other significant arrivals in Bergen-Belsen that autumn, not least in connection with the camp's designation as an *Erholungslager*, or "recuperation camp." As many as eight thousand female prisoners were transferred from Auschwitz, ostensibly as part of the ongoing evacuation of the Auschwitz camp complex but also so that these prisoners might recover from disease and once again prove useful as labor. Among them was the German Jewish teenager Anne Frank, who had been captured in hiding in Amsterdam earlier that year and had been deported to Auschwitz in September 1944, before being transferred to Belsen because she was suffering from scabies. Mirjam Wiener, who had attended the same school as Frank in Amsterdam, remembered seeing her soon after her arrival: "We waved to each other across the wire," she recalled.[59]

Anne Frank would soon find other familiar faces in Belsen. Hanneli Goslar had been one of her close childhood friends and a regular visitor to the family home before the war. While the Franks went into hiding, however, the Goslar family—father Hans and his daughters Hanneli and Rachela—managed to source a Paraguayan passport for the family, using an uncle in Switzerland as an intermediary. Hanneli's father had to explain to her that Paraguay was a country in South America, before showing it to her on a map. He pointed out the capital, Asunción, and told her to remember it in case anyone asked. Hans Goslar and his two daughters were arrested in June 1943 and sent to Westerbork, before being sent to Bergen-Belsen in February of the following year as Exchange Jews. Despite her own suffering, Hanneli found her friend, and they exchanged a few words through the straw-packed fence. She was shocked. "It was not Anne," she recalled, "the nice little girl I knew from Amsterdam. [She was] a sad little girl." She listened as Anne explained that the Germans had shaved her head and taken from her everything she had; she was cold and plagued by lice, and, following the loss of her family, she said she no longer wanted to live.[60]

For many of those arriving that autumn in Bergen-Belsen, life was scarcely better than the hell they had experienced in

Auschwitz. Throughout 1944, conditions in the camp had deteriorated markedly, with poor food supply, overcrowding, and disease becoming ever more commonplace. At first, the primary challenge was that of tuberculosis, which—along with diarrhea—racked the already weakened prisoners. At the end of 1944, however, an outbreak of typhus would compound their misery, cutting a swath through the emaciated and the overworked. "It gets worse and worse," Renata Laqueur wrote in her diary.

> There are no toilets, and there is no water. The chaos and filth are beyond comprehension, they are the worst hygienic conditions that one can possibly imagine. At night, when it is pitch dark in the barrack, one has to be careful not to trip over someone doing their business over a bucket or a frying pan, because they can no longer manage the 400m walk to the latrine. The stench is revolting!

Suffering from diarrhea herself, Laqueur lost the will to continue her diary a few days later. But, even in her fevered reveries, she couldn't have imagined that it was all merely a foreshadowing of the horrors that the New Year would bring.[61]

In early December 1944, conditions in Belsen would be exacerbated still further by the arrival of a new camp commandant. *SS-Hauptsturmführer* Josef Kramer was a thickset brute of a man who had already served in many of the Third Reich's most odious establishments, including Dachau, Sachsenhausen, Mauthausen, and Auschwitz. Promoted to commandant of Natzweiler in October 1942, he had then proved his mettle by personally carrying out the gassing of some eighty prisoners.[62]

Under his command, Bergen-Belsen was intended to be transformed into a camp for sick prisoners, where they could recuperate before being returned to hard labor. However, Kramer's brutal instincts left little room for compassion. Instead, he set about transforming Belsen into a regular concentration camp, bringing many of the peculiarities that had previously existed there to a swift end. In the *Sternlager*, the leadership of the Jewish Council was abolished and replaced by the brutal rule of the "Kapos," the same thuggish trustee-prisoners who ran the barrack blocks in the remainder of the concentration camp system. The Kapos were given the task of "cleaning up" the *Sternlager*, and punishments were meted out for every infraction, real or imagined. As one female inmate wrote, "The camp regime gets more atrocious by the day. Beatings are commonplace; punishments that in the past were given to individuals and meant depriving one person of food, are now collective measures meted out to the camp as a whole." Kramer was "a villain and an avowed anti-Semite," she wrote. "Absolute master of the camp, he is subordinate to no-one. No authority exists for us, except him. God himself is powerless here."[63]

Almost overnight, all the petty privileges that Exchange Jews had enjoyed over other camp inmates were revoked. They were expelled from the "cozier" jobs, such as working in the camp kitchens, and instances of harassment and violence against them multiplied. In addition, as one of his first punitive orders, the new commandant decreed that all Jewish inmates had to go without food for an entire day. If it were possible to imagine, life for the remaining Exchange Jews in Bergen-Belsen was about to get even worse.[64]

"MY GOD, WHY HAVE YOU FORSAKEN ME?"

THE NEW YEAR BEGAN MUCH AS 1944 HAD ENDED—WITH despair. As Louis Tas wrote in his diary on January 2, "Never been so despondent as I am now, even thought about suicide. A temporary collapse? I believe neither in an exchange, nor in the swift end to the war, but I tell mother that I do." His depression was understandable. Conditions in Belsen were deteriorating rapidly. The supply of food had dwindled and become erratic, exacerbated by the increasing volume and ferocity of Allied air raids, which had destroyed the bakery in Celle that supplied the camp. As a consequence, bread rations—which were already miserly—were cut by 50 percent. The prisoners were reduced to living on scraps. "The turnip soup always came at different times," Renata Laqueur noted. "It could be at eight in the morning, and then nothing until seven the following evening. All we had in the thirty-six hours in between was the bread we had kept aside."[1]

The arrival of numerous evacuation transports from other camps further east over the previous few months had posed another profound challenge to the fading morale of the exchange prisoners. Though they were separated by a barbed-wire fence, it was still possible to glimpse the new prisoners and sometimes to hear their laments. One internee recalled a group of female inmates who had come from Auschwitz, looking "utterly pitiful," and remembered how they would "sing and cry out" in prayer, a favorite being the recitation of Psalm 22: "My God, my God, why have you forsaken me?" It was a bitter reminder that, however bad Belsen became, life outside could still be worse.[2]

The new arrivals also led to a catastrophic increase in overcrowding, with inmates forced to share bunks with the newcomers. As one prisoner noted, "We are submerged in an ocean of germs, lice and fleas, of mould and stench . . . but there is nothing we can do about it."[3] The result was an outbreak of dysentery that swept through the overcrowded barrack blocks: "There's no way to stop it and no cure. It literally devours the body and everything reeks, soiled and vile—the floors, the beds, the sinks, the yards, the toilets—a deluge. . . . So many exhausted, famished, half-dead bodies reduced to skeletons. And so much excrement."[4]

The barrack blocks were littered with emaciated bodies. Every morning revealed a few more who had died in the night. The dead were supposed to be gathered up by the block seniors to be cremated, but because of the volume of bodies and the exhaustion of those still living, the system of disposal broke down, leaving the corpses on gruesome display. "Death no longer affected us," Henryk Schönker remembered. "We were used to it, but we hadn't seen anything like that before. Those faces distorted in some convulsive effort, those eye sockets with glassy eyes, those twisted bodies, tangled together, one on top of the other—dead, desecrated human remains."[5]

Often, the dead were indistinguishable from those still living, the latter similarly immobile and silent and betrayed by only a groan or the flicker of a half-opened eye. The camp's rudimentary hospital could do nothing for them. Renata Laqueur spent a month confined to the infirmary and remembered, with particular clarity, the wife of a doctor, suffering from diarrhea, whose sunken cheeks and swollen legs betrayed the seriousness of her condition.

Sometimes she groaned, then lay unmoving for hours, until she was wracked again with cramps. She tried to eat the little food that we had, but the diarrhoea worsened. Every day, her husband came, but he didn't have the strength to climb up onto her bunk. They talked about food, about the special rations that were promised, and about the possibility of exchange—but the diarrhoea remained, until one morning she lay motionless in the bed.[6]

Rumors of exchange—whether they were believed or not—had never really abated. Indeed, the worse conditions got in Belsen, the more desperately they were held on to. The comings and goings to the camp of the previous autumn—the recuperation cases and the thousands of forced laborers shipped into Belsen and then out to fresh horrors elsewhere—must at least have maintained the hope of an eventual escape, however fleeting. More than that, the example of the so-called Kasztner train—in which more than 1,600 Hungarian Jews had been brought into Belsen the previous summer, before being transported to Switzerland, and freedom, in early December, following payment of a ransom—demonstrated that escape was still possible if the conditions were right.

Nonetheless, the announcement of a new transport list on January 19 came as a surprise to many in the camp. When an SS officer read out the names of 450 Latin American passport holders, Louis Tas at first thought that it was related to a new labor detail, but he was shocked to learn that they were being called for a possible exchange. Given that the prisoners were to endure a long journey, however, they had to undergo a cursory medical examination prior to departure. Bearing in mind the health crisis in the camp, with the typhus epidemic then raging, this presented a fundamental problem. Irene Hasenberg remembered the announcement being greeted with a flurry of questions. Was it real? Would the Germans actually carry it through? And, most pertinently, what was to be done with those—like her mother—who were on the list but were too sick to walk? In Irene's case, the medical examination was farcical: the SS doctor failed to notice either that Irene—aged fourteen—had stood in for her ill mother or that her father could barely stand. The family was cleared for exchange.[7]

Others were not so lucky. When Renata Laqueur failed the selection procedure, she and her husband were devastated: "For a day and a half we had blossomed, as Paul and I belonged to the selected few. We fantasized about Switzerland, about warm food, a bath, a cigarette, a woolen blanket. . . . Then the transport left, and we were struck from the list at the last moment." Louis Tas was also left off the final list, but he was rather unconcerned at the outcome. Unable to believe in the promise of liberation, he felt himself "a wise man among idiots" and later claimed that he would have swapped the possibility of exchange for a job in the bakery. Such a pessimistic assessment was not uncommon. Irene Hasenberg recalled that the consensus in her barrack block was that no train had ever left Belsen for a better place: "It was all just a Nazi lie."[8]

Nonetheless, at dawn on January 21, 1945, those cleared for exchange were woken by their block leaders. Of the 450 "Latin Americans" initially listed by the SS, only 301 were considered healthy enough to travel. They were lined up, in rows of five, with their few remaining belongings, to be taken by truck to the railway station at Celle. On arrival there, many were relieved to see not only a passenger train but one bearing the emblems of the Red Cross. It caused a rush of optimism. "We didn't know where we were really being taken," Mirjam Wiener recalled, "except that there seemed a possibility of something good coming out of it."[9]

The journey began in hope. Irene Hasenberg remembered being served a bowl of thick, hot stew—she called it the best of her life—before being lulled to sleep by the rhythmic motion of the train as it chugged southward. However, her troubles were far from over. For one thing, some of those aboard the train were thrown off en route, as the Germans prioritized other prisoner groups for evacuation. Forty Belsen inmates were forced to leave the train at Biberach in southwestern Germany, while numerous others were unloaded at Ravensburg, with both groups being replaced by other, presumably more valuable, prisoners. It seems that the "Latin Americans" were close to the bottom of the prisoner food chain as far as the Germans were concerned.[10]

What's more, despite having passed the obligatory medical examination before departure, many of the Belsen prisoners were still in fragile health. Irene Hasenberg's father, who had been badly beaten shortly before leaving Belsen, began to fade on the journey. Irene tried to feed him some soup and told him they would soon be out of Germany, but he sank back onto the seat and apologized weakly, before telling her that he was not going to make it. Soon after, he died. His body was simply left on a bench on the station platform at Biberach, with a card bearing his name pinned to his lapel.[11]

Two days later, after a journey interrupted by air raids and unwanted siding sojourns in devastated German towns, the train finally arrived at Kreuzlingen, on the Swiss shore of Lake Constance, where it drew to a halt alongside another locomotive. The 301 "Latin American" prisoners who had left Belsen a few days before had been whittled down to just 136. Irene Hasenberg remembered the moment:

This was it, the exchange that we had dreamed about. The Germans ordered us off the train that would soon be heading back into Germany, and the Swiss ordered us onto the other train that would take us farther into their country. In the snow and cold between the two tracks, we passed the newly freed German civilian prisoners. These people were what we were worth. One of them equaled one of us. I looked at their clean coats, full suitcases, shiny shoes and full faces. Like us, they may have recently been prisoners, but it was obvious that the Allies hadn't treated them the way we had been treated.

As the train pulled away, she realized that her ordeal was finally over.[12]

Freedom came too late for some, however. Mirjam Wiener's mother, Margarethe, who had sustained her three daughters throughout their time in Westerbork and Bergen-Belsen, was now so weak that she was unable to leave the train. At Kreuzlingen, the family was handed to the care of the Red Cross and escorted to a large barrack block, where they were fed and provided with clothing. But, for Margarethe Wiener, it was all too late. As Mirjam recalled, "She saw us into freedom. I think she knew that her children . . . were in freedom and she could let go, and she died that night."[13]

FOR THOSE WHO REMAINED IN BELSEN, THE HORRORS GOT worse. Overcrowding, the root of Belsen's considerable malaise, became untenable that spring. When Kramer had been appointed commandant in early December, the camp's population had numbered a little over fifteen thousand; by the end of March 1945, there were forty-four thousand inmates in Belsen. That month, Kramer complained to his superior, *SS-Gruppenführer* Richard Glücks, the "inspector" of concentration camps. He reminded Glücks that, earlier in the year, he had placed the occupancy limit in the camp at thirty-five thousand prisoners, yet this number had already been exceeded, and a further 6,200 new arrivals were on the way. "The consequence of this," Kramer wrote,

is that all barracks are overcrowded by at least 30 percent. The detainees cannot lie down to sleep, but must sleep in a sitting position on the floor. . . . In addition to this, a spotted fever and typhus epidemic has now begun, which increases in extent every day. The daily mortality rate, which was in the region of 60–70 at the beginning of February, has in the meantime attained a daily average of 250–300 and will increase still further in view of the conditions which at present prevail.[14]

Morale among the prisoners—fragile at best—collapsed, and any solidarity that they had felt for one another began to fracture. There was a surge in theft and violence. "Our hut is like a madhouse," one inmate wrote that spring. "Only a few are capable of controlling themselves. The slightest incident leads to vicious arguments, threats, insults and abuse. Everyone is irritable, on edge, waiting to be provoked, ready to assume a personal animosity on the part of the next person. Everyone's mind is full of suspicion and deceitfulness. It makes one shudder." Diarist Abel Herzberg recalled the "bitter disappointment" and "flat, low spirit" that descended over the camp following the departure of the transport that January, and it wasn't long before there were suicides—a mother taking veronal, a man cutting his wrists. "The days pass in an endless, endless frustrating sequence," Herzberg wrote. "Days of dying."[15]

In the accelerating breakdown of the camp, Belsen's Exchange Jews were in a better situation than most: having been permitted to retain some of their possessions, many of them still had something to barter. One Dutch Jew remembered her father trading his wedding ring that spring for a sandwich. Sexual exploitation was rife. Another prisoner agreed to an "arrangement" with one of the Kapos to ensure that her sick husband would not be dragged out for a work detail. To her relief, their meeting was interrupted by an air raid. "Never again," she recalled, "did I savor the sound of the siren so much as in those few seconds."[16]

Rumors of new transports did not abate. Many of those who had been rejected from the January transport, such as Renata Laqueur, were assured that they would be included in the next one, which was supposed to leave four weeks later. Even Louis

Tas managed to muster some enthusiasm, noting that "this time I have the feeling, even if we're not on the list, that we'll be going too." Hanneli Goslar had pleaded with the camp doctors to include her father, Hans, in the next transport, as his health was rapidly deteriorating, and on February 24 she was astonished to hear that she and her sister, father, and grandmother would all be on the train departing the following day. She rushed to share the good news with her father in the camp infirmary, and he was soon propped up in the bed and dressed in his old suit, ready for departure. When she returned the following morning, however, she was told that he had died in the night. She consoled herself with the thought that he had, at least, died with the knowledge that his daughters would be on an exchange transport "out of hell." Later that day, Hanneli, her sister, and grandmother lined up with several hundred other people outside the administration block awaiting their departure. After four hours in the freezing cold, they were informed that the exchange had been canceled and that they were to return to their barracks.[17]

In March, conditions deteriorated still further, as food supplies collapsed and disease ravaged those prisoners who remained. That month, the death toll at Belsen exceeded that of any other concentration camp in the greater German Reich, with 18,168 prisoners registered as deceased. Among them were Anne Frank and her sister, Margot, both of whom succumbed to typhus. As if to compound the horror, the camp was equipped with only one crematorium, meaning that the large numbers of dead could not be adequately disposed of. As one eyewitness recalled, the result was chaos:

> The dead were then gathered into piles and burned in the open but this was discontinued when military personnel in [the nearby] barracks objected to the smell. Large pits were then bulldozed out and the dead were dragged to them for burial. . . . But as the death rate and the physical incapacity of the internees increased . . . the dead were simply dragged as far away

from the huts as possible and dumped. As exhaustion increased, the distance the corpses were dragged diminished and the piles around the huts grew.[18]

Spurred by the parlous state of the camp, Himmler's deputy *SS-Obergruppenführer* Oswald Pohl arrived in Belsen to see conditions for himself. Horrified, he agreed to the evacuation of the Exchange Jews into the ever-shrinking heart of the Reich, not only to make room for new arrivals that were still expected, but also because those foreign Jews were still considered to have some value as human bargaining chips. To this end, three transports were arranged in the second week of April, and 6,800 Exchange Jews, many of them Dutch, were ordered to prepare themselves for departure. For Henryk Schönker, it was a desperate attempt "to escape from a sinking ship."[19]

Józef Gitler-Barski was among those selected for the first train to depart, numbering some 2,500 Jews, including 200 from Poland. "We set out on foot to Celle station," he wrote in his diary. "Lovely weather. We look at the free world: roads, forests, the lovely homes of the Germans. But we have little strength to walk." That evening, they were loaded onto freight wagons, but there was no engine available, so they sat in the station. After they departed, the train passed through Stendal, west of Berlin, thereby shattering the dreams of some of the prisoners who had imagined that they were being sent to Hamburg to be exchanged. Instead, the rumor circulated that they were being sent to Theresienstadt.[20]

Their journey to Bohemia ground to a halt on the night of April 12, not far from Magdeburg. They had been stopped by an air raid and forced to disembark from the train and lie in the ditch along the rail lines, waiting for the bombers to pass. That night, Gitler-Barski overheard a conversation between the SS guards, who criticized their commander for having failed to exterminate the prisoners. When he asked, "What do you intend to do with us?" he received no reply. The following day, the SS escort left, having bartered tins of food for civilian clothes. They told the prisoners to remain where they were until they returned. Their instincts dulled by starvation and the forced regimen of camp life, most of the prisoners complied, wondering why no guard detail had been left behind. After half an hour, the bravest among them, realizing that their tormentors had abandoned them, wandered off to the nearby villages to forage for food. Later that morning, they were approached by "four dusty soldiers" in an unfamiliar vehicle. As one prisoner remembered, "They stopped the jeep and came up to us hesitantly, looking at the motley group. Women and children dressed in rags; a few men. Pitiful scarecrows. They asked, 'Who are you?' and we shrieked, in English, 'Hello! Friends! We love America!'" Józef Gitler-Barski wrote, "The long-awaited hour of liberation! People are crying, kissing the soldiers. The Americans look at our human skeletons with terror."[21]

While Gitler-Barski was savoring his moment of liberation, two other trains were carrying the remaining Exchange Jews from Belsen to Theresienstadt. The first departed Celle with 1,712 individuals on April 9, arriving in Bohemia on April 21. No accounts have survived from the prisoners aboard that train, and their fate is unknown, but it can be safely surmised—given their fragile state of health—that many of them did not survive the trip.

The last of the three trains is somewhat better documented. It consisted of forty-six wagons, both third-class passenger carriages and cattle cars, into which some 2,400 people had been crammed, including Louis Tas, Renata Laqueur, and Hanneli Goslar. Abel Herzberg remembered the scene as he arrived at the station after an exhausting walk from Belsen camp:

When we arrive, [the train] is already packed. It was to hold a total of two thousand four hundred people. Of these two thousand four hundred people, two thousand four hundred have dysentery. Besides that, seven hundred of them are also sick: typhus, paratyphoid, spotted fever. . . . Not counting edema.

It is crawling with lice. And all that is setting out on a journey together, around the world.[22]

The train departed Celle on April 11, proceeding first north, toward Hamburg, before turning east, its journey punctuated throughout by air raids and interminable delays in sidings, where the dead would be unloaded. The prisoners had little idea of where they were headed. "Theresienstadt, Switzerland, Sweden?" Renata Laqueur wondered. "Were we en route to our extermination, or were we to be exchanged? We could not find out, but it seemed to be the intention of the SS to take us to Theresienstadt . . . where—according to the pessimists—the gas chambers were waiting for us."[23]

On departure, the prisoners were provided with only meager amounts of food and water for the journey, although the frequent stops did at least allow them to forage by the rail lines for nourishment and to collect water from ponds and puddles. Hanneli Goslar traded jewelry, gathered from the prisoners in her carriage, with a German soldier, who gave her a freshly killed rabbit in return, which they cooked on a makeshift fire. Louis Tas remembered that on one occasion the appearance of RAF Typhoons sent their German guards scurrying for cover, allowing the fittest among the prisoners to loot a goods train that was parked alongside them in the sidings. "When the all-clear sounded," Tas wrote, "I had to fight myself free, like a rugby player, to preserve my loot from the hands of those who had been too passive to rob the train themselves."[24]

Many of the prisoners were already too ill to stand. One of them described the scene in her carriage, a converted goods wagon into which fifty-seven people had been forced, and that—unusually—contained a toilet. "Here lay sick people with typhus, pleurisy, tuberculosis and open, suppurating wounds," she noted. "All of them, more or less, were disfigured by edema, all of them were riddled with lice. Thirty of us could lie on the floor, the remainder had to sit. It would be fourteen endless days."[25]

Their journey would come to an end near the town of Trö-bitz, south of Berlin, where a railway bridge destroyed by Allied bombing blocked the line. For two days and nights, the train was stationary as the front line approached. The prisoners endured oc-casional air attacks and listened helplessly to the distant rumble of artillery. Then the able-bodied among them were ordered to a roll call, presumably with the intention that they would be marched onward to their destination. Only a couple of hundred were able—and willing—to obey the order. By now, though, German soldiers were fleeing past them. "German officers ran, in a small group, through the woods," Renata Laqueur noticed. "Some of them pushed bicycles, upon which cases and bags had been tied. I recognised a colonel and a captain who passed by our train with sullen expressions. It had to mean something! Was the enemy that close? But was it Americans or Russians?" The answer came on the morning of April 23, when the prisoners realized that their German guards had fled and that Red Army soldiers, in their fa-miliar olive uniforms, were approaching.[26]

Renata Laqueur jumped up to embrace the first Soviet soldier she saw: "A Russian, a friend, the liberator from our torment! I had so much to say; he smiled, he didn't understand." She might have been more cautious. Louis Tas remembered the Red Army as peculiar liberators. On the day after his liberation, he encountered a group of "very hospitable" Soviet soldiers who offered him the "honour" of being first with a young German woman whom they were going to rape. He declined, disappointed that they hadn't offered him any bread instead. In the final reckoning, 198 prison-ers are thought to have died on the journey; dozens more were so weakened by disease that they would not survive their liberation.[27]

For those who had remained in Belsen, the end came swiftly after the departure of the three transports. Already on April 10, SS-Standartenführer Kurt Becher, whom Himmler had appointed as a Reich special commissar for Jewish affairs, arrived in Belsen to consult with commandant Kramer. Becher was told of the spiraling death rates—by then at over five hundred per day—and the parlous lack of food, with only a few days' supply remaining. The two men agreed that they had no alternative but to seek to hand the camp over to the British without delay, and a car carrying two Wehrmacht officers and bearing a white flag was duly dispatched to the Allied lines. Five days later, on the afternoon of April 15, forward units of the British Eleventh Armored Division arrived outside the camp, causing both joy and consternation among those still sentient enough to realize what was going on. As German Jew Anita Lasker recalled:

> For days we had heard the rumbling noises of heavy artillery, but we hadn't known who was firing. We had no idea what was happening to us. The noise came closer . . . and then . . . a voice through a loud-hailer . . . first in English, then in German. At the beginning we were too confused and excited to take anything in. But the announcements kept being repeated, again and again. At last we understood. BRITISH TROOPS ARE STANDING BY THE CAMP GATES. . . PLEASE KEEP CALM. . . YOU ARE LIBERATED.[28]

Belsen was the only one of Hitler's main concentration camps that was formally handed over to Allied troops. That gesture would not spare the camp's commandant, however. Arrested by the British, Josef Kramer would be tried before a military tribunal in Lüneburg later that year, charged with crimes against humanity. His defense, that he was merely a soldier following the orders of his superiors and that he had never personally killed anyone, failed to convince the court. Found guilty, Kramer was sentenced to death and hanged in the prison at Hamelin on December 13, 1945.[29]

WHILE THE END OF THE WAR IN MAY 1945 BROUGHT A close to the fighting, it did not bring an end to the pain endured by many of the former camp prisoners. For the liberated, a cruel twist in their tale of suffering came with the first days of freedom, because—starved as they were—they could barely tolerate being fed, especially when well-meaning Allied soldiers indiscriminately distributed army rations and chocolate. Though typhus and tuberculosis would continue to kill prisoners in the days after their liberation, one of the biggest killers was the inability of the weakened and malnourished prisoners to tolerate a normal diet. The British were aware of the problem, and army medics experimented with various concoctions of "Bengal mixture"—a gruel of powdered milk, sugar, and flour resembling a thick, white soup— with inconclusive results. Tragically, in the weeks after liberation, a further thirteen thousand of Belsen's prisoners would perish.[30]

There was also scant comfort to be had for many of those desperately seeking their loved ones. Until a formal system was established to register concentration camp and Holocaust survivors, relatives were dependent on receiving messages by post or through the Red Cross. For many, those messages never came. One of those waiting for news was Saul Weingort, who had been a key player in the development of the passport forgery network. That summer, Weingort wrote to a friend expressing his hope that both his parents and his brother Leo might, by some miracle, have survived. "When one hears of the hundreds of thousands of liberated survivors who have not yet made contact, one still has some hope," he said. In time, it would transpire that his parents and brother—who had all been prisoners in Vittel—had been deported to Auschwitz in the spring of 1944, where they are thought to have been murdered upon arrival.

While waiting for news of his family, Weingort pondered the successes—and failures—of the passport operation. Though he laid the primary blame for the failure to save more lives on the "malevolence" of the Germans, he was also highly critical of both the Latin American governments and their proxies in Europe. "When I think about the Vittel matter," he wrote to a friend that summer, "I place the blame on the slow action of the South American states and the protecting powers, who waited until after the deportation [to recognize the passports]. . . . We worked feverishly," he lamented, but to no avail.[31]

For the diplomats of the Ładoś Group, too, the summer of 1945 proved to be one of disappointments. They would have been temporarily buoyed, perhaps, by the messages of thanks that arrived from representatives of the Jewish organizations with which they had collaborated. Already in January, the London office of Agudath Israel had written to the Polish Ministry of Foreign Affairs to thank them for the "very active assistance and rescue work" of their colleagues in Bern: "Legation Counsellor Ryniewicz, attaché Juliusz Kühl, Minister Aleksander Ładoś [and] Consul Rokicki." The Union of Orthodox Rabbis, meanwhile, sent its thanks that summer directly to Juliusz Kühl, stating that "it is through your generous help in the production of documents, with God's help, that thousands of lives were saved." The letter closed by expressing the belief that "these actions will forever be written as a particular chapter in the history of this most terrible tragedy."[32]

Nonetheless, despite the Allied victory and those expressions of gratitude, the mood in Polish political and diplomatic circles was downbeat. That summer, Moscow's takeover of Poland—which had been in the offing since the previous autumn—accelerated, leaving many Polish diplomats and others facing either an uncomfortable accommodation with the Soviets or a life in exile. The pressure had been building for some time. Diplomatic relations between the Polish government-in-exile and the Soviets had been difficult for most of the war. Formally restored after the German invasion of the USSR in 1941, relations had been broken off by Moscow following the discovery, in the spring of 1943, of the mass graves of the Polish officers murdered by the Soviets at Katyń—a crime that the Kremlin attempted to blame on the Germans. Consequently, by the summer of 1944—when Red Army forces were already on the territory of the prewar Polish Repub-lic—the Soviet Union and the Polish government-in-exile still lacked direct diplomatic representation. From that point on, then, all discussions of Poland's frontiers and political future would take place without Polish participation.

By the summer of 1945, therefore, Poland's new frontiers had already been fixed—de facto on the ground and de jure by the Grand Alliance—with the Polish government-in-exile able to do nothing more than protest against the high-handed redrawing of its territory. Worse still, a treaty of friendship, mutual aid, and co-operation had been signed in April between Moscow and its proxy provisional government in Poland, which committed the new Pol-ish state to joining the Soviet camp for twenty years. This treaty, little remarked upon at the time, made a nonsense of the ambi-tion—solemnly aired by the big three at the Yalta Conference in February 1945—that "free and unfettered elections," with universal suffrage and a secret ballot, were to be held in Poland "as soon as possible." Regardless of how any such elections—or the pretense thereof—would play out, Poland's fate had already been sealed.

If Polish diplomats and politicians in exile had thus far been able to suppress the thought that the country they represented was slipping from their grasp, the events of the summer of 1945 would have been a rude awakening. In mid-June, the sixteen leaders of the Polish underground state—the most senior representatives of the Polish government-in-exile in Poland itself—appeared in a Moscow courtroom. In March, they had been invited—with a promise of safe conduct—to a meeting in Warsaw with NKVD general Ivan Serov, where they had been kidnapped, interrogated, and secretly flown to the Soviet capital. Indicted on fictitious charges of terrorism and collaborating with Nazi Germany, most would receive long sentences in the gulag, a fate from which three of the defendants would never return. With that, not only was the Polish underground state rendered lame, but the idea of peaceful cooperation with the Soviets was exposed as a dangerous fiction.

Despite these setbacks, there were some Polish politicians who were still determined to take Soviet assurances of good faith at face value, pressing for the creation of a genuinely representative provisional government and the holding of those promised "free and unfettered elections." The most prominent among them was Stanisław Mikołajczyk, the former leader of the center-left Polish People's Party and a former prime minister of the Polish government-in-exile. Returning to Poland in June 1945, Mikołajczyk was appointed to the provisional government as deputy prime minister and enjoyed a fanfare of popular enthusiasm, which at one point saw him carried shoulder high through the streets of Kraków. Any hope he had for democracy vanished, however, when it became apparent where the real power lay. As he later recalled, the Communist members of the government met with their Soviet handler—an anonymous NKVD colonel—every Thursday morning to receive their orders. It would take Mikołajczyk the best part of two years to realize that he had been cast in the role of a fig leaf—the democratic gloss on a totalitarian seizure of power.[33]

Though Soviet control over Poland was not finally and unequivocally cemented until 1947, the die was already cast in the summer of 1945, when the Western powers effectively abandoned the Polish government-in-exile in London and shifted their official recognition to the pro-Moscow provisional government then newly installed in Warsaw. With that, the primary rival power base able to oppose the Communist takeover was removed. In his intemperate protest to the British government over the decision, the Polish ambassador in London, Edward Raczyński, explained that the territory of Poland remained under a foreign military occupation—that of the Soviets—and that his government remained the "sole constitutional and independent representative of Poland." In such circumstances, he said, he refused either to recognize the new regime "unilaterally enacted in Poland" or to delegate his functions to any "imposter" pretending to be authorized to claim his position. He concluded with a blunt history lesson:

Once more . . . the Polish Nation is being deprived of its independence, though this time not as a result of events which took place in Eastern Europe alone, but after a war which the United Nations waged in defense of law and justice. Notwithstanding the recognition by other powers of its present subjugation, the Polish Nation will never give up its right to independent existence and will never cease to struggle for it.[34]

Despite the righteous anger on display, it was the end of the line for the Polish government-in-exile, and though it would remain in existence until 1989—with cabinet meetings and prime ministers and party politics—the country that it claimed to rule was now dancing to Moscow's tune. For Polish diplomats, meanwhile, there could be no business as usual, and though a few found an easy segue into exile politics—Raczyński, for instance, served as president of the government-in-exile in the 1980s—for the vast majority of diplomatic staff, the new realities of the summer of 1945 presented something of an existential crisis. So it was with the staff of the Polish legation in Bern.

That summer, Aleksander Ładoś found himself replaced. Prior to the arrival of his successor, the writer and Communist activist Jerzy Putrament, all of the embassy staff were asked whether they were willing to serve the new provisional government in Warsaw. Given that most of them still felt a professional and political loyalty to the government-in-exile, the majority refused. Juliusz Kühl, Konstanty Rokicki, and Stefan Ryniewicz all resigned their posts and settled, temporarily at least, in Switzerland. Ładoś, too, resigned after discussion with his colleagues and with Swiss officials. Decisive, it seems, was the attitude of the Swiss foreign minister, Max Petitpierre, who informed him that the Swiss government had decided to recognize the new provisional government in Poland and would also recognize its appointed representatives in Bern. Ładoś, it seemed, was surplus to requirements.[35]

A few members of Ładoś's staff were rather more equivo-
cal, even enthusiastic. In his memoir, Stanisław Nahlik, who had
overseen the legation's radio correspondence, would express the
widespread conviction that the world had changed by 1945, with
the terrible destruction caused by the war, and that the priority
should be reconstruction rather than political factionalism. In his
opinion, the straitened circumstances in which Poland found itself demanded a compromise with communism and an acceptance
of "the inevitability of certain fundamental changes in the future
form of the Polish state." These opinions were highly controversial in the diplomatic circles in which Nahlik moved. Indeed, he
noted, many of his fellow Poles shunned him for expressing them,
calling him a defeatist and a pessimist; one former friend even
"threatened him with the gallows."[36]

The attitude of Aleksander Ładoś to the new Communist government has been the subject of some scrutiny, not least because
he was criticized in 1945 in a report, prepared for the minister
of foreign affairs of the government-in-exile in London, Adam
Tarnowski, as someone who had a "positive stance" toward the
Communist government. Ładoś had certainly given his blessing
to Nahlik traveling to Paris to meet representatives of the Polish provisional government that summer, and he himself had
met with Warsaw's new Communist ambassador to Paris, Stefan
Jędrychowski, outside Bern. However, in the fevered atmosphere
of the time, it seems that the political context might have been lost.
Ładoś refused to cooperate with the new Communist-led government; rather, he supported the efforts of Polish People's Party
leader Stanisław Mikołajczyk to find a workable compromise
with the Soviets. And it was to this end that he agreed to remain
in Switzerland as a special envoy for Mikołajczyk. In answer to
the accusation that he was sympathetic to communism, one might
cite a speech he made to a congress of peasant parties in Paris in
1947, in which he stated that Poland was "ruled by violence, terror

and lawlessness" and complained that "the best sons of our nation are perishing in prisons or who knows where . . . without trial or evidence, thousands are persecuted only because they will not march to the music of those currently in power."[37]

By that time, of course, Poland was firmly in the grip of the Communists, and Mikołajczyk's cause—and that of Ładoś—was already lost. Ładoś had moved to the Paris suburbs, where he lived on what remained of his savings with his mother and his sister. Later, he moved to a small farm north of Paris, where he pursued the life of a smallholder, raising chickens and growing strawberries. Facing financial ruin, he returned to Poland in 1960, where he received a modest pension from the Communist regime. He died in Warsaw in 1963.[38]

By that time, the group he had led in Bern during the war had been scattered to the four winds. Juliusz Kühl had left Switzerland in 1949 for Canada, where he established a construction company. Stefan Ryniewicz—the linchpin of the passport operation—emigrated to France and later to Argentina, where he was active in Polish émigré circles. Three of the group had already passed away by the time of Ładoś's death. Chaim Eiss had died in the autumn of 1943, and Abraham Silberschein—who had settled in Geneva after the war—passed away in 1951, aged sixty-nine. Most tragic of all, perhaps, was the fate of Konstanty Rokicki, in whose hand most of the Ładoś passports had been written. After leaving diplomatic service in 1945, he had remained in Switzerland, but—lacking the business instincts of his former colleagues—he fell on hard times, being declared bankrupt in 1951. Thereafter he lived in a succession of hostels before dying of lung cancer in Lucerne in 1958. He would be buried in a pauper's grave.

EPILOGUE

THE ŁADOŚ GROUP CARRIED OUT ONE OF THE MOST AMBI-
tious rescue operations of the Holocaust. Until very recently, its
story was unknown, confined—at best—to the archives and to
the footnotes of the wider narrative, its members condemned by
circumstances to obscurity. Sidelined by the political upheavals of
the postwar period, and by the durability of the shadows in which
they had once sought to operate, they died unknown and unrec-
ognized. They sought no reward and received none. They did what
they did, not for personal gain, but—as Aleksander Ładoś stated
in 1943—as a "humanitarian operation," an attempt "to save as
many people as possible."[1]

They were not alone in that ambition, of course. Most fam-
ously, perhaps, the German industrialist Oskar Schindler saved
almost 1,100 Jews who were part of the workforce at his enamel
factory in occupied Kraków. Or there was the Swedish diplomat
Raoul Wallenberg, who is thought to have saved as many as nine
thousand Hungarian Jews by issuing false Swedish identity papers
and providing safe houses while in Budapest in the last months of
the war.[2]

There were also more controversial examples. As is detailed here, the Swiss politician Jean-Marie Musy managed to secure the release of 1,200 Jews from Theresienstadt in 1944, in return for the promise of a payment of one million US dollars to the Germans, an action that was frowned upon by many in Jewish circles, even though the money was never paid. Most dubious of all, perhaps, is that of Rudolf Kasztner, the Hungarian journalist who bought the release of some 1,600 Jews from the Germans in 1944 at a price of $1,000 per head, to be paid in gold and diamonds. It was a deal that would ultimately cost Kasztner his life. Such was the fury of some on the Israeli right at his wartime dealings with Adolf Eichmann that he was assassinated at his Tel Aviv home in 1957.[3]

The efforts of the Ladoś Group lack that element of controversy, of course, yet they may have helped to save similar numbers of people. The total number of recipients of Ladoś passports is not known, but it was estimated by Abraham Silberschein in 1944 at around ten thousand, a figure that is borne out by the available statistical data. Scholars who have been investigating the story over the past few years have unearthed the names of some 3,282 individuals who are known to have been recipients of passports and identity documents supplied by the Ladoś Group in Bern. Assuming that the partial and incomplete lists of passports that have been discovered were complete provides an estimated total of between 3,800 and 5,300 documents issued. Bearing in mind that passports and identity documents of that time were routinely issued for more than one individual and often for entire families, and that the available data suggests that the average number of individuals entered on Paraguayan and Honduran passports issued by the Ladoś Group was 2.2 people, one arrives at an estimate of between 8,300 and 11,400 individuals.[4]

The question of how many of those people survived requires another statistical exercise. It is known that, from the sample of 3,282 known recipients of Ladoś documents, some 868 survived the war. Given that survivors are most likely overrepresented among those whose fates can be established, it can be assumed that a realistic estimate for a survival rate—based on these figures—might be between 30 and 35 percent. On this basis, bearing in mind a conservative estimate of between eight thousand and ten thousand recipients, it is thought that between two thousand and three thousand of those people who received Ładoś documents may have survived the Holocaust.[5]

While those assumptions are entirely sensible, we must resist the temptation of assuming that those who survived with a Ładoś passport did so *because of* a Ładoś passport. Though there are doubtless many examples where that is the case—such as that of Heinz Lichtenstern, which opened this book—there are other instances where the securing of a Paraguayan passport or a Honduran *promesa* was merely one of a number of survival measures undertaken, alongside going underground, adopting a new "Aryan" identity, or securing immigration papers for Palestine. In the murderous chaos of the Holocaust, it was sometimes difficult to ascertain which measure, if any, was decisive.

Moreover, it should be clear from the foregoing chapters that possession of a Ładoś passport was no guarantee of survival. Far from it. At best, perhaps, it represented a reprieve, a stay of execution, giving its bearers the opportunity to escape, at least temporarily, the deadly process that ended in the gas chambers of Birkenau or Treblinka. The passport holders, if they were lucky, then found themselves consigned to German internment camps, such as Bergen-Belsen or Vittel, where maltreatment, disease, or exhaustion could still spell their end.

Furthermore, it is clear from the available statistics that Polish Jews had a worse chance of survival than their non-Polish fellows. Though they made up more than 70 percent of passport holders, for instance, they account for only 41 percent of the identified survivors. This disparity is partly due to the generally harsher conditions experienced in the German occupation of Poland, but it can also be attributed to the deliberate shift in German policy, in which western European Jews were to be favored in the Exchange Jews program, because Polish and eastern European Jews were considered to have seen too much. In addition to all that, the fraught issue of the recognition of the passports by the Latin American governments added another layer of potential jeopardy. One is tempted to conclude that, even when in possession of a Ładoś passport, one needed a miracle to survive.[6]

Given that only a "small lucky handful" of Polish Jews survived Bergen-Belsen with Latin American passports, some have considered that the Ładoś operation—for all its effort and ingenuity—was a disappointment. This, I suggest, is mistaken. The passport forgery operation represented the limit of what, in the circumstances, was possible, and initially it functioned as was intended: reasserting a legal obstacle to the nefarious machinery of the Holocaust. Abraham Silberschein estimated that, in January 1944, the vast majority of the ten thousand Ładoś passport holders were still alive, being held by the Germans in internment camps. Their tragedy, of course, is that they then had to survive a further eighteen months of privation and ill-treatment at German hands, while distant bureaucrats in Washington and Asunción discussed whether they should be permitted to abuse the sanctity of official documents.[7]

In this discussion, of course, Ładoś and his compatriots could persuade, cajole, and plead—and they did—but they could do no more to help; so the fact that most of the Ładoś passport holders did not survive to the end of the war cannot be fairly blamed on them. Consequently, I suggest that it would be invidious to judge the Ładoś Group purely by the number of individuals whom it enabled to survive. It should be judged on its intentions, on the principled stand that Aleksander Ładoś, his staff, and their Jewish colleagues took to do what was right—to try to assist those in desperate need. There is honor in that intention, regardless of the numbers saved.

What's more, who else was willing to assist on this scale? As we have seen, international, government-sponsored attempts to rescue Jews from the Holocaust were few and far between. As the deliberations at Évian and later at Bermuda demonstrated all too clearly, there was vanishingly little desire or intention to provide material assistance to Europe's Jews. Other considerations always seemed to take precedence: British concerns about Palestine, Swiss worries about the sanctity of official documents, American fears about espionage, not to mention the oldest prejudice of all, the latent anti-Semitism that routinely relegated the Jews to the category of somebody else's problem or an issue to be addressed further down the line. Before we criticize the efforts that *were* made, therefore—however flawed or ineffective they may have been—we should perhaps contemplate the alternative. In such circumstances, the actions of the Ładoś Group and of the diplomats of the Polish government-in-exile, both in alerting the world to the truth of the ongoing Holocaust and later in trying to secure the international recognition of Ładoś passports, stand out as a beacon of moral clarity.

Of course, it may surprise some readers that Poland should be the source of this attempt at rescue. Polish-Jewish relations during World War II were immensely difficult and fraught, marred on both sides by mistrust and prejudice. It didn't help, of course, that Poland was, to a large extent, damned by association—given that the majority of the killing in the Holocaust, though carried out by the Germans, nonetheless took place on Polish soil. Moreover, accusations of wartime Polish anti-Semitism persist, spurred by the checkered record of minority relations in the prewar Polish Republic and by the many rejections and betrayals at Polish hands that Holocaust memoirs sometimes demonstrate.

Such episodes cannot and must not be denied, yet they should also be viewed within a wider context, a context in which the unimaginable suffering of ordinary Polish Jews under German occupation is understood alongside that of their non-Jewish neighbors. One in which it is appreciated that—despite Poland being the only area of German-occupied Europe in which the death penalty was imposed for those assisting Jews—more Poles have been awarded the honorific title Righteous Among the Nations—for non-Jews who risked their own lives during the Holocaust to save Jews—than any other nationality. This should not be a zero-sum game, where one side of the equation is weaponized to erase the other; rather, both sides should be acknowledged and understood as being integral to a complex and painful shared history.

The Ładoś Group is part of that history. They were moved to help, primarily on purely humanitarian grounds, but more than that they saw their task as that of assisting Polish citizens in need, regardless of what religion those citizens professed to adhere to. Though the members of the group—Aleksander Ładoś, Stefan Ryniewicz, Konstanty Rokicki, Juliusz Kühl, Abraham Silberschein, and Chaim Eiss—disappeared into postwar obscurity, their legacy was to be those whom they endeavored to rescue.

Heinz Lichtenstern, whose story opened this book, never knew where his Paraguayan passport had come from, and he always considered it to be a last resort, a final throw of the dice. Yet it would undoubtedly save not only his life but also those of his wife and children. In the more than four decades that remained to him, he would continue his career as a metals trader and become a grandfather and a great-grandfather. He was but one of the many the Ładoś Group helped to save. Others would go on to be academics, rabbis, engineers, politicians, mathematicians, historians, and journalists—and in their time mothers and fathers, grandmothers and grandfathers—every one of them living proof of the Talmud saying that "he who saves one life, saves the world entire."[8]

ACKNOWLEDGMENTS

I was first alerted to the story of the Ładoś Group in the winter of 2018. At the time, I was working on the final draft of my previous book *Poland 1939* when I received an email from a Polish friend giving the outline of the story. By that point, much of the preliminary research had already been done, and the Ładoś story had already broken in the Swiss and Polish press, but a full treatment—placing the episode in the wider context of the Holocaust and of German policy of the period—was still outstanding. In due course, I was asked if I would be interested in taking it on.

Consequently, my first debt of gratitude must be to those who did so much in that early phase to research and contextualize the subject, foremost among them the Polish honorary consul in Zürich, Markus Blechner, and the then Polish ambassador to Switzerland, Dr. Jakub Kumoch. No less significantly, I have benefitted hugely from the knowledge and insight of the two primary authorities on the subject of the Ładoś Group: Jędrzej Uszyński of the Polish Foreign Ministry and Monika Maniewska of the Pilecki Institute. Without their expertise and boundless generosity this book would simply not have been possible.

In preparing this volume, I was assisted by the Pilecki Institute in Warsaw, which generously granted me a research fellowship. My sincere thanks go to Wojciech Kozłowski and John Cornell for the smooth running of that cooperation. My own research was carried out at a number of locations, including the Wiener Library, the National Archives, the German Historical Institute, London, and the Sikorski Institute. Sonia Bacca at the Wiener and Jadwiga Kowalska at the Sikorski Institute went beyond the call of duty in assisting. Honorable mention must also be made of the excellent Sugihara House in Kaunas, Lithuania, where I was privileged to give a lecture—and hear the story of Chiune Sugihara—in those far-off days before Covid-19. Due to the restrictions imposed by the pandemic, my visits to the archives of the US Holocaust Memorial Museum in Washington, DC, and Yad Vashem in Tel Aviv were restricted to the virtual realm.

As I developed my ideas for the book, I was honored to be given the opportunity to speak at a number of locations—among them JW3 in London, Trinity College in Dublin, and the London History Festival—where I could road test my findings and hone my thoughts. Thanks are due to all those who made those outings—so precious after the interminable lockdowns—so enlightening and enjoyable, foremost among them Judy Trotter at JW3 and Agnieszka Skolimowska of the Polish embassy in Dublin.

In addition, thanks must go—as always—to my agent, Georgina Capel, for her tireless enthusiasm and solid good sense, and to her brilliant codirector Rachel Conway, for her unfussy handling of financial and administrative matters. Of my publishers, huge thanks are due to Lara Heimert of Basic Books in the US, and in the UK to Stuart Williams of Bodley Head, who showed their customary perspicacity in commissioning the book. My editor Jörg Hensgen was as patient and eagle-eyed as ever.

Numerous individuals also gave their time, advice, expertise, or precious family stories, including Dr. Paul Bartrop, Louisa

Clein, Jeffrey Cymbler, Prof. Norman Davies, Slawomir Dębski, Lord Finkelstein, Heidi Fishman, Dr. Claire Hubbard-Hall, Sara Kadosh, Neil Kaplan, Fabian Krougman, Michael Leventhal, Rachel Marcus, Alina Nowobilska, Prof. Ewa Pałasz-Rutkowska, Prof. Antony Polonsky, Alexandra Reiter, Hephzibah Rudofsky, Prof. Arkady Rzegocki, Sjoerd Schelvis, Linas Venclauskas, Anna Whitty, and Dr. Joshua Zimmerman.

Special thanks must also go to my brilliant and long-suffering research assistant, Anastazja Pindor, and lastly to my wife, Melissa, for the endless cups of tea and understanding. Apologies to those whom I have inevitably forgotten; you know who you are . . .

ROGER MOORHOUSE

SELECTED BIBLIOGRAPHY

Adelson, Alan, ed. *The Diary of Dawid Sierakowiak* (London, 1996).

Adler, H. G. *Theresienstadt 1941–1945* (Cambridge, 2017).

Aly, Götz. *Endlösung* (Frankfurt am Main, 1998).

Ammann, Thomas, and Stefan Aust. *Hitlers Menschenhändler* (Berlin, 2013).

Bartov, Omer, ed. *The Holocaust: Origins, Implementation, Aftermath* (London, 2000).

Bartrop, Paul R. *The Evian Conference of 1938 and the Jewish Refugee Crisis* (Basingstoke, UK, 2018).

Berg, Mary. *The Diary of Mary Berg: Growing Up in the Warsaw Ghetto* (London, 2006).

Blanken, I. J. *The History of Philips Electronics N.V.* Vol. 4 (Zaltbommel, Netherlands, 1999).

Blatman, Daniel. *The Death Marches: The Final Phase of Nazi Genocide* (London, 2011).

Blum, Aleksander, et al. *Zwyciężeni, ale nie pokonani* (Warsaw, 2000).

Böhler, Jochen. *Auftakt zum Vernichtungskrieg: Die Wehrmacht in Polen 1939* (Frankfurt am Main, 2006).

———. *Der Überfall: Deutschlands Krieg gegen Polen* (Frankfurt am Main, 2009).

Bornstein, Heini. *Insel Schweiz: Hilfs- und Rettungsaktionen sozialistisch-zionistischer Jugendorganisationen 1939–1946* (Zürich, 2000).

Bosch, Gideon, et al. *Die Wannsee-Konferenz und der Völkermord an den europäischen Juden* (Berlin, 2006).

Braham, Randolph L. "Rescue Operations in Hungary: Myths and Realities." *East European Quarterly* 34, no. 2 (2004).

Brechtken, Magnus. *"Madagaskar für die Juden": Antisemitische Idee und politische Praxis 1885–1945* (Oldenburg, Germany, 1998).

Breitman, Richard. *Hitler's Shadow: Nazi War Criminals, U.S. Intelligence, and the Cold War* (Washington, DC, 2011).

———. *Official Secrets: What the Nazis Planned, What the British and Americans Knew* (New York, 1998).

Browning, Christopher R. "A Final Hitler Decision for the 'Final Solution'? The Riegner Telegram Reconsidered." *Holocaust and Genocide Studies* 10, no. 1 (Spring 1996).

———. *The Origins of the Final Solution: The Evolution of Nazi Jewish Policy, 1939– 1942* (London, 2005).

———. *Remembering Survival: Inside a Nazi Slave-Labor Camp* (New York, 2010).

Butter, Irene. *Shores Beyond Shores: From Holocaust to Hope* (London, 2018).

Celnikier, Feliks. *Żyd, czyli kto? Pojęcie Żyda w doktrynie i hitlerowskich poczynaniach prawodawczych. Studium absurdu i mistyfikacji* (Warsaw, 2014).

Cesarani, David. *Final Solution: The Fate of the Jews, 1933–1949* (New York, 2016).

Czech, Danuta. *Auschwitz Chronicle 1939–1945* (London and New York, 1990).

Datner, Szymon. *55 dni Wehrmachtu w Polsce: zbrodnie dokonane na polskiej ludności cywilnej w okresie 1 IX-25 X 1939 r.* (Warsaw, 1967).

Davies, Norman. *God's Playground: A History of Poland*. Vol. 2, *1795 to the Present* (Oxford, 1981).

Dawidowicz, Lucy. *The War Against the Jews 1933–1945* (London, 1987).

Długołęcki, Piotr, ed. *Confronting the Holocaust: The Polish Government-in-Exile's Policy Concerning Jews 1939–1945* (Warsaw, 2022).

Dobroszycki, Lucjan, ed. *The Chronicle of the Łódź Ghetto, 1941–1944* (New Haven, CT, and London, 1984).

Documents on German Foreign Policy 1918–1945. Series D, Vol. 9 (Washington, DC, 1956).

Domarus, Max. *Hitler: Reden und Proklamationen, 1932–1945*. Vol. 1, part 2 (Wiesbaden, Germany, 1973).

Donat, Alexander. *The Holocaust Kingdom: A Memoir* (London, 1965).

Dwork, Deborah, and Robert Jan van Pelt. *Flight from the Reich: Refugee Jews, 1933–1946* (New York, 2009).

Eck, Nathan. "The Rescue of Jews with the Aid of Passports and Citizenship Papers of Latin American States." *Yad Vashem Studies* 1 (Jerusalem, 1957).

Engel, David. *In the Shadow of Auschwitz: The Polish Government-in-Exile and the Jews, 1939–1942* (Chapel Hill, NC, and London, 1987).

Feingold, Henry. *The Politics of Rescue* (New Brunswick, NJ, 1970).

Flanagan, Ben, and Donald Bloxham, eds. *Remembering Belsen* (London, 2005).

Friedenson, Joseph, and David Kranzler. *Heroine of Rescue* (New York, 1984).

Friedländer, Saul. *The Years of Extermination: Nazi Germany and the Jews, 1939– 1945* (London, 2007).

Friedman, Max Paul. "The U.S. State Department and the Failure to Rescue: New Evidence on the Missed Opportunity at Bergen-Belsen." *Holocaust and Genocide Studies* 19, no. 1 (Spring 2005).

Fröhlich, Elke, ed. *Die Tagebücher von Joseph Goebbels*. Part 1, Vol. 6 (Munich, 1998).

Fry, Helen. *Spymaster: The Man Who Saved MI6* (London, 2021).

Fry, Varian. *Assignment Rescue: An Autobiography* (New York, 1968).

Fulbrook, Mary. *A Small Town Near Auschwitz: Ordinary Nazis and the Holocaust* (Oxford, 2013).

Garliński, Józef. *Poland in the Second World War* (Basingstoke, UK, 1985).

Gerwarth, Robert. *Hitler's Hangman: The Life of Heydrich* (London, 2011).

Gilbert, Martin. *The Holocaust* (London, 1986).

———. *Kristallnacht: Prelude to Destruction* (London, 2006).

Gitler-Barski, Józef. *Przeżycia i wspomnienia z lat okupacji* (Warsaw, 1986).

Gottwald, Alfred, and Diana Schulle. *Die "Judendeportationen" aus dem Deutschen Reich 1941–1945* (Stuttgart, 2005).

Gross, Jan T. *Revolution from Abroad: The Soviet Conquest of Poland's Western Ukraine and Western Byelorussia* (Princeton, NJ, and Oxford, 2002).

Grunwald-Spier, Agnes. *Women's Experiences in the Holocaust: In Their Own Words* (Stroud, UK, 2018).

Grynberg, Michał, ed. *Words to Outlive Us: Eyewitness Accounts from the Warsaw Ghetto* (London, 2003).

Gutschow, Niels, and Barbara Klain. *Vernichtung und Utopie. Stadtplanung Warschau 1939–1945* (Hamburg, 1994).

Haska, Agnieszka. *Hotel Polski w Warszawie, 1943* (Warsaw, 2006).

Herrmann, Simon Heinrich. *Austauschlager Bergen-Belsen* (Tel Aviv, 1944).

Herzberg, Abel. *Between Two Streams: A Diary from Bergen-Belsen* (London, 1997).

Hilberg, Raul. *The Destruction of the European Jews*. Vol. 2 (New York, 1985).

———, ed. *The Warsaw Diary of Adam Czerniaków* (Chicago, 1979).

Hillesum, Etty. *Etty: A Diary 1941–1943* (London, 1985).

Hoess, Rudolf. *Commandant of Auschwitz* (London, 2000).

Kadosh, Sara. *We Think of You as an Angel* (Jerusalem, 2019).

Karski, Jan. *Story of a Secret State: My Report to the World* (London, 2011).

Kassow, Samuel D., ed. *In Those Nightmarish Days: The Ghetto Reportage of Peretz Opoczynski and Josef Zelkowicz* (New Haven, CT, and London, 2015).

Kirsch, Jonathan. *The Short, Strange Life of Herschel Grynszpan* (New York, 2014).

Kitade, Akira. *Visas of Life and the Epic Journey* (Tokyo, 2014).

Klarsfeld, Serge. *Memorial to the Jews Deported from France, 1942–1944* (New York, 1983).

Klemperer, Victor. *I Shall Bear Witness: The Diaries of Victor Klemperer, 1933–41* (London, 1998).

Klinger, Chajka. *"I Am Writing These Words to You": The Original Diaries, Będzin, 1943* (Jerusalem, 2017).

Kochański, Halik. *The Eagle Unbowed: Poland and the Poles in the Second World War* (London, 2012).

Kohn, Zahava. *Fragments of a Lost Childhood* (London, 2009).

Kolb, Eberhard. *Bergen-Belsen: From "Detention Camp" to Concentration Camp: 1943 to 1945* (Göttingen, Germany, 1985).

———. *Bergen-Belsen: Geschichte des "Aufenthaltslagers" 1943–1945* (Hannover, Germany, 1962).

Kranzler, David. *The Man Who Stopped the Trains to Auschwitz* (Syracuse, NY, 2000).

———. *Thy Brother's Blood: The Orthodox Jewish Response to the Holocaust* (New York, 1987).

Kreis, Georg, ed. *Switzerland and the Second World War* (London, 2000).

Kumoch, Jakub, et al. *The Ładoś List* (Warsaw, 2020).

Ładoś, Aleksander. *Polska w latach 1918–1939: Relacje, Wspomnienia.* 3 vols. (unpublished).

Ładoś, Sebastian. *Zanim Bóg odwróci wzrok* (Wrocław, Poland, 2019).

Laqueur, Renata. *Bergen-Belsen Tagebuch, 1944/1945* (Hannover, Germany, 1983).

Lasker-Wallfisch, Anita. *Inherit the Truth 1939–1945* (London, 1996).

Levine, Hillel. *In Search of Sugihara* (New York, 1996).

Lévy-Hass, Hannah. *Diary of Bergen-Belsen* (Minneapolis, MN, 2009).

Lewin, Abraham. *A Cup of Tears: A Diary of the Warsaw Ghetto* (Oxford, 1988).

Longerich, Peter. *Goebbels: A Biography* (London, 2015).

———. *Heinrich Himmler* (Oxford, 2012).

———. *Holocaust* (Oxford, 2010).

Lukas, Richard C. *The Forgotten Holocaust: The Poles Under German Occupation 1939–1944* (New York, 1986).

MacDonogh, Giles. *1938: Hitler's Gamble* (New York, 2009).

Manes, Philipp. *As If It Were Life: A WWII Diary from the Theresienstadt Ghetto* (New York, 2009).

Marguerat, Philippe, and Louis-Edouard Roulet, eds. *Diplomatic Documents of Switzerland.* Vol. 15 (Bern, 1992).

Markowska, Marta, ed. *The Ringelblum Archive: Annihilation—Day by Day* (Warsaw, 2008).

Mechanicus, Philip. *Waiting for Death: A Diary* (London, 1968).

Meed, Vladka. *On Both Sides of the Wall* (Washington, DC, 1993).

Moczarski, Kazimierz. *Conversations with an Executioner* (Hoboken, NJ, 1981).

Moorhouse, Roger. *First to Fight: The Polish War 1939* (London, 2019).

———. *Poland 1939: The Outbreak of World War II* (New York, 2020).

Müller, Filip. *Eyewitness Auschwitz: Three Years in the Gas Chambers* (New York, 1979).

Nahlik, Stanisław. *Przesiane przez pamięć.* Vol. 2 (Kraków, 2002).

Noakes, J., and G. Pridham, eds. *Nazism 1919–1945.* Vol. 2, *State, Economy and Society 1933–39* (Exeter, UK, 1984).

———. *Nazism 1919–1945.* Vol. 3, *Foreign Policy, War and Racial Extermination* (Exeter, UK, 1988).

Obremski, Tadeusz. *Wśród zatrutych nozy: Zapiski z getta i okupowanej Warszawy* (Warsaw, 2017).

Ogilvie, Sarah A., and Scott Miller. *Refuge Denied: The* St. Louis *Passengers and the Holocaust* (London, 2006).

Paldiel, Mordechai. *Diplomat Heroes of the Holocaust* (Jersey City, NJ, 2007).

Pankiewicz, Tadeusz. *The Kraków Ghetto Pharmacy* (Kraków, 2013).

Paulsson, Gunnar. *Secret City: The Hidden Jews of Warsaw, 1940–1945* (New Haven, CT, 2002).

Perechodnik, Calel. *Am I a Murderer? Testament of a Jewish Ghetto Policeman* (Boulder, CO, 1996).

Pivnik, Sam. *Survivor: Auschwitz, the Death March and My Fight for Freedom* (London, 2012).

Presser, Jacob. *Ashes in the Wind: The Destruction of Dutch Jewry* (London, 2010).

Przemsza-Zieliński, Jan, ed. *Żydzi w Zagłębiu* (Sosnowiec, Poland, 1993).

Rees, Laurence. *The Holocaust: A New History* (London, 2017).

Reilly, Jo, et al., eds. *Belsen in History and Memory* (London, 1997).

Reitlinger, Gerald. *The Final Solution: The Attempt to Exterminate the Jews of Europe, 1939–1945* (London, 1953).

Rhodes, Richard. *Masters of Death* (Oxford, 2002).

Ronen, Avihu. "The Cable That Vanished." *Yad Vashem Studies* 41, no. 2 (2013).

Rossino, Alexander B. *Hitler Strikes Poland: Blitzkrieg, Ideology and Atrocity* (Lawrence, KS, 2003).

Schönker, Henryk. *Dotknięcie anioła* (Warsaw, 2011).

Shatyn, Bruno. *A Private War: Surviving in Poland on False Papers, 1941–1945* (Detroit, MI, 1985).

Shephard, Ben. *After Daybreak: The Liberation of Belsen, 1945* (London, 2005).

Shulman, Abraham. *The Case of the Hotel Polski* (New York, 1982).

Skipwith, Sofka. *Sofka: The Autobiography of a Princess* (London, 1968).

Sloan, Jacob, ed. *Notes from the Warsaw Ghetto: The Journal of Emmanuel Ringelblum* (New York, 2006).

Snyder, Timothy. *Black Earth: The Holocaust as Warning and History* (London, 2015).

Stein, A., ed. *Pinkes Bendin* (Tel Aviv, 1959).

Steinbacher, Sybille. *Auschwitz: A History* (London, 2005).

Sterling, Eric J., ed. *Life in the Ghettos During the Holocaust* (Syracuse, NY, 2005).

Sternbuch, Gutta, and David Kranzler. *Gutta: Memories of a Vanished World* (Jerusalem, 2005).

Stola, Dariusz. "Early News of the Holocaust from Poland." *Holocaust and Genocide Studies* 11, no. 1 (Spring 1997).

Stone, Dan. *The Liberation of the Camps: The End of the Holocaust and Its Aftermath* (New Haven, CT, and London, 2015).

Sword, Keith, ed. *The Soviet Takeover of the Polish Eastern Provinces, 1939–41* (Basingstoke, UK, 1991).

Szpilman, Władysław. *The Pianist* (London, 2002).

Tarulis, Albert N. *Soviet Policy Toward the Baltic States: 1918–1940* (Notre Dame, IN, 1959).

Taylor, Frederick, ed. *The Goebbels Diaries 1939–41* (London, 1982).

Tokayer, Marvin, and Mary Swartz. *The Fugu Plan* (London, 1979).

Ullrich, Volker. *Hitler: Downfall 1939–45* (London, 2020).

Urynowicz, Marcin. *Adam Czerniaków, Prezydent Getta Warszawskiego* (Warsaw, 2009).

Venclauskas, Linas, ed. *Casablanca of the North: Refugees and Rescuers in Kaunas 1939–1940* (Kaunas, Lithuania, 2017).

Vogel, Loden. *Tagebuch aus einem Lager* (Göttingen, Germany, 2002).

Wachsmann, Nikolaus. *KL: A History of the Nazi Concentration Camps* (London, 2015).

Wasserstein, Bernard. *The Ambiguity of Virtue: Gertrude van Tijn and the Fate of the Dutch Jews* (London, 2014).

Wenck, Alexandra-Eileen. "Das 'Sonderlager' im Konzentrationslager Bergen-Belsen." *Dachauer Hefte* 14 (1998).

———. *Zwischen Menschenhandel und "Endlösung": Das Konzentrationslager Bergen-Belsen* (Paderborn, Germany, 2000).

Winstone, Martin. *The Dark Heart of Hitler's Europe: Nazi Rule in Poland Under the General Government* (London, 2015).

Wood, E. Thomas, and Stanisław M. Jankowski. *Karski: How One Man Tried to Stop the Holocaust* (New York, 1994).

Wyman, David. *The Abandonment of the Jews: America and the Holocaust, 1941–1945* (New York, 1984).

Zariz, Ruth. "Attempts at Rescue and Revolt—Attitude of Members of the Dror Youth Movement in Bedzin to Foreign Passports as Means of Rescue." *Yad Vashem Studies* 20 (1990).

Zariz, Ruth, et al. *From Bergen Belsen to Freedom* (Jerusalem, 1986).

Zimmerman, Joshua D. *The Polish Underground and the Jews, 1939–1945* (Cambridge, 2015).

PICTURE CREDITS

Évian Conference	Narodowe Archiwum Cyfrowe, Warsaw
St. Louis in Havana harbor	Bettmann/Getty Images
Jews queuing in Kaunas	Yad Vashem
Chiune Sugihara	Sugihara House Museum, Kaunas
Jan Zwartendijk	Sugihara House Museum, Kaunas
Sugihara visa	Sugihara House Museum, Kaunas
Tadeusz Romer	Narodowe Archiwum Cyfrowe, Warsaw
Bern embassy building	Narodowe Archiwum Cyfrowe, Warsaw
Ładoś with Second Rifle Division	Narodowe Archiwum Cyfrowe, Warsaw
Pierre Mendès-France portrait	Public Domain
Jean Lemberg card	Courtesy of Joan Mendès France
Weingort family	Courtesy of the Weingort family
Dr. Heinrich Rothmund	Public Domain
Aleksander Ładoś	Public Domain
Stefan Ryniewicz	Swiss Federal Archive
Konstanty Rokicki	Public Domain
Juliusz Kühl	Public Domain
Abraham Silberschein	Public Domain
Chaim Eiss	Public Domain
Ładoś passport	United States Holocaust Memorial Museum, courtesy of Zvi Rosenwein
Promesa	Yad Vashem Archive, Dr. Abraham Silberschein collection, file no. M20/174

Warsaw ghetto street scene	Yad Vashem Archive
Szmul Zygielbojm	United States Holocaust Memorial Museum, courtesy of Aveda Ayalon
Simcha Korngold	Ghetto Fighters' House Museum, Israel/Archive
Deportation	Ullstein Bild/The Granger Collection/Imagno/AKG Images
Będzin families	United States Holocaust Memorial Museum, courtesy of Siegmund Pluznik
Vittel camp	Public Domain
Yitzhak Katzenelson and son	United States Holocaust Memorial Museum, courtesy of Anne Wolfe
Belsen	United States Holocaust Memorial Museum, courtesy of National Archives and Records Administration, College Park
Westerbork	Public Domain
Tittmoning camp	United States Holocaust Memorial Museum, courtesy of Greg & Helen Hiestand
Group in Tittmoning	United States Holocaust Memorial Museum, courtesy of Zvi Rosenwein
Heinz Lichtenstern	Courtesy of Heidi Fishman (Fishman, K. Heidi, *Tutti's Promise: A novel based on a family's true story of courage and hope during the Holocaust*, MB Publishing, 2017.)
"Ausgeschieden"	Courtesy of Heidi Fishman (Fishman, K. Heidi, *Tutti's Promise: A novel based on a family's true story of courage and hope during the Holocaust*, MB Publishing, 2017.)
Frumka Płotnicka	Ghetto Fighters' House Museum, Israel/Archive
Nathan Eck	Ghetto Fighters' House Museum, Israel/Archive
Liberation of Belsen	AKG Images
Evacuation train	United States Holocaust Memorial Museum, courtesy of Mark Nusbaum

NOTES

PROLOGUE: "HE WHO SAVES ONE LIFE . . ."

1. Original text is reproduced in H. G. Adler, *Theresienstadt 1941–1945* (Cambridge, 2017), p. 245.

2. Original notice is from the "Mitteilungen der Jüdischen Selbstverwaltung Theresienstadt," September 24, 1944, Jewish Museum in Prague, https://collections.jewishmuseum.cz/index.php/Detail/Object/Show/object_id/133781. Additional information from Philipp Manes, *As If It Were Life: A WWII Diary from the Theresienstadt Ghetto* (New York, 2009), p. 233.

3. Account given at K. Heidi Fishman, "History of the Lichtenstern Family," Passports for Life, http://passportsforlife.pl/historie/.

4. Adler, op. cit., p. 247; Manes, op. cit., p. 235.

5. Adler, op. cit., p. 243.

6. Author correspondence with Heidi Fishman, granddaughter of Heinz Lichtenstern.

7. Alfred Gottwald and Diana Schulle, *Die "Judendeportationen" aus dem Deutschen Reich 1941–1945* (Stuttgart, 2005), p. 435.

8. Jakub Kumoch et al., *The Ładoś List* (Warsaw, 2020), p. 47.

CHAPTER 1: EMPTY SYMPATHIES

1. Quoted in Henry Feingold, *The Politics of Rescue* (New Brunswick, NJ, 1970), p. 27; Paul R. Bartrop, *The Evian Conference of 1938 and the Jewish Refugee Crisis* (Basingstoke, UK, 2018), p. 23.

2. *Proceedings of the Intergovernmental Committee, Evian, July 6th to 15th, 1938: Verbatim Record of the Plenary Meetings of the Committee, Resolutions, and Reports* (Chambéry, France, 1938), pp. 12–13.

3. Ibid., pp. 19, 22, 34–35.

4. Ibid., pp. 27–28, 30–31.

5. Ibid., pp. 37–38.

6. Ibid., p. 32.

7. Bartrop, op. cit., pp. 96–97; The National Archives, London (hereafter "TNA"), CAB 23/94/6, Minutes of Cabinet Meeting, July 20, 1938, p. 7.

8. Bartrop, op. cit., p. 49; *Proceedings*, op. cit., p. 42.

9. *Proceedings*, op. cit., p. 42.

10. Menu from July 11, 1938, courtesy of the Hotel Royal, Évian; quoted in Bartrop, op. cit., p. 97.

11. Golda Meir, *My Life* (New York, 1975), pp. 158–159.

12. *Time*, July 18, 1938, p. 16; William Shirer, entry for July 7, 1938, in *Berlin Diary 1934–1941*, illustrated ed. (London, 1997), p. 67.

13. *Völkischer Beobachter*, July 13, 1938; Adolf Hitler, "Speech on 12th September, 1938," in Max Domarus, *Hitler: Reden und Proklamationen, 1932–1945*, vol. 1, part 2 (Wiesbaden, Germany, 1973), p. 899.

14. Quoted in Giles MacDonogh, *1938: Hitler's Gamble* (New York, 2009), p. 137; Helen Fry, *Spymaster: The Man Who Saved MI6* (London, 2021), pp. 110–112, 114.

15. Helen Fry, op. cit., pp. 116, 121, 124.

16. Arieh Tartakower and Kurt R. Grossman, *The Jewish Refugee* (New York, 1944), p. 36; Martin Gilbert, *The Holocaust* (London, 1986), p. 65.

17. Quoted in *Documents on German Foreign Policy, 1918–1945* (hereafter "DGFP"), series D, vol. 5, doc. 642 (Washington, DC, 1953), p. 896; see, for instance, "1944 Swiss Refugee ID," September 13, 2019, *Our Passports*, http://our passports.com/1944-swiss-refugee-id/; DGFP, series D, vol. 5, doc. 642, p. 897; see also Salomon Adler-Rudel, "The Evian Conference on the Refugee Question," *Leo Baeck Institute Yearbook* 13, no. 1 (January 1968), p. 250.

18. Peter Longerich, *Holocaust* (Oxford, 2010), pp. 109–110; quoted in Gilbert, op. cit., p. 68.

19. Jonathan Kirsch, *The Short, Strange Life of Herschel Grynszpan* (New York, 2014), pp. 108–110.

20. Entry for November 10, 1938, in *Die Tagebücher von Joseph Goebbels*, ed. Elke Fröhlich, part 1, vol. 6 (Munich, 1998), p. 180.

21. Quoted in Martin Gilbert, *Kristallnacht: Prelude to Destruction* (London, 2006), p. 29; Kim Wünschmann, *Before Auschwitz: Jewish Prisoners in the Prewar Concentration Camps* (Cambridge, MA, 2015), p. 168.

22. For more, see "Feng-Shan Ho," Righteous Among the Nations, Yad Vashem, www.yadvashem.org/righteous/stories/ho.html.

23. Eric Sanders, quoted in Helen Fry, op. cit., p. 118.

24. Eric Lucas, *The Sovereigns: A Jewish Family in the German Countryside* (Evanston, IL, 2001), pp. 146–147.

25. Sarah A. Ogilvie and Scott Miller, *Refuge Denied: The St. Louis Passengers and the Holocaust* (London, 2006), p. 19; testimony of Oscar Schwarz, Wiener Holocaust Library, London, p. 4, www.testifyingtothetruth.co.uk/viewer/meta data/104908/1/.

26. Gilbert, *Kristallnacht*, op. cit., pp. 214–215; Schwarz testimony, op. cit., pp. 4, 24.

27. Ogilvie and Miller, op. cit., p. 25.

28. See Miklós Zeidler, "Gyula Gömbös: An Outsider's Attempt at Radical Reform," and Andreas Kossert, "Founding Father of Modern Poland and Nationalist Antisemite: Roman Dmowski," in *In the Shadow of Hitler: Personalities of the Right in Central and Eastern Europe*, eds. Rebecca Haynes and Martyn Rady (London, 2011).

29. See the example of Eric Goldstaub in Gilbert, *Kristallnacht*, op. cit., pp. 161–162.

CHAPTER 2: THE BLOOD-SOAKED EARTH

1. Account of Hinda Turbin, held in the archive of the Jewish Historical Institute, Warsaw (hereafter ZIH), ref: 301/3301.

2. Account of Marian Bień, ZIH, ref: 301/1938.

3. Jochen Böhler, *Der Überfall: Deutschlands Krieg gegen Polen* (Frankfurt am Main, 2009), p. 200.

4. Bruno Shatyn, *A Private War: Surviving in Poland on False Papers, 1941–1945* (Detroit, MI, 1985), p. 121.

5. Ibid., p. 122.

6. Most sources cite a figure of five hundred to six hundred victims at Przemyśl, but Szymon Datner gives a figure of nine hundred killed at Przekopana alone. Szymon Datner, *55 dni Wehrmachtu w Polsce: zbrodnie dokonane na polskiej ludności cywilnej w okresie 1 IX–25 X 1939 r.* (Warsaw, 1967), p. 489; Böhler, *Überfall*, op. cit., p. 203.

7. See Jochen Böhler, *Auftakt zum Vernichtungskrieg: Die Wehrmacht in Polen 1939* (Frankfurt am Main, 2006), p. 213; Datner, op. cit., pp. 358–389.

8. Mary Berg, *The Diary of Mary Berg: Growing Up in the Warsaw Ghetto* (London, 2006), p. 10; testimony of Stanisław Sznapman in *Words to Outlive Us: Eyewitness Accounts from the Warsaw Ghetto*, ed. Michał Grynberg (London, 2003), p. 19.

9. Akira Kitade, *Visas of Life and the Epic Journey* (Tokyo, 2014), p. 96.

10. Martin Gilbert, *The Holocaust* (London, 1986), p. 93.

11. DGFP, series D, vol. 8, document 419, p. 489, Memorandum by State Secretary Weizsäcker, December 5, 1939; Christopher R. Browning, *Remembering Survival: Inside a Nazi Slave-Labor Camp* (New York, 2010), p. 27.

12. Eichmann quoted in Gilbert, *Holocaust*, op. cit., p. 94.

13. Alexander B. Rossino, *Hitler Strikes Poland: Blitzkrieg, Ideology and Atrocity* (Lawrence, KS, 2003), p. 234; Donna Gawell, ed., *Poland Under Nazi Rule 1939–1941: A Report Written by Thaddeus H. Chylinski, Vice Consul at the US Consular Office in Warsaw, November 13, 1941* (London, 2019), pp. 22–23; *Nowy Kurier Warszawski*, no. 25 (November 8, 1939), p. 3.

14. Testimony of Wacław Klemensiewicz, Archive of the Institute of National Remembrance, Warsaw (hereafter IPN), ref: G.K. 196/62, available at www.chron iclesofterror.pl; Testimony of Stanisław Krupka, IPN, ref: G.K. 196/62.

15. Richard C. Lukas, *The Forgotten Holocaust: The Poles Under German Occupation, 1939–1944* (New York, 1986), p. 8.

16. Martin Winstone, *The Dark Heart of Hitler's Europe: Nazi Rule in Poland Under the General Government* (London, 2015), p. 58.

17. Maria Wardzyńska, *Był rok 1939: Operacja niemieckiej policji bezpieczeństwa w Polsce 'Intelligenzaktion'* (Warsaw, 2009), p. 74.

18. Christopher R. Browning, *The Origins of the Final Solution: The Evolution of Nazi Jewish Policy, 1939–1942* (London, 2005), p. 111; Gilbert, *Holocaust*, op. cit., p. 96.

19. Berg, op. cit., p. 16.

20. Roger Moorhouse, *Poland 1939: The Outbreak of World War II* (New York, 2020), p. 164.

21. Jan T. Gross, *Revolution from Abroad: The Soviet Conquest of Poland's Western Ukraine and Western Byelorussia* (Princeton, NJ, and Oxford, 2002), p. 37.

22. Author interview with Artur Rynkiewicz, London, September 2011.

23. Zbigniew Siemaszko, "The Mass Deportations of the Polish Population to the USSR, 1940–1941," in *The Soviet Takeover of the Polish Eastern Provinces, 1939–41*, ed. Keith Sword (Basingstoke, UK, 1991), p. 224.

24. Nikita Khrushchev, *Khrushchev Remembers* (Boston, 1970), p. 141; quoted in Gross, op, cit., p. 206.

25. Stanley Seidner, "Reflections from Rumania and Beyond: Marshal Śmigły-Rydz in Exile," *Polish Review* 22, no. 2 (1977), p. 45; Julian Bussgang, "Haunting Memories," in Carole Garbuny Vogel (ed.), *We Shall Not Forget: Memories of the Holocaust* (Lexington, MA, 1994), p. 238.

26. For the full story, see Moorhouse, op. cit., pp. 253–235.

27. Lukas, op. cit., p. 43.

28. Jan Karski, *Story of a Secret State: My Report to the World* (London, 2011), pp. 178–179.

29. Gross, op. cit., pp. 139, 148.

30. Józef Garliński, *Poland in the Second World War* (Basingstoke, UK, 1985), pp. 50–51; Karski, op. cit., pp. 118–135.

31. Original text is cited in David Engel, "An Early Account of Polish Jewry Under Nazi and Soviet Occupation Presented to the Polish Government-in-Exile, February 1940," *Jewish Social Studies* 45, no. 1 (1983), pp. 1–16.

32. David Engel, *In the Shadow of Auschwitz: The Polish Government-in-Exile and the Jews, 1939–1942* (London, 1987), p. 52.

33. Aleksander Ładoś, *Polska w latach 1918–1939: Relacje, Wspomnienia*, vol. 1 (unpublished), Archiwum Wojskowe Biuro Historyczne (Archives of the Military Historical Bureau), inv. no. IX.1.2.18, p. 248.

34. Zbigniew Rene, "Trzy życiorysy," *Palestra* 40/11–12 (467–468), (1996), pp. 134–135.

35. Karski, op. cit., p. 130.

36. Danuta Drywa, *Sieć dyplomatyczna rządu RP na uchodźstwie w akcji ratowniczej na rzecz polsko-żydowskich uchodźców w latach II wojny światowej. Ze szczególnym uwzględnieniem Poselstwa RP w Bernie* (unpublished), p. 55.

37. Stanisław Nahlik, *Przesiane przez pamięć*, vol. 2 (Kraków, 2002), pp. 240–242.

38. Willi Gautschi, *General Henri Guisan: Commander-in-Chief of the Swiss Army in World War II* (New York, 2003), p. 144.

39. DGFP, series D, vol. 9, document 189, pp. 270–271, Memorandum by Foreign Minister Ribbentrop, May 2, 1940.

40. Drywa, op. cit., p. 58.

41. Nahlik, op. cit., p. 231.

42. Ładoś, vol. 2, op. cit., p. 33.

43. Ładoś, vol. 1, pp. 44–45; Ładoś, vol. 2, op. cit., p. 32.

CHAPTER 3: "IN A SHORT TIME, IT WILL BE TOO LATE"

1. Alfred Erich Senn, *Lithuania 1940: Revolution from Above* (New York, 2007), p. 20.

2. Jane Degras, ed., *Soviet Documents on Foreign Policy*, vol. 3, *1933–1941* (Oxford, 1953), p. 455.

3. Albert N. Tarulis, *Soviet Policy Toward the Baltic States: 1918–1940* (Notre Dame, IN, 1959), p. 233; V. Stanley Vardys, "The Baltic States Under Stalin: The First Experiences, 1940–41," in *The Soviet Takeover of the Polish Eastern Provinces, 1939–41*, ed. Keith Sword (Basingstoke, UK, 1991), pp. 268–290.

4. Quoted in Hillel Levine, *In Search of Sugihara* (New York, 1996), p. 239. The five murdered were Deputy Prime Minister Kazys Bizauskas, Interior Minister Kazys Skučas, Justice Minister Antanas Tamošaitis, Trade Minister Jonas Masiliūnas, and Education Minister Kazimieras Jokantas.

5. Edward Kossoy, "Ziarno i plewy (przyczynek do działalności Poselstwa RP w Bernie w latach II wojny światowej)," in *Zeszyty Historyczne*, vol. 114 (Paris, 1995), p. 90. For more on Sir Thomas Preston, see British Embassy Vilnius, "UK's Special Envoy for Post-Holocaust Issues Visited Lithuania," Gov.uk, October 18, 2019, www.gov.uk/government/news/uks-special-envoy-for-post-holocaust-issues-visited-lithuania.

6. Levine, op. cit., pp. 125, 132.

7. Ibid., pp. 193–194.

8. There are a number of accounts of the origin of the Sugihara operation, but that with Nathan Gutwirth is the most common, so it is cited here. See Marvin Tokayer and Mary Swartz, *The Fugu Plan* (London, 1979), pp. 20–31. A similar account is given by Alyza Lewin, "How My Grandmother Helped the 'Japanese Schindler' Save Thousands of European Jews," *Haaretz*, April 26, 2016, www .haaretz.com/jewish/how-my-grandmother-helped-save-thousands-of-european -jews-1.5441445. Levine, op. cit., p. 161.

9. Levine, op. cit., p. 161.

10. Ilya Altman, "The Issuance of Visas to War Refugees by Chiune Sugihara as Reflected in the Documents of Russian Archives," in *Casablanca of the North: Refugees and Rescuers in Kaunas 1939–1940*, ed. Linas Venclauskas (Kaunas, Lithuania, 2017), p. 136.

11. Mordechai Paldiel, *Diplomat Heroes of the Holocaust* (Jersey City, NJ, 2007), p. 43; Lucille Szepsenwol-Camhi, quoted in Levine, op. cit., p. 255.

12. The list of recipients of Sugihara visas is at www.sugihara-museum.jp /shared/pdf/about/issued_list.pdf; Tokayer and Swartz, op. cit., p. 80.

13. Tadeusz Romer, "The Problem of the Polish Refugees Coming to the Far East," January 15, 1941, Hoover Institute Archive, ref: 800/42/0/536-829; Samuil Manski, *With God's Help* (Madison, WI, 1990), p. 45.

14. Akira Kitade, *Visas of Life and the Epic Journey* (Tokyo, 2014), p. 106.

15. Dr. Ewa Pałasz-Rutkowska, "Polish-Japanese Secret Cooperation During World War II: Sugihara Chiune and Polish Intelligence" (Asiatic Society of Japan lecture, March 1995).

16. Chaim Kaplan, quoted in David Cesarani, *Final Solution: The Fate of the Jews, 1933–1949* (New York, 2016), pp. 263–264.

17. Jan Przemsza-Zieliński, ed., *Żydzi w Zagłębiu* (Sosnowiec, Poland, 1993), pp. 89–91.

18. Jacob Sloan, ed., *Notes from the Warsaw Ghetto: The Journal of Emmanuel Ringelblum* (New York, 2006), p. 32; Martin Gilbert, *The Holocaust* (London, 1986), pp. 148–149.

19. Mary Fulbrook, *A Small Town Near Auschwitz: Ordinary Nazis and the Holocaust* (Oxford, 2013), pp. 143–144.

20. Sam Pivnik, *Survivor: Auschwitz, the Death March and My Fight for Freedom* (London, 2012), p. 50.

21. Jewish Historical Institute, Warsaw (hereafter ZIH), Representation of the Population of the City of Będzin (Bendsburg), various testimonies.

22. For more on the Pabst Plan, see Niels Gutschow and Barbara Klain, *Vernichtung und Utopie. Stadtplanung Warschau 1939–1945* (Hamburg, 1994).

23. Magnus Brechtken, *"Madagaskar für die Juden": Antisemitische Idee und politische Praxis 1885–1945* (Oldenburg, Germany, 1998), p. 121.

24. Deborah Dwork and Robert Jan van Pelt, *Flight from the Reich: Refugee Jews, 1933–1946* (New York, 2009), p. 103.

25. Peter Longerich, *Heinrich Himmler* (Oxford, 2012), pp. 508–509.

26. Peter Longerich, *Goebbels: A Biography* (London, 2015), p. 465; Volker Ullrich, *Hitler: Downfall 1939–45* (London, 2020), p. 251; Gilbert, *Holocaust*, op. cit., p. 130.

27. Brechtken, op. cit., p. 237; Victor Klemperer, *I Shall Bear Witness: The Diaries of Victor Klemperer, 1933–41* (London, 1998), p. 332; Raul Hilberg, ed., *The Warsaw Diary of Adam Czerniaków* (Chicago, 1979), p. 169.

28. Christopher R. Browning, *The Origins of the Final Solution: The Evolution of Nazi Jewish Policy, 1939–1942* (London, 2005), p. 89.

29. Helena Gutman-Staszewska, quoted in *Words to Outlive Us: Eyewitness Accounts from the Warsaw Ghetto*, ed. Michał Grynberg (London, 2003), p. 26; Gilbert, *Holocaust*, op. cit., pp. 127–129.

30. Lucy Dawidowicz, *The War Against the Jews 1933–1945* (London, 1987), pp. 254–255.

31. Chaim Kaplan, quoted in ibid., p. 257; Mary Berg, *The Diary of Mary Berg: Growing Up in the Warsaw Ghetto* (London, 2006), pp. 27–29; Diane Plotkin, "Smuggling in the Ghettos," in *Life in the Ghettos During the Holocaust*, ed. Eric J. Sterling (Syracuse, NY, 2005), p. 102.

32. Yehuda Elberg, quoted in Dawidowicz, op. cit., p. 262.

33. Władysław Szpilman, *The Pianist* (London, 2002), p. 68.

34. See Amos Goldberg, "A Fool or a Prophet: Rubinstein the Warsaw Ghetto Jester" (2019 J. B. and Maurice C. Shapiro Annual Lecture at the United States Holocaust Memorial Museum, March 13, 2019), www.academia.edu/38809091/A _Fool_or_a_Prophet_Rubinstein_the_Warsaw_Ghetto_Jester; Samuel Puterman in Grynberg, op. cit., p. 29.

35. Editorial commentary in Grynberg, op. cit., pp. 97–104.

36. Szpilman, op. cit., pp. 63–64.

37. Dawidowicz, op. cit., p. 259.

38. Berg, op. cit., p. 49.

39. Sloan, op. cit., p. 330; Mojżesz Passenstein, quoted in *The Ringelblum Archive: Annihilation—Day by Day*, ed. Marta Markowska (Warsaw, 2008), pp. 69–70.

40. Calel Perechodnik, *Am I a Murderer? Testament of a Jewish Ghetto Policeman* (Boulder, CO, 1996), pp. 45, 191.

41. Norman Davies, *Rising '44: The Battle for Warsaw* (London, 2003), p. 98; Sloan, op. cit., p. 115.

42. Sloan, op. cit., p. 114.

43. J. Noakes and G. Pridham, eds., *Nazism 1919–1945*, vol. 2, *State, Economy and Society 1933–39* (Exeter, UK, 1984), p. 539.

44. Roger Moorhouse, *Poland 1939: The Outbreak of World War II* (New York, 2020), p. 137; Regulation of the Warsaw District, November 22, 1939, cited in Feliks Celnikier, *Żyd, czyli kto? Pojęcie Żyda w doktrynie i hitlerowskich poczynaniach prawodawczych. Studium absurdu i mistyfikacji* (Warsaw, 2014), p. 108; cited in Amos Elon, *The Pity of It All: A Portrait of the German-Jewish Epoch, 1743–1933* (London, 2004), p. 224; Himmler to Gottlob Berger, July 28, 1942, cited in J. Noakes and

G. Pridham, eds., *Nazism 1919–1945*, vol. 3, *Foreign Policy, War and Racial Extermination* (Exeter, UK, 1988), p. 1160.

45. Sebastian Piątkowski, "'Aryan Papers': On the Help Provided by Poles in Legalising False Identities for Jews in the Territory of the General Governorate for the Occupied Polish Regions," *Polish-Jewish Studies* 1 (2020), p. 440.

46. "Verordnung über die Deutsche Volksliste und die deutsche Staatsangehörigkeit in den eingegliederten Ostgebieten," *Reichsgesetzblatt*, part 1 (1941), pp. 118–120; Karski Report, February 1940, in *Confronting the Holocaust: The Polish Government-in-Exile's Policy Concerning Jews 1939–1945*, ed. Piotr Długołęcki (Warsaw, 2022), doc. 27, p. 40.

47. David Engel, *In the Shadow of Auschwitz: The Polish Government-in-Exile and the Jews, 1939–1942* (London, 1987), p. 160; Sloan, op. cit., p. 39n; Stanisław Sznapman, quoted in Grynberg, op. cit., p. 19.

48. Joshua D. Zimmerman, *The Polish Underground and the Jews, 1939–1945* (Cambridge, 2015), p. 79.

49. Engel, op. cit., p. 65.

50. Stańczyk declaration, quoted in ibid., p. 80.

51. Testimony of Jan Kobryner, in Aleksander Blum et al., *Zwyciężeni, ale nie pokonani* (Warsaw, 2000), p. 38.

52. Stanisław Nahlik, *Przesiane przez pamięć*, vol. 2 (Kraków, 2002), pp. 249–250.

53. Leszek Puchała, "Zawsze wierny," *Tygodnik Sanocki* no. 26, 764 (June 30, 2006), p. 6; Joseph Friedenson and David Kranzler, *Heroine of Rescue* (New York, 1984), p. 64; Aleksander Ładoś, *Polska w latach 1918–1939. Relacje, Wspomnienia*, vol. 3 (unpublished), Wojskowe Biuro Historyczne, inv. no. IX.1.2.20, p. 96.

54. Sebastian Ładoś, *Zanim Bóg odwróci wzrok* (Wrocław, Poland, 2019), p. 323; communication between Kühl and Jewish aid agencies, 1940, in Wiener Library Archive, London, Kühl papers, ref. 615/2/1.

55. Varian Fry, *Assignment Rescue: An Autobiography* (New York, 1968), p. 39.

56. Telegram from Kunicki, Istanbul, to the Ministry of Foreign Affairs, No. 41, sent October 26, 1940, Hoover Institution Archive, Polish Ministry of Foreign Affairs Collection, ref. no. 800/42/0/-/518, folder 5.

57. Ellen Meth, *Kaleidoscope* (private publication, 1998), p. 146–147; Eldad Beck, "The Angel from Istanbul," *Israel Hayom*, December 11, 2020, www.israelhayom.com/2020/12/11/the-angel-from-istanbul/.

58. Romer to Polish Ministry of Foreign Affairs, London, October 10, 1940, Hoover Institution Archive, ref: 800/42/0/-/518, folder 14.

59. Romer report on "The Problem of the Polish Refugees Coming to the Far East," Tokyo, January 18, 1941, Hoover Institution Archive, ref: 800/42/0/-/526.

60. Oskar Schenker, quoted in Pałasz-Rutkowska, "The Polish Ambassador Tadeusz Romer: A Rescuer of Refugees in Tokyo," in Venclauskas, op. cit., p. 154.

61. Sara Kadosh, *We Think of You as an Angel* (Jerusalem, 2019), p. 114; Stanisław Różycki, quoted in Markowska, op. cit., p. 82.

62. Kadosh, op. cit., p. 117.

63. Gilbert, *Holocaust*, op. cit., p. 131.

64. Kadosh, op. cit., p. 121.

65. Protocol of Police Interview with Saul Weingort, dated May 11, 1943, Montreux, located at Swiss Federal Archive, Bern E 4320 [B] 1987/187, pp. 3–4.

66. Kadosh, op. cit., p. 122; Hügli to Leo Weingort, dated May 9, 1941, ZIH, sig: Ring.II/312.

CHAPTER 4: A CRIME WITHOUT A NAME

1. Sebastian Ładoś, *Zanim Bóg odwróci wzrok* (Wrocław, Poland, 2019), pp. 336–337.

2. John Colville, *The Fringes of Power: Downing Street Diaries*, vol. 1, *1939–October 1941* (London, 1985), p. 481; Frederick Taylor, ed., *The Goebbels Diaries 1939–41* (London, 1982), pp. 424–425; quoted in Constantine Pleshakov, *Stalin's Folly: The Secret History of the German Invasion of Russia, June 1941* (London, 2005), p. 6.

3. Władysław Szpilman, *The Pianist* (London, 2002), p. 62; Mary Berg, *The Diary of Mary Berg: Growing Up in the Warsaw Ghetto* (London, 2006), p. 67; Christopher R. Browning, *The Origins of the Final Solution: The Evolution of Nazi Jewish Policy, 1939–1942* (London, 2005), pp. 253–254.

4. Szymon Datner cited by Martin Gilbert, *The Holocaust* (London, 1986), pp. 160–161; David Engel, *In the Shadow of Auschwitz: The Polish Government-in-Exile and the Jews, 1939–1942* (London, 1987), p. 173.

5. Diary entry of Stanisław Różycki, quoted in *The Ringelblum Archive: Annihilation—Day by Day*, ed. Marta Markowska (Warsaw, 2008), p. 84.

6. Richard Breitman, *Hitler's Shadow: Nazi War Criminals, U.S. Intelligence, and the Cold War* (Washington, DC, 2011), p. 75.

7. John-Paul Himka, "The Lviv Pogrom of 1941: The Germans, Ukrainian Nationalists, and the Carnival Crowd," *Canadian Slavonic Papers* 53, nos. 2–4 (2011), pp. 210–211.

8. Ibid., pp. 213, 217–218, 220–221; Richard Breitman, "Himmler and the 'Terrible Secret' Among the Executioners," *Journal of Contemporary History* 26, no. 3 (1991), pp. 431–451.

9. Quoted in Sara Kadosh, *We Think of You as an Angel* (Jerusalem, 2019), pp. 125–126.

10. Witold Babiński, *Przyczynki historyczne do okresu 1939–1945* (London, 1967), p. 583, Sosnkowski to Sikorski, June 22, 1941.

11. Peter Longerich, *Holocaust* (Oxford, 2010), p. 181; Andreas Hillgruber, "War in the East and the Extermination of the Jews," in *The Nazi Holocaust*, ed. Michael Marrus, part 3, vol. 1 (Westport, CT, 1989), pp. 94–95.

12. Longerich, *Holocaust*, op. cit., p. 200.

13. Richard Rhodes, *Masters of Death* (Oxford, 2002), pp. 129–130.

14. Quoted in ibid., p. 152; quoted in Browning, *Origins*, op. cit., p. 353.

15. Rudolf Hoess, *Commandant of Auschwitz* (London, 2000), p. 185.

16. K. Smoleń, *Auschwitz-Birkenau State Museum in Oświęcim* (Oświęcim, Poland, 2014), p. 23; Sybille Steinbacher, *Auschwitz: A History* (London, 2005), p. 94.

17. Alfred Gottwaldt and Diana Schulle, *Die "Judendeportationen" aus dem Deutschen Reich 1941–1945* (Stuttgart, 2005), pp. 68–83.

18. Lucjan Dobroszycki, ed., *The Chronicle of the Łódź Ghetto, 1941–1944* (New Haven, CT, and London, 1984), pp. 83, 165; David Cesarani, *Final Solution: The Fate of the Jews, 1933–1949* (New York, 2016), p. 323.

19. Roger Moorhouse, *Berlin at War: Life and Death in Hitler's Capital, 1939–1945* (London, 2010), p. 169.

20. Ibid., pp. 163–164; Timothy Snyder, *Black Earth: The Holocaust as Warning and History* (London, 2015), p. 255.

21. Saul Friedländer, *The Years of Extermination: Nazi Germany and the Jews, 1939–1945* (London, 2007), p. 310.

22. Dobroszycki, op. cit., p. 124; Testimony of Michael Etkind, in Lyn Smith, *Forgotten Voices of the Holocaust* (London, 2006), p. 120.

23. Testimony of Szlamek Winer, in Markowska, op. cit., p. 137.

24. Ibid., pp. 137, 139, 142.

25. Text of the Wannsee Protocol, in Gideon Bosch et al., *Die Wannsee-Konferenz und der Völkermord an den europäischen Juden* (Berlin, 2006), pp. 115–119.

26. Browning, *Origins*, op. cit., p. 421.

27. Dobroszycki, op. cit., pp. 141, 145.

28. Ibid., pp. 160, 167.

29. Dariusz Stola, "Early News of the Holocaust from Poland," *Holocaust and Genocide Studies* 11, no. 1 (Spring 1997), p. 4.; cited in Joshua D. Zimmerman, *The Polish Underground and the Jews, 1939–1945* (Cambridge, 2015), p. 98.

30. Zimmerman, op. cit., p. 99; David Kelly to Frank Roberts, November 19, 1941, TNA, ref: FO371/26515; Walter Laqueur, "Hitler's Holocaust: Who Knew What, When and How?," in *The Nazi Holocaust*, ed. Michael R. Marrus, part 8, vol. 1 (Westport, CT, 1989), p. 70.

31. Cited in Gunnar Paulsson, *Secret City: The Hidden Jews of Warsaw, 1940–1945* (New Haven, CT, 2002), p. 67; Richard C. Lukas, *Forgotten Holocaust: The Poles Under German Occupation 1939–1944* (New York, 1986), p. 330.

32. For details, see "Names and Numbers of Righteous Among the Nations—per Country and Ethnic Origin, as of January 1, 2022," Yad Vashem, www.yadvashem.org/righteous/statistics.html.

33. Zimmerman, op. cit., pp. 81, 100.

34. Cited in Richard Breitman, *Official Secrets: What the Nazis Planned, What the British and Americans Knew* (New York, 1998), p. 93.

35. Cited in Zimmerman, op. cit., p. 115.

36. Gutta Sternbuch and David Kranzler, *Gutta: Memories of a Vanished World* (Jerusalem, 2005), pp. 67, 73.

37. Kadosh, op. cit., pp. 70, 87.

38. Ibid., p. 90.

39. Rechenschaftsbericht for 1941, dated April 30, 1942, in Wiener Library Archive, London, Kühl papers, ref: 615/5; Sternbuch and Kranzler, op. cit., p. 96.

40. Jakub Kumoch et al., *The Ładoś List* (Warsaw, 2020).

41. *Polskie Radio*, "Instytut Pileckiego odkryliśmy ślady najstarszego paszportu wydanego przez Grupę Ładosia, by ratować Żydów," February 8, 2021. It should be mentioned that the dating of the Goldberger passport is disputed.

42. Eric Roussel, *Pierre Mendès France* (Paris, 2007), pp. 139–140.

43. Luc Weibel, *Charles Rosselet (1893–1946); un homme de raison au "temps des passions"* (Geneva, 1997), p. 107.

44. Edward Kossoy, "Ziarno i plewy (przyczynek do działalności Poselstwa RP w Bernie w latach II wojny światowej)," in *Zeszyty Historyczne*, vol. 114 (Paris, 1995), p. 93.

45. Sternbuch and Kranzler, op. cit. p. 96.

46. Ibid., p. 97.

47. Peter Kamber, "Der Verrat von Vittel," *Basler Magazin*, no. 16, April 24, 1999, p. 7.

48. Kossoy, op. cit., p. 93; Hügli's Testimony to Swiss Police, 1943, Swiss Federal Archive, Hügli files, ref. E20001E#1000-1571#657#27. Also Kamber, op. cit; Sebastian Ładoś, op. cit., p. 330.

49. Letter from Rudolf Hügli to the Paraguayan Embassy, Berlin, October 12, 1941, in Wiener Library Archive, London, Kühl papers, ref. 615/2.

50. Hügli correspondence with Leo Weingort and Henryk Goldberger, October 12, 1941, in Wiener Library Archive, London, Kühl papers, ref. 615/2.

51. Kühl papers, op. cit., ref. 615/2.

52. Assorted correspondence, Kühl papers, op. cit., ref. 615/2.

53. Sternbuch and Kranzler, op. cit., p. 97; Kadosh, op. cit., p. 131; Kumoch et al., op. cit., p. 170.

54. Abraham Lewin, *A Cup of Tears: A Diary of the Warsaw Ghetto* (Oxford, 1988), p. 81.

55. Sternbuch and Kranzler, op. cit. p. 96; Jacob Sloan, ed., *Notes from the Warsaw Ghetto: The Journal of Emmanuel Ringelblum* (New York, 2006), p. 271; Nathan Eck, "The Rescue of Jews with the Aid of Passports and Citizenship Papers of Latin American States," *Yad Vashem Studies* 1 (Jerusalem, 1957), p. 135.

56. Eck, op. cit., p. 136; Sloan, op. cit., p. 267; Kadosh, op. cit., p. 137.

57. Sternbuch and Kranzler, op. cit., pp. 98–99.

58. Berg, op. cit., p. 134; Dobroszycki, op. cit., pp. 140, 194; Sloan, op. cit., p. 260.

59. Quoted in Kadosh, op. cit., p. 140.

CHAPTER 5: "THEY ARE DYING. THAT'S ALL."

1. Callum MacDonald, *The Killing of SS Obergruppenführer Reinhard Heydrich* (London, 1989), p. 172.

2. Quoted in Robert Gerwarth, *Hitler's Hangman: The Life of Heydrich* (London, 2011), p. 279.

3. MacDonald, op. cit., pp. 186–187.

4. Gerwarth, op. cit., p. 285.

5. Ibid., p. 286.

6. Entry of June 2, 1942, in *Die Tagebücher von Joseph Goebbels*, ed. Elke Fröhlich, part 2, vol. 4 (Munich, 1995); Alfred Gottwaldt and Diana Schulle, *Die "Judendeportationen" aus dem Deutschen Reich 1941–1945* (Stuttgart, 2005), p. 224.

7. Quoted in Peter Longerich, *Heinrich Himmler* (Oxford, 2012), pp. 573, 909n74; Gerwarth, op. cit., p. 286.

8. Raul Hilberg, ed., *The Warsaw Diary of Adam Czerniaków* (Chicago, 1979), p. 382.

9. Testimony of Józef Gitler-Barski (July 12, 1948, Warsaw), Chronicles of Terror, www.chroniclesofterror.pl/Content/1238/Gitler_Jozef_en.html; Mary Berg, *The Diary of Mary Berg: Growing Up in the Warsaw Ghetto* (London, 2006), p. 158.

10. Berg, op. cit., pp. 160–161.

11. Hilberg, op. cit., pp. 384–385.

12. Czerniaków's suicide note, from Nathan Eck Collection, Yad Vashem Archive, part 3, record group P. 22, file no. 28, item ID 10570389.

13. Gerald Reitlinger, *The Final Solution: The Attempt to Exterminate the Jews of Europe, 1939–1945* (London, 1953), p. 260; Marcin Urynowicz, *Adam Czerniaków, Prezydent Getta Warszawskiego* (Warsaw, 2009), p. 330.

14. Gutta Sternbuch and David Kranzler, *Gutta: Memories of a Vanished World* (Jerusalem, 2005), p. 102.

15. Władysław Szpilman, *The Pianist* (London, 2002), pp. 98–99.

16. David Cesarani, *Final Solution: The Fate of the Jews, 1933–1949* (New York, 2016), p. 507; Peter Longerich, *Holocaust* (Oxford, 2010), p. 339.

17. Sternbuch and Kranzler, op. cit., p. 100; Gunnar Paulsson, *Secret City: The Hidden Jews of Warsaw, 1940–1945* (New Haven, CT, 2002), p. 74.

18. Abraham Lewin, *A Cup of Tears: A Diary of the Warsaw Ghetto* (Oxford, 1988), pp. 143, 157; Marta Markowska, ed., *The Ringelblum Archive: Annihilation—Day by Day* (Warsaw, 2008), p. 189.

19. Szpilman, op. cit., pp. 101–102.

20. Jacob Sloan, ed., *Notes from the Warsaw Ghetto: The Journal of Emmanuel Ringelblum* (New York, 2006), pp. 309–310; Paulsson, op. cit., p. 75; Markowska, op. cit., pp. 187–188.

21. Szpilman, op. cit., p. 93; Lewin, op. cit., p. 270n158.

22. Tadeusz Pankiewicz, *The Kraków Ghetto Pharmacy* (Kraków, 2013), p. 110.

23. Ibid., p. 119.

24. See David M. Crowe, *Oskar Schindler: The Untold Account of His Life, Wartime Activities, and the True Story Behind the List* (Cambridge, MA, 2004).

25. Lucjan Dobroszycki, ed., *The Chronicle of the Łódź Ghetto, 1941–1944* (New Haven, CT, and London, 1984), p. 207; Alan Adelson, ed., *The Diary of Dawid Sierakowiak* (London, 1996), p. 215; Samuel D. Kassow, ed., *In Those Nightmarish Days: The Ghetto Reportage of Peretz Opoczynski and Josef Zelkowicz* (New Haven, CT, and London, 2015), pp. 215–217.

26. Rumkowski quoted in Kassow, op. cit., p. 218; Cesarani, op. cit., p. 570.

27. Etty Hillesum, *Etty: A Diary 1941–1943* (London, 1985), p. 253.

28. Cesarani, op. cit., p. 561; Etty Hillesum letter, quoted in Bernard Wasserstein, *The Ambiguity of Virtue: Gertrude van Tijn and the Fate of the Dutch Jews* (London, 2014), p. 191; Rudolf Hoess, *Commandant of Auschwitz* (London, 2000), p. 208.

29. Hillesum, *Etty*, op. cit., p. 252; Wasserstein, op. cit., p. 196.

30. Jakub Kumoch et al., *The Ładoś List* (Warsaw, 2020), p. 127. Additional material thanks to Louisa Clein.

31. Primo Levi, *The Drowned and the Saved* (London, 1988), pp. 1–2.

32. David Engel, *In the Shadow of Auschwitz: The Polish Government-in-Exile and the Jews, 1939–1942* (London, 1987), pp. 175–176.

33. Ibid., p. 176; quoted in Dariusz Stola, "Early News of the Holocaust from Poland," *Holocaust and Genocide Studies* 11, no. 1 (Spring 1997), p. 8.

34. Christopher R. Browning, "A Final Hitler Decision for the 'Final Solution'? The Riegner Telegram Reconsidered," *Holocaust and Genocide Studies* 10, no. 1 (Spring 1996), pp. 3–4, 8.

35. Richard Breitman, *Official Secrets: What the Nazis Planned, What the British and Americans Knew* (New York, 1998), pp. 139, 142.

36. Stanisław Nahlik, *Przesiane przez pamięć*, vol. 2 (Kraków, 2002), p. 202; David Kranzler, *Thy Brother's Blood: The Orthodox Jewish Response to the Holocaust* (New York, 1987), pp. 202–203.

37. Joseph Friedenson and David Kranzler, *Heroine of Rescue* (New York, 1984), pp. 87–88; Breitman, op. cit., p. 142.

38. Zofia Kossak-Szczucka, quoted in Joshua D. Zimmerman, *The Polish Underground and the Jews, 1939–1945* (Cambridge, 2015), pp. 175–176.

39. This was noted in Calel Perechodnik, *Am I a Murderer? Testament of a Jewish Ghetto Policeman* (Boulder, CO, 1996), pp. 99–100.

40. Halik Kochański, *The Eagle Unbowed: Poland and the Poles in the Second World War* (London, 2012), p. 320; Richard C. Lukas, *The Forgotten Holocaust: The Poles Under German Occupation, 1939–1944* (New York, 1986), p. 148; Paulsson, op. cit., p. 103.

41. Testimony of Jan Karski recorded for Claude Lanzmann's *Shoah* (1985), transcript of interview held at the US Holocaust Memorial Museum, Washington, DC, p. 27, https://collections.ushmm.org/film_findingaids/RG-60.5006_01_trs _en.pdf.

42. Jan Karski, *Story of a Secret State: My Report to the World* (London, 2011), p. 385; Breitman, op. cit., p. 145.

43. "Annihilation Commission in Poland," *The Times*, November 24, 1942, p. 3.

44. Polish Ministry of Foreign Affairs, *The Mass Extermination of Jews in German Occupied Poland*, reprint ed. (London, 2019), pp. 16–24.

45. "11 Allies Condemn Nazi War of Jews," *New York Times*, December 18, 1942, p. 1.

46. Martin Gilbert, *The Holocaust* (London, 1986), p. 485.

47. Hillel Seidman, *The Warsaw Ghetto Diaries* (Southfield, MI, 1997), p. 133.

48. Sara Kadosh, *We Think of You as an Angel* (Jerusalem, 2019), p. 145.

49. Letter from Isaac Domb to Yitzchak Sternbuch, September 4, 1942, Wiener Library Archive, London, Kühl papers, ref. 615/2/1; explained in Friedenson and Kranzler, op. cit., pp. 91–92.

50. See, for instance, the example of Leon Blat: Nathan Eck Collection, Yad Vashem Archive, P.22, file no. 22, item ID 10572948; Kumoch et al., op. cit., pp. 14–15.

51. Seidman, op. cit., p. 133; Saul Weingort deposition, Swiss Police, May 11, 1943, p. 6, Swiss Federal Archive (hereafter SFA), ref. E4320B#1990-266#4140#89.

52. Elia Boczko deposition, Swiss Police, May 11, 1943, p. 2, SFA, ref. E4320B#1990-266#4140#78; Nathan Eck, "The Rescue of Jews with the Aid of Passports and Citizenship Papers of Latin American States," in *Yad Vashem Studies* 1 (Jerusalem, 1957), p. 145.

53. Eck, op. cit., p. 138; Agnieszka Haska, *Hotel Polski w Warszawie, 1943* (Warsaw, 2006), p. 52.

54. Arie Liwer, "That Which Will Not Be Forgotten," in *Pinkes Bendin*, ed. A. Stein (Tel Aviv, 1959), p. 353; Eck, op. cit., p. 145n32; Ruth Zariz, "Attempts at Rescue and Revolt—Attitude of Members of the Dror Youth Movement in Bedzin to Foreign Passports as Means of Rescue," *Yad Vashem Studies* 20 (1990), p. 220.

55. Kumoch et al., op. cit., pp. 68–69; Thomas Ammann and Stefan Aust, *Hitlers Menschenhändler* (Berlin, 2013), p. 93.

56. Seidman, op. cit., pp. 135–136.

57. Eck, op. cit., p. 145; Kadosh, op. cit., p. 237.

58. Władysław Szlengel, "The Passports," trans. Halina Birenbaum, displayed in the *Passports for Life* exhibition, Clapham Library, London, January 25, 2022. A shortened version is cited at the Ulma Family Museum, Markowa, Poland, https://muzeumulmow.pl/en/temporary-exhibition/passports/.

59. Valdis Lumans, *Himmler's Auxiliaries: The Volksdeutsche Mittelstelle and the German National Minorities of Europe* (London, 1993), p. 161; Ben Flanagan and Donald Bloxham, eds., *Remembering Belsen* (London, 2005), p. 133.

60. Max Paul Friedman, "The U.S. State Department and the Failure to Rescue: New Evidence on the Missed Opportunity at Bergen-Belsen," *Holocaust and Genocide Studies* 19, no. 1 (Spring 2005), pp. 30, 32; Alexandra-Eileen Wenck, *Zwischen*

Menschenhandel und "Endlösung": Das Konzentrationslager Bergen-Belsen (Paderborn, Germany, 2000), p. 78.

61. Friedman, op. cit., pp. 32, 36.

62. Raul Hilberg, *The Destruction of the European Jews*, vol. 2 (New York, 1985), p. 446.

63. Eberhard Kolb, *Bergen-Belsen: From "Detention Camp" to Concentration Camp: 1943 to 1945* (Göttingen, Germany, 1985), pp. 21–22.

64. Ammann and Aust, op. cit., p. 63.

CHAPTER 6: ASKING AFTER AUNT DARKA

1. Foreign Office Memorandum, February 4, 1943, and RSHA Memorandum, February 3, 1943, Nathan Eck Collection, Yad Vashem, part 12, record group P.22, file no. 37, item NG 2586 and NG 2652A.

2. Eberhard Kolb, *Bergen-Belsen: From "Detention Camp" to Concentration Camp: 1943 to 1945* (Göttingen, Germany, 1985), p. 22; Alexandra-Eileen Wenck, *Zwischen Menschenhandel und "Endlösung": Das Konzentrationslager Bergen-Belsen* (Paderborn, Germany, 2000), p. 80.

3. Kolb, op. cit., p. 24.

4. Mary Berg, *The Diary of Mary Berg: Growing Up in the Warsaw Ghetto* (London, 2006), p. 208.

5. Ibid., p. 212; Gutta Sternbuch and David Kranzler, *Gutta: Memories of a Vanished World* (Jerusalem, 2005), p. 111.

6. Sternbuch and Kranzler, op. cit., p. 112.

7. Charles Glass, *Americans in Paris: Life and Death Under Nazi Occupation* (London, 2009), pp. 253–234; Sternbuch and Kranzler, op. cit., pp. 112–113.

8. Berg, op. cit., p. 216; Sofka Skipwith, *Sofka: The Autobiography of a Princess* (London, 1968), pp. 222–223.

9. Bericht, report on Hügli's activities, June 1, 1943, pp. 3–4, Swiss Federal Archive (hereafter SFA), Hügli files, ref. E2001E#1000/1571#657#28.

10. Letter, Swiss Justice Department to Political Department, July 21, 1943, pp. 2–3, SFA, Hügli files, ref. E2001E#1000-1571#657#26.

11. Hügli Bericht, June 1, 1943, pp. 4–5.

12. Notiz on Hügli Interrogations, August 9, 1943, pp. 8–10, 15, SFA, Hügli files, ref. E2001E#1000-1571#657#27.

13. Ibid., pp. 13–14.

14. Ibid., p. 10.

15. SFA, Löri files, ref. E4301#1992/36#3631; Elia Boczko deposition, May 1, 1943, pp. 4–5, SFA, ref. E4320B#1990-266#4140#78.

16. Weingort witness statement, July 13, 1943, SFA.

17. Löri statement, June 1, 1943, p. 3, SFA.

18. Martin Gilbert, *The Holocaust* (London, 1986), p. 522; Abraham Lewin, *A Cup of Tears: A Diary of the Warsaw Ghetto* (Oxford, 1988), p. 242.

19. Chajka Klinger, *"I Am Writing These Words to You": The Original Diaries, Będzin, 1943* (Jerusalem, 2017), p. 152; Vladka Meed, *On Both Sides of the Wall* (Washington, DC, 1993), p. 120; Władysław Szpilman, *The Pianist* (London, 2002), p. 130.

20. Quoted in Gilbert, *Holocaust*, op. cit., p. 524.

21. Józef Gitler-Barski, *Przeżycia i wspomnienia z lat okupacji* (Warsaw, 1986), p. 47; Jan Mawult, quoted in *Words to Outlive Us: Eyewitness Accounts from the Warsaw Ghetto*, ed. Michał Grynberg (London, 2003), pp. 251–252.

22. Reports of the Council for the Aid of Jews (Żegota) to the Government Delegation for Poland, February 12, 1943, and July 21, 1943, in Archiwum Akt Nowych (hereafter AAN), Warsaw, ref. 2/1325/0/202/XV-2, vol. 4; correspondence between Zygmunt Gepner and Abraham Silberschein, April–May 1943, Abraham Silberschein Collection, Yad Vashem Archive, record group M. 20, file no. 163, item ID 3687364.

23. Klinger, op. cit., p. 9; see Georg Kreis, "Swiss Refugee Policy, 1933–45" in *Switzerland and the Second World War*, ed. Georg Kreis (London, 2000), p. 112; Heini Bornstein, *Insel Schweiz: Hilfs- und Rettungsaktionen sozialistisch-zionistischer Jugendorganisationen 1939–1946* (Zürich, 2000), pp. 202–203.

24. Zivia Lubetkin, extract from her testimony at the Eichmann Trial, Jerusalem, 1961, available at "Fighters in the Warsaw Ghetto," Yad Vashem, YouTube, March 21, 2013, www.youtube.com/watch?v=pin_H8rcfPQ.

25. Kazimierz Moczarski, *Conversations with an Executioner* (Hoboken, NJ, 1981), p. 176; Feigele Peltel, quoted in Gilbert, *Holocaust*, op. cit., p. 562.

26. Testimony of Heinz Polke in *Dem Wahnsinn Entkommen: Soldatenschicksale im Zweiten Weltkrieg*, ed. Klaus Förg (Rosenheim, Germany, 2022), pp. 23–24; Alexander Donat, *The Holocaust Kingdom: A Memoir* (London, 1965), p. 146.

27. Jürgen Stroop, report to Berlin, April 26, 1943, quoted in *The Nazi Germany Sourcebook: An Anthology of Texts*, eds. Roderick Stackelberg and Sally A. Winkle (London, 2002), p. 368.

28. Agnes Grunwald-Spier, *Women's Experiences in the Holocaust: In Their Own Words* (Stroud, UK, 2018), pp. 226–228; Jakub Kumoch et al., *The Ładoś List* (Warsaw, 2020), p. 106.

29. Bornstein, op. cit., p. 203.

30. Moczarski, op. cit., p. 164; see "The Stroop Report," in Roger Moorhouse, *The Third Reich in 100 Objects* (Barnsley, UK, 2017), pp. 219–222.

31. Richard Breitman, *Official Secrets: What the Nazis Planned, What the British and Americans Knew* (New York, 1998), p. 184.

32. Henry Feingold, *The Politics of Rescue* (New Brunswick, NJ, 1970), p. 198.

33. Ibid., p. 206; quoted in Breitman, op. cit., p. 184.

34. E. Thomas Wood and Stanisław M. Jankowski, *Karski: How One Man Tried to Stop the Holocaust* (New York, 1994), p. 152.

35. Jan Karski, interviewed by Claude Lanzmann, at "Jan Karski About the Indifference of the Free World and Szmul Zygielbojm," JanKarskiProgram, YouTube, March 23, 2012, www.youtube.com/watch?v=hHJ7TI3qqjU.

36. Dispatches between the Polish legation in Bern and the Ministry of Foreign Affairs in London, Book of Coded Correspondence, Bern to London dispatch no. 187, May 12, 1943, a request to forward dispatch no. 11 to Washington, AAN, ref. 0002-AAN/2/495/0/-/330/0127.

37. Dispatch from the Ministry of Foreign Affairs in London to the Polish legation in Bern, May 19, 1943, AAN, ref. 001-AAN/2/495/0/404/0003.

38. Dispatches between the Polish legation in Bern and the Ministry of Foreign Affairs in London, Book of Coded Correspondence, Bern to London dispatch no. 257 ref. dispatch no. 276, June 30, 1943, description of the recipients of the Latin American passports, AAN, ref. 0006-AAN/2/495/0/327/0150.

39. Polish Foreign Ministry to the Polish legation in Rio de Janeiro, June 29, 1943, and to Buenos Aires, July 3, 1943, and reply of August 6, both from Hoover Institution Archive, ref: MSZ, 616; and all in *Confronting the Holocaust: The Polish Government-in-Exile's Policy Concerning Jews 1939–1945*, ed. Piotr Długołęcki (Warsaw, 2022), pp. 667, 670.

40. Madonne's concerns were noted in a letter from Robert Jezler to Heinrich Rothmund on April 27, 1943, SFA, Hügli files, ref. E2001E#1000/1571#657, Piece 1000/1571_47; Max Paul Friedman, "The U.S. State Department and the Failure to Rescue: New Evidence on the Missed Opportunity at Bergen-Belsen," *Holocaust and Genocide Studies* 19, no. 1 (Spring 2005), p. 38.

41. Jacob Presser, *Ashes in the Wind: The Destruction of Dutch Jewry* (London, 2010), pp. 202–205.

42. Transcript of an interview with Mirjam Finkelstein, in the British Library, London, ref: C410/093.

43. See Zahava Kohn, *Fragments of a Lost Childhood* (London, 2009), and author interview with Hephzibah Rudofsky, London, May 2022.

44. Philip Mechanicus, *Waiting for Death: A Diary* (London, 1968), p. 83.

45. Alison Leslie Gold, *Hannah Goslar Remembers: A Childhood Friend of Anne Frank* (London, 1998), p. 51; Mechanicus, op. cit., p. 193.

46. I. J. Blanken, *The History of Philips Electronics N.V.*, vol. 4 (Zaltbommel, Netherlands, 1999), p. 274.

47. Unpublished manuscript on the Dutch side of the passport operation, written by Gerard van den Berg, kindly supplied to the author by Mr. Sjoerd Schelvis.

48. Material supplied to the author by Mr. Sjoerd Schelvis. Eva and David van Amerongen are listed as recipients of a Ładoś passport. Kumoch et al., op. cit., p. 143.

49. Presser, op. cit., p. 227–228; Irene Butter, *Shores Beyond Shores: From Holocaust to Hope* (London, 2018), p. 60.

50. Presser, op. cit., p. 227; Bernard Wasserstein, *The Ambiguity of Virtue: Gertrude van Tijn and the Fate of the Dutch Jews* (London, 2014), p. 200, 225; Simon Heinrich Herrmann, *Austauschlager Bergen-Belsen* (Tel Aviv, 1944), pp. 26–27.

51. See Mirjam Finkelstein, in the British Library, London, ref: C410/093; Kumoch et al., op. cit., p. 148; author interview with Lord Finkelstein, London, January 2020; obituary for Mirjam Finkelstein, *The Times*, February 2, 2017.

52. Mechanicus, op. cit., p. 236.

53. Mary Fulbrook, *A Small Town Near Auschwitz: Ordinary Nazis and the Holocaust* (Oxford, 2013), pp. 233, 289.

54. Klinger, op. cit., pp. 118–119.

55. Kumoch et al., op. cit., pp. 40–41, 71, 108–109, 146.

56. Bornstein, op. cit., pp. 206, 211.

57. Quoted in Ruth Zariz, "Attempts at Rescue and Revolt—Attitude of Members of the Dror Youth Movement in Bedzin to Foreign Passports as Means of Rescue," *Yad Vashem Studies* 20 (1990), pp. 225–226.

58. Bornstein, op. cit., p. 208.

59. Klinger, op. cit., p. 116.

60. Both quotes from Zariz, op. cit., p. 222.

61. Arie Liwer, "That Which Will Not Be Forgotten," in *Pinkes Bendin*, ed. A. Stein (Tel Aviv, 1959), pp. 353–354; Bornstein, op. cit., p. 207.

CHAPTER 7: NO TIME TO LOSE

1. Agnieszka Haska, *Hotel Polski w Warszawie, 1943* (Warsaw, 2006), p. 54.

2. Quoted in David Cesarani, *Final Solution: The Fate of the Jews, 1933–1949* (New York, 2016), p. 665.

3. Gerald Reitlinger, *The Final Solution: The Attempt to Exterminate the Jews of Europe, 1939–1945* (London, 1953), p. 339.

4. Abraham Shulman, *The Case of the Hotel Polski* (New York, 1982), p. 39; Haska, op. cit., p. 56.

5. Shulman, op. cit., pp. 132–133; Yitzhak Katzenelson, *The Song of the Massacred Jewish People*, trans. Jack Hirschman (Berkeley, CA, 2021), p. 21.

6. Quoted in Haska, op. cit., p. 68.

7. Gunnar Paulsson, *Secret City: The Hidden Jews of Warsaw, 1940–1945* (New Haven, CT, 2002), p. 109.

8. Symcha Binem Motyl, *Do moich ewentualnych cztelników. Wspomnienia z czasu wojny* (Warsaw, 2011), p. 205; Vladka Meed, *On Both Sides of the Wall* (Washington, DC, 1993), pp. 91–92.

9. Haska, op. cit., p. 76; Calel Perechodnik, *Am I a Murderer? Testament of a Jewish Ghetto Policeman* (Boulder, CO, 1996), p. 180.

10. Armia Krajowa III—105/50, Archiwum Akt Nowych, Warsaw (hereafter AAN), quoted in Haska, op. cit., p. 60.

11. Testimony of Mina Tomkiewicz, in Shulman, op. cit., p. 67.

12. Józef Gitler-Barski, *Przeżycia i wspomnienia z lat okupacji* (Warsaw, 1986), p. 75; Meed, op. cit., p. 176.

13. Tuvia Borzykowski, quoted in Shulman, op. cit., p. 44.

14. Hela Schüpper, quoted in Haska, op. cit., p. 80; Tomkiewicz testimony, in Shulman, op. cit., p. 67; Meed, op. cit., p. 177.

15. Jakub Kumoch et al., *The Ładoś List* (Warsaw, 2020), pp. 98, 132, 152. See also Haska, op. cit., p. 61.

16. Testimony of Bernard Goldstein, in Shulman, op. cit., p. 42; Government Delegation for Poland XV—2/343, AAN, quoted in Haska, op. cit., p. 66; testimony of Helena Citrynik, in Shulman, op. cit., p. 91; testimony of Simcha Korngold, in Shulman, op. cit., p. 59; quoted in Haska, op. cit., p. 82.

17. Haska, op. cit., p. 66; testimony of Henryk Zamoszowski, in Shulman, op. cit., p. 82.

18. Testimony of Anna Szpiro, in Shulman, op. cit., p. 85; testimony of Ber Baskind, in ibid., p. 74.

19. Sofka Skipwith, *Sofka: The Autobiography of a Princess* (London, 1968), p. 224.

20. Meed, op. cit., p. 178; Thomas Ammann and Stefan Aust, *Hitlers Menschenhändler* (Berlin, 2013), p. 115.

21. Testimony of Ella Sendowska, in Shulman, op. cit., p. 87; Tadeusz Obremski, *Wśród zatrutych nozy: Zapiski z getta i okupowanej Warszawy* (Warsaw, 2017), pp. 218–219.

22. Cited in Report of the Council for the Aid of Jews (Żegota) to the Government Delegation for Poland, July 21, 1943, AAN, ref. 2/1325/0/202/XV-2, vol. 4.

23. Ber Baskind, in Shulman, op. cit., p. 77; Armia Krajowa III—105/39, AAN, quoted in Haska, op. cit., p. 75.

24. Testimony of Barbara Rucinska, in Shulman, op. cit., p. 97.

25. Korngold, in ibid., p. 63.

26. Motyl, op. cit., p. 211.

27. Simcha Korngold, in Shulman, op. cit., p. 167.

28. Tomkiewicz, in ibid., p. 142.

29. Gitler-Barski, op. cit., p. 76.

30. Tomkiewicz in Shulman, op. cit., pp. 143–144.

31. Korngold, in ibid., p. 168; Gitler-Barski, op. cit., p. 76.

32. Gitler-Barski, quoted in Shulman, op. cit., p. 159.

33. Tomkiewicz in ibid., p. 153.

34. Henryk Schönker, *Dotknięcie anioła* (Warsaw, 2011), p. 215.

35. Alexandra-Eileen Wenck, "Das 'Sonderlager' im Konzentrationslager Bergen-Belsen," *Dachauer Hefte* 14 (1998), p. 268.

36. Meed, op. cit., p. 179.

37. Archivum Żydowski Instytut Historyczny, Warsaw, ref. 301/5941, quoted in Haska, op. cit., p. 90.

38. Testimony of Rudolf Sawicki, in Haska, op. cit., p. 94; testimony of Stanisław Wróblewski, in "Documentation and Correspondence Regarding the Rescue of Jews Through the Use of Foreign Travel Documents," Nathan Eck Collection, Yad Vashem Archive, record group P.22, file no. 21, item: 10572948.

39. Avihu Ronen, "The Cable That Vanished," *Yad Vashem Studies* 41, no. 2 (2013), p. 17; Chajka Klinger, *"I Am Writing These Words to You": The Original Diaries, Będzin, 1943* (Jerusalem, 2017), p. 120.

40. See Eck's story at Passports of Life, https://paszportyzycia.pl.

41. Arie Liwer, "That Which Will Not Be Forgotten," *Pinkes Bendin*, ed. in A. Stein (Tel Aviv, 1959), p. 358; Mary Fulbrook, *A Small Town Near Auschwitz: Ordinary Nazis and the Holocaust* (Oxford, 2013), p. 291.

42. Klinger, op. cit., pp. 120–121.

43. Quoted in Fulbrook, op. cit., p. 291; Danuta Czech, *Auschwitz Chronicle 1939–1945* (London and New York, 1990), pp. 424, 426.

44. Fulbrook, op. cit., p. 294.

45. Quoted in Ruth Zariz, "Attempts at Rescue and Revolt—Attitude of Members of the Dror Youth Movement in Bedzin to Foreign Passports as Means of Rescue," *Yad Vashem Studies* 20 (1990), p. 236; Fulbrook, op. cit., p. 294; Czech, op. cit., pp. 452–457.

46. Neville Wylie, "Pilet-Golaz and the Making of Swiss Foreign Policy: Some Remarks," *Schweizerische Zeitschrift für Geschichte* 47, no. 4. (1997), pp. 608–611.

47. Sara Kadosh, *We Think of You as an Angel* (Jerusalem, 2019), p. 234.

48. Ibid., pp. 237–238.

49. Silberschein Testimony, September 1, 1943, Swiss Federal Archive (hereafter SFA), ref. BAR#E4320B#1990-266#2164; Note on an interview between Mr. Stefan Ryniewicz and Chief of Alien Police, Heinrich Rothmund, September 6, 1943, in *Diplomatic Documents of Switzerland*, eds. Philippe Marguerat and Louis-Edouard Roulet, vol. 15 (Bern, 1992), doc. 20, pp. 53–54, dodis.ch/11958.

50. Report of the Federal Political Department, August 16, 1943, SFA, ref. BAR#E2001E#1000-1571#657#25.

51. Wylie, op. cit., p. 615.

52. Note on an interview between Mr. Aleksander Ładoś and M. Marcel Pilet-Golaz, October 13, 1943, in Marguerat and Roulet, op. cit., pp. 52–53, dodis .ch/47624.

53. Nikolaus Wachsmann, *KL: A History of the Nazi Concentration Camps* (London, 2015), p. 335.

54. Eberhard Kolb, *Bergen-Belsen: Geschichte des "Aufenthaltslagers" 1943–1945* (Hannover, Germany, 1962), p. 67.

55. Korngold in Shulman, op. cit., p. 168; Schönker, op. cit., p. 220.

56. Tomkiewicz, in Shulman, op. cit., p. 145; Gitler-Barski, op. cit., p. 78; Schönker, op. cit., pp. 210, 215; Helena Goldberg, quoted in Shulman, op. cit., p. 177.

57. Schönker, op. cit., pp. 229–239.

58. Ruth Zariz, in Ruth Zariz et al., *From Bergen Belsen to Freedom* (Jerusalem, 1986), p. 17; Eberhard Kolb, *Bergen-Belsen: From "Detention Camp" to Concentration Camp: 1943 to 1945* (Göttingen, Germany, 1985), p. 21.

59. Alexandra-Eileen Wenck, *Zwischen Menschenhandel und "Endlösung": Das Konzentrationslager Bergen-Belsen* (Paderborn, Germany, 2000), p. 150.

60. David Kranzler, *The Man Who Stopped the Trains to Auschwitz* (Syracuse, NY, 2000), p. 36; Gutta Sternbuch and David Kranzler, *Gutta: Memories of a Vanished World* (Jerusalem, 2005), p. 121n; see Kadosh., op. cit., pp. 241–242, and David Wyman, *The Abandonment of the Jews: America and the Holocaust, 1941–1945* (New York, 1984), p. 277.

61. Ryniewicz to Silberschein, August 17, 1943, AAN, Delegatura Rządu RP na Kraj, 202/XV/2; telegram from the Polish legation in Bern to Lima, telegram no. 1, 17.08.1943: request to Lima to recognize the passports of Peru issued at the behest of the Polish legation in Bern, AAN, ref. AAN/2/495/330/0152.

62. Brunner to Eichmann, August 23, 1943, Bundesarchiv, Berlin, ref. R 58/7658.

63. Korngold, in Shulman, op. cit., p. 169.

64. Gitler-Barski, op. cit., p. 79; Schönker, op. cit., p. 226; Tomkiewicz, in Shulman, op. cit., p. 155.

65. Tomkiewicz, in Shulman, op. cit., p. 155.

66. Gideon Greif, *"...płakaliśmy bez lez..."* (Warsaw and Oświęcim, Poland, 2001), p. 149.

67. Filip Müller, *Eyewitness Auschwitz: Three Years in the Gas Chambers* (New York, 1979), pp. 82–84.

68. Ibid., pp. 86–87.

69. Greif, op. cit., pp. 149–150. This discussion of the available evidence is useful: Kim LaCapria, "Did a Jewish Ballerina Shoot an SS Guard at Auschwitz?," *Snopes*, March 9, 2017, www.snopes.com/fact-check/franceska-mann/. Müller does not name the woman, but gives the more lurid account of the attack in Müller, op. cit., p. 87; Czech, op. cit., p. 513.

70. Müller, op. cit., p. 89.

71. Quoted in Wenck, *Zwischen*, op. cit., p. 160; Nathan Eck, "The Rescue of Jews with the Aid of Passports and Citizenship Papers of Latin American States," *Yad Vashem Studies* 1 (Jerusalem, 1957), p. 143.

72. Sternbuch and Kranzler, op. cit., pp. 120–121; Kadosh, op. cit., p. 242.

73. Sternbuch and Kranzler, op. cit., p. 122.

74. Skipwith, op. cit., p. 228; Anonymous Memorandum, September 20, 1944, "Documentation and Correspondence Regarding the Rescue of Jews Through the Use of Foreign Travel Documents," Nathan Eck Collection, Yad Vashem Archive, record group P.22, file no. 21, item: 10572948.

75. Skipwith, op. cit., pp. 225–226.

76. Kumoch et al., op. cit., p. 12.

77. Andrzej Kunert, ed., *Kazimierz Moczarski: Zapiski* (Warsaw, 1990), p. 152; Anna Rószkiewicz-Litwinowiczowa, *Trudne decyzje. Kontrwywiad Okręgu Warszawa AK 1943–1944. Więzienie 1949–1954* (Warsaw, 1991), p. 32.

78. Mary Berg, *The Diary of Mary Berg* (London, 2006), p. 240; Kadosh, op. cit., p. 247.

79. Sebastian Ładoś, *Zanim Bóg odwróci wzrok* (Wrocław, Poland, 2019), p. 333; Ładoś to Polish Foreign Ministry, London, December 18, 1943, telegram no. 583, AAN, ref. AAN/2/495/327/0321.

80. Ładoś to Polish Foreign Ministry, London, December 19, 1943, telegram no. 584, AAN, ref. AAN/2/495/327/0322; Romer circular to Polish missions in Latin America, December 21, 1943, in *Confronting the Holocaust: The Polish Government-in-Exile's Policy Concerning Jews 1939–1945*, ed. Piotr Długołęcki (Warsaw, 2022), doc. 417, pp. 790–791.

81. Weingort correspondence cited in Kadosh, op. cit., pp. 248–249; letter from Abraham Silberschein, January 7, 1944, Abraham Silberschein Collection, Yad Vashem Archive, record group M. 20, file no. 161, item ID 3687362.

82. Cable from the Consul General in New York to the Polish Foreign Ministry, London, January 4, 1944, in Długołęcki, op. cit., doc. 421, p. 795; Envoy in Havana to the ambassador in Washington, DC, January 5, 1944, in ibid., doc. 422, p. 796.

83. Washington to Bern, January 26 and February 4, 1944, telegrams no. 4 and 5, AAN, refs. AAN/2/495/331/0012-0013 and AAN/2/495/331/0017; Envoy in Bogotá to the Polish Ministry of Foreign Affairs in London, February 12, 1944, in Długołęcki, op. cit., doc. 435, p. 814.

CHAPTER 8: DEATH CASTS ITS SHADOW

1. Mina Tomkiewicz, in Abraham Shulman, *The Case of the Hotel Polski* (New York, 1982), pp. 151–152.

2. Józef Gitler-Barski, *Przeżycia i wspomnienia z lat okupacji* (Warsaw, 1986), p. 80.

3. Eberhard Kolb, *Bergen-Belsen: From "Detention Camp" to Concentration Camp: 1943 to 1945* (Göttingen, Germany, 1985), p. 26.

4. Alexandra-Eileen Wenck, *Zwischen Menschenhandel und "Endlösung": Das Konzentrationslager Bergen-Belsen* (Paderborn, Germany, 2000), p. 210.

5. Philip Mechanicus, *Waiting for Death: A Diary* (London, 1968), p. 225.

6. Ibid.; from the transcript of an interview with Mirjam Finkelstein, in the British Library, London, ref. C410/093; quoted in Eberhard Kolb, *Bergen-Belsen: Geschichte des "Aufenthaltslagers" 1943–1945* (Hannover, Germany, 1962), p. 61.

7. Irene Butter, *Shores Beyond Shores: From Holocaust to Hope* (London, 2018), p. 100; Renata Laqueur, *Bergen-Belsen Tagebuch, 1944/1945* (Hannover, Germany, 1983), p. 9.

8. Mechanicus, op. cit., p. 239.

9. Interview testimony of Mr. Charles Siegman, "Oral History Interview with Charles Siegman," July 24, 2003, US Holocaust Memorial Museum, https:// collections.ushmm.org/search/catalog/irn513365. Siegman is on the Ładoś List, see Jakub Kumoch et al., *The Ładoś List* (Warsaw, 2020), p. 131.

10. Butter, op. cit., p. 105.

11. Laqueur, op. cit., p. 12; Bernard Wasserstein, *The Ambiguity of Virtue: Gertrude van Tijn and the Fate of the Dutch Jews* (London, 2014), p. 203.

12. Gitler-Barski, op. cit., p. 84.

13. Interview with Mirjam Finkelstein, op. cit.; Butter, op. cit., p. 123.

14. Gitler-Barski, op. cit., p. 83.

15. Tomkiewicz, in Shulman, op. cit., pp. 146–147.

16. Butter, op. cit., p. 129; Korngold, in Shulman, op. cit., pp. 171–172.

17. Tomkiewicz, in Shulman, op. cit., p. 149; Henryk Schönker, *Dotknięcie anioła* (Warsaw, 2011), p. 220.

18. Mary Berg, *The Diary of Mary Berg* (London, 2006), p. 242.

19. Gutta Sternbuch and David Kranzler, *Gutta: Memories of a Vanished World* (Jerusalem, 2005), p. 124; Sofka Skipwith, *Sofka: The Autobiography of a Princess* (London, 1968), p. 230.

20. Max Paul Friedman, "The U.S. State Department and the Failure to Rescue: New Evidence on the Missed Opportunity at Bergen-Belsen," *Holocaust and Genocide Studies* 19, no. 1 (Spring 2005), pp. 38–39; Henry Feingold, *The Politics of Rescue* (New Brunswick, NJ, 1970), p. 226.

21. David Wyman, *The Abandonment of the Jews: America and the Holocaust, 1941–1945* (New York, 1984), p. 278.

22. Quoted in Friedman, op. cit., p. 39.

23. Washington to Bern, March 3, 1944, telegram no. 11, Archiwum Akt Nowych, Warsaw (hereafter AAN), ref. AAN/2/495/0/-/331/0028.

24. See, for instance, Washington to Bern, March 17, 1944, telegram no. 10, AAN, ref. AAN/2/495/331/0037.

25. Lewin to Arciszewski, March 24, 1944, in *Confronting the Holocaust: The Polish Government-in-Exile's Policy Concerning Jews 1939–1945*, ed. Piotr Długołęcki (Warsaw, 2022), doc. 454, pp. 852–854.

26. Polish Ministry of Foreign Affairs note, June 19, 1944, in Długołęcki, op. cit., doc. 486, pp. 917–920.

27. Quoted in Wyman, op. cit., p. 279.

28. Sara Kadosh, *We Think of You as an Angel* (Jerusalem, 2019), p. 272.

29. Bern to Washington, April 6, 1944, telegram no. 25, AAN, ref. AAN/2/495/331/0046; Romer to Polish missions in Latin America, April 11, 1944, in Długołęcki, op. cit., doc. 459, pp. 864–865.

30. Skipwith, op. cit., p. 230; Sternbuch and Kranzler, op. cit., p. 126.

31. Sternbuch and Kranzler, op. cit., pp. 126–127.

32. Serge Klarsfeld, *Memorial to the Jews Deported from France, 1942–1944* (New York, 1983), pp. 544, 548, 550–551. Cross-reference with Kumoch et al., op. cit., pp. 75, 119–120.

33. Skipwith, op. cit., pp. 230–231; Kadosh, op. cit., pp. 274–275; Kumoch et al., op. cit., p. 57. The height from which she jumped is disputed, see Skipwith, op. cit., p. 231, and Kadosh, op. cit., p. 275.

34. Sternbuch and Kranzler, op. cit., pp. 128–130.

35. A similar situation occurred in wartime Berlin, where a fugitive Jew who was injured in escaping the Gestapo had to be nursed back to health before she could be deported to Auschwitz. Fortunately for her, her doctors delayed her treatment and exaggerated her injuries for nearly two years, thereby staving off her deportation and saving her life. See the example of Ursula Finke in Roger Moorhouse, *Berlin at War: Life and Death in Hitler's Capital, 1939–1945* (London, 2010), p. 305.

36. Sternbuch to Agudath Israel, April 27, 1944, in Długołęcki, op. cit., doc. 484, p. 914n; Danuta Czech, *Auschwitz Chronicle 1939–1945* (London, 1990), p. 617.

37. Kermenić to Polish Ministry of Foreign Affairs, London, May 1, 1944, in Długołęcki, op. cit., doc. 469, pp. 882–883; Dębicki to Polish embassy, Washington, May 8, 1944, in ibid., doc. 470, pp. 883–885.

38. Arciszewski to Polish Ministry of Foreign Affairs, London, May 31, 1944, in ibid., doc. 481, pp. 909–910; Letter from Klara Eck to Abraham Silberschein, May 3, 1944, Abraham Silberschein Collection, Yad Vashem Archive, record group M.20, file no. 162, item ID 3687363.

39. Skipwith, op. cit., p. 233.

40. Sternbuch and Kranzler, op. cit., p. 134.

41. Anonymous handwritten account (thought to be from Róża Frankiel), Nathan Eck Collection, Yad Vashem Archive, record group P. 22, file no. 20, item ID 10569134.

42. See Kadosh, op. cit., pp. 288–289, and anonymous typed account, Nathan Eck Collection, op. cit.

43. Klarsfeld, op. cit., pp. 570, 572–573; Czech, op. cit., p. 638.

44. Gitler-Barski, op. cit., pp. 95–96.

45. Christine Lattek, "Bergen-Belsen: From 'Privileged' Camp to Death Camp," in *Belsen in History and Memory*, eds. Jo Reilly et al. (London, 1997), p. 50; Walter Guttmann, quoted in Thomas Ammann and Stefan Aust, *Hitlers Menschenhändler* (Berlin, 2013), p. 134.

46. Michael Gelber, quoted in Ammann and Aust, op. cit., p. 135; Butter, op. cit., pp. 153–154.

47. Loden Vogel, *Tagebuch aus einem Lager* (Göttingen, Germany, 2002), pp. 23, 29–30, 68.

48. Abel Herzberg, *Between Two Streams: A Diary from Bergen-Belsen* (London, 1997), p. 163.

49. Gitler-Barski, op. cit., pp. 80, 83–84, 89, 94.

50. Butter, op. cit., p. 161; Vogel, op. cit., p. 82.

51. Ciechanowski to Strakacz, June 13, 1944, in Długołęcki, op. cit., doc. 484, pp. 914–915.

52. Eyewitness report to the Polish legation in Lisbon, July 26, 1944, in ibid., doc. 502, pp. 956–958.

53. Note from the Polish legation in Lisbon to the Polish Ministry of Foreign Affairs, London, August 9, 1944, in ibid., doc. 506, pp. 963–964; Saul Weingort letter, quoted in Kadosh, op. cit., p. 296.

54. Joseph Friedenson and David Kranzler, *Heroine of Rescue* (New York, 1984), pp. 117, 119.

55. David Kranzler, *Thy Brother's Blood: The Orthodox Jewish Response During the Holocaust* (New York, 1987), pp. 40, 110.

56. Walter Schellenberg, *Schellenberg* (London, 1965), p. 167; Friedenson and Kranzler, op. cit., p. 129; Kranzler, *Thy Brother's Blood*, op. cit., p. 114.

57. Kolb, *Geschichte*, op. cit., p. 67.

58. Gitler-Barski, op. cit., p. 93.

59. Melissa Müller, *Anne Frank: The Biography* (London, 1998), p. 252; Mirjam Finkelstein deposition, op. cit.

60. Alison Leslie Gold, *Hannah Goslar Remembers: A Childhood Friend of Anne Frank* (London, 1998), pp. 24–25; Interview with Hanneli Goslar, "'That's What I Hope': The Story of Holocaust Survivor Hannah Pick," Yad Vashem, www.yadvashem.org/education/testimony-films/hannah-pick.html; Müller, op. cit., p. 258.

61. Laqueur, op. cit., pp. 86, 88–89.

62. Kolb, *Geschichte*, op. cit., p. 123.

63. Laqueur, op. cit., p. 89; Hannah Lévy-Hass, *Diary of Bergen-Belsen* (Minneapolis, MN, 2009), p. 96.

64. Wenck, *Zwischen*, op. cit., pp. 281–282; Lattek in Reilly et al., op. cit., p. 55.

CHAPTER 9: "MY GOD, WHY HAVE YOU FORSAKEN ME?"

1. Loden Vogel, *Tagebuch aus einem Lager* (Göttingen, Germany, 2002), p. 85; Józef Gitler-Barski, *Przeżycia i wspomnienia z lat okupacji* (Warsaw, 1986), p. 100; Renata Laqueur, *Bergen-Belsen Tagebuch, 1944/1945* (Hannover, Germany, 1983), p. 96.

2. Zahava Kohn, *Fragments of a Lost Childhood* (London, 2009), p. 89.

3. Hannah Lévy-Hass, *Diary of Bergen-Belsen* (Minneapolis, MN, 2009), p. 97.

4. Ibid., pp. 102–103.

5. Henryk Schönker, *Dotknięcie anioła* (Warsaw, 2011), p. 248.

6. Lévy-Hass, op. cit., p. 104; Laqueur, op. cit., p. 96.

7. Vogel, op. cit., p. 89; Irene Butter, *Shores Beyond Shores: From Holocaust to Hope* (London, 2018), pp. 172–177.

8. Laqueur, op. cit., pp. 91–92; Vogel, op. cit., pp. 89–90; Butter, op. cit., p. 180.

9. Eberhard Kolb, *Bergen-Belsen: Geschichte des "Aufenthaltslagers" 1943–1945* (Hannover, Germany, 1962), p. 102; Interview with Mirjam Finkelstein, in the British Library, London, ref: C410/093.

10. Kolb, *Geschichte*, op. cit., p. 102.

11. Butter, op. cit., pp. 194, 196, 199.

12. Kolb, *Geschichte*, op. cit., p. 102; Butter, op. cit., p. 201.

13. Finkelstein, op. cit.

14. Quoted in Daniel Blatman, *The Death Marches: The Final Phase of Nazi Genocide* (London, 2011), pp. 133–134.

15. Hannah Lévy-Hass, quoted in Christine Lattek, "Bergen-Belsen: From 'Privileged' Camp to Death Camp," in *Belsen in History and Memory*, eds. Jo Reilly et al. (London, 1997), p. 51; Abel Herzberg, *Between Two Streams: A Diary from Bergen-Belsen* (London, 1997), pp. 194, 197.

16. Ben Shephard, *After Daybreak: The Liberation of Belsen, 1945* (London, 2005), p. 16; Laqueur, op. cit., pp. 94–95.

17. Laqueur, op. cit., p. 92; Vogel, op. cit., p. 98; Alison Leslie Gold, *Hannah Goslar Remembers: A Childhood Friend of Anne Frank* (London, 1998), pp. 104–106.

18. Nikolaus Wachsmann, *KL: A History of the Nazi Concentration Camps* (London, 2015), p. 567; quoted in Shephard, op. cit., p. 15.

19. Schönker, op. cit., p. 249.

20. Gitler-Barski, op. cit., p. 104; Józef Gitler-Barski postwar testimony from 1948, "Chronicles of Terror" archive, Pilecki Institute, Warsaw, ref. 1238.

21. Alexandra-Eileen Wenck, *Zwischen Menschenhandel und "Endlösung": Das Konzentrationslager Bergen-Belsen* (Paderborn, Germany, 2000), p. 370; Testimony of Hilde Huppert in Lattek in Reilly et al., op. cit., p. 60; Gitler-Barski, op. cit., pp. 105–106, and Gitler-Barski testimony, op. cit.

22. Abel Herzberg, quoted in Lattek in Reilly et al., op. cit., p. 60.

23. Laqueur, op. cit., p. 103.

24. Hanneli Goslar's testimony in Jacek Papis's documentary *Polmission* (Warsaw, 2021); Gold, op. cit., pp. 115–116; Vogel, op. cit., p. 163.

25. Laqueur, op. cit., pp. 101–102.

26. Herzberg, op. cit., p. 218; Laqueur, op. cit., p. 129.

27. Laqueur, op. cit., pp. 129–130; Vogel, op. cit., pp. 167–168; Wenck, *Zwischen*, op. cit., p. 371.

28. Anita Lasker-Wallfisch, *Inherit the Truth 1939–1945* (London, 1996), p. 95.

29. Karin Orth, *Das System der nationalsozialistischen Konzentrationslager* (Hamburg, 2002), p. 310.

30. Dan Stone, *The Liberation of the Camps: The End of the Holocaust and Its Aftermath* (New Haven, CT, and London, 2015), p. 104.

31. Quoted in Sara Kadosh, *We Think of You as an Angel* (Jerusalem, 2019), pp. 299–300.

32. Goodman to Polish Ministry of Foreign Affairs, January 2, 1945, in *Confronting the Holocaust: The Polish Government-in-Exile's Policy Concerning Jews 1939–1945*, ed. Piotr Długołęcki (Warsaw, 2022), doc. 537, pp. 1019–1020; letter from Union of Orthodox Rabbis to Juliusz Kühl, June, 3, 1945, Wiener Library Archive, London, Kühl papers, ref. 615/1/1/92.

33. Anne Applebaum, *Iron Curtain: The Crushing of Eastern Europe, 1944–1956* (London, 2012), p. 211; Norman Davies, *God's Playground: A History of Poland*, vol. 2, *1795 to the Present* (Oxford, 1981), p. 568.

34. Raczyński to Eden, July 6, 1945, in Długołęcki, op. cit., doc. 554, pp. 1050–1052.

35. Sebastian Ładoś, *Zanim Bóg odwróci wzrok* (Wrocław, Poland, 2019), p. 360.

36. Stanisław Nahlik, *Przesiane przez pamięć*, vol. 2 (Kraków, 2002), pp. 361–362.

37. Sebastian Ładoś, op. cit., pp. 367–368; Nahlik, op. cit., p. 364.

38. Sebastian Ładoś, op. cit., pp. 371–372.

EPILOGUE

1. Note on an interview between Mr. Aleksander Ładoś and M. Marcel Pilet-Golaz, October 13, 1943, in *Diplomatic Documents of Switzerland*, eds. Philippe Marguerat and Louis-Edouard Roulet, vol. 15 (Bern, 1992), pp. 52–53, dodis .ch/47624.

2. See David M. Crowe, *Oskar Schindler: The Untold Account of His Life, Wartime Activities, and the True Story Behind the List* (Cambridge, MA, 2004), and Randolph L. Braham, "Rescue Operations in Hungary: Myths and Realities," *East European Quarterly* 34, no. 2 (2004), pp. 183–184.

3. See Ronald W. Zweig, *The Gold Train: The Destruction of the Jews and the Looting of Hungary* (London, 2002).

4. Abraham Silberschein Collection, Yad Vashem Archive, file ref: record group M.20, file no. 161, item ID 3686816, cited in Jakub Kumoch et al., *The Ładoś List*, 2nd ed. (Warsaw, 2020), p. 41n52; the statistical methodology is explained in Kumoch et al., op. cit., pp. 41–46.

5. Kumoch et al., op. cit., pp. 55–56.

6. Ibid., pp. 48, 50–51.

7. Edward Kossoy, "Ziarno i plewy (przyczynek do działalności Poselstwa RP w Bernie w latach II wojny światowej)," in *Zeszyty Historyczne*, vol. 114 (Paris, 1995), p. 103; letter from Abraham Silberschein, January 7, 1944, Abraham Silberschein Collection, Yad Vashem Archive, record group M.20, file no. 161, item ID 3687362.

8. Author correspondence with Heidi Fishman, January 2023.

INDEX

Roger Moorhouse studied history at the University of London and is a visiting professor at the College of Europe in Warsaw. He is the author of several books on World War II history, including *Poland 1939* (winner of the Polish Foreign Ministry History Prize), *Berlin at War* (short-listed for the Hessell-Tiltman Prize), and *The Devils' Alliance*. He lives in the United Kingdom.